Putting Poetry First

Putting Poetry First

A LIFE OF
ROBERT NICHOLS
1893–1944

———

ANNE & WILLIAM
CHARLTON

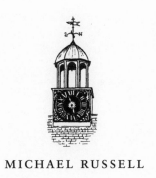

MICHAEL RUSSELL

First published in Great Britain 2003
by Michael Russell (Publishing) Ltd
Wilby Hall, Wilby, Norwich NR16 2JP

Typeset in Sabon by Waveney Typesetters,
Wymondham, Norfolk
Printed and bound in Great Britain
by Biddles Ltd, Guildford and King's Lynn

Contents

Authors' Note and Acknowledgements

Robert Nichols left his books and papers to his wife Norah, and she left them to his niece Anne, one of the present writers. Since he was unwilling to throw anything away, they form a considerable mass of source material. Conspicuous among them are journals Nichols kept between 1934 and 1944, the last ten years of his life, and collections of letters from him which the recipients returned. There are some 475 letters (averaging some 8 pages of foolscap) to the neurologist Sir Henry Head and his wife, and nearly 200 to Sir Edward Marsh, the personal secretary to Winston Churchill and fashionable litterateur. There are also many letters written to Nichols, some by friends, some by relatives, and about 240 from his lover Vivienne Wilkinson. We have drawn deeply on this correspondence for this biography, while realising that Nichols did not speak his full mind either to the Heads (who were perhaps a little puritanical) or to Marsh (whom he regarded more as a literary than as a personal friend), and that he received many important letters that have not come down to us. Norah, who although divorced from Nichols remained attached to him, may have done some censoring; certainly there is a notable absence of correspondence between herself and him.

Besides the correspondence, the journals and the manuscripts, we have been able to draw on the memories of Vivienne Wilkinson. Towards the end of her life, assisted by her niece Susanna Webb, she wrote an autobiography running to 100 pages of typescript, (referred to here as her Recollections), and Mr Richard Andersen made several tapes of conversations she had with him. Her great-niece Helen Schell has also provided useful information.

The Nichols family had hoped that Mr Andersen might himself write Robert Nichols's life, and he worked on the project for many years; but other commitments prevented him from completing it. He has most generously, however, placed the results of his work at our disposal and commented on a draft of this book. Mr Richard Tolson also collected material for a biography and had some meetings with Norah Nichols, and we are grateful for his assistance too. Some interesting photographs were supplied by Norah Nichols's cousins Robin Miller and James Denny. Several people have kindly read drafts of this book and sent useful comments, including Mr David Bradshaw and Mr Layton Ring. Our own researches started only when nearly everyone who knew Nichols well was already dead, but his nephews Francis Nichols and Anthony Gater and his niece Sally Roberts (née Strauss) have told us what they remember hearing about him.

In addition we should like to thank the following – and apologise for any omissions: Michael Bristow-Smith of the Sheila Kaye-Smith Society for information about Robert Nichols's friendship with Sheila Kaye-Smith; The British Library and also Condé Nast Publications Ltd for permission to reproduce the photograph from *Vogue* 'Studded Elegance', shelfmark Ld 89 *Vogue* 23.6.1937; The Carcanet Press Ltd for permission to quote from Robert Graves, *Fairies and Fusiliers* (1917), *Goodbye To All That* (1929) and *In Broken Images* (ed. Paul O'Prey, 1982); Faber and Faber Ltd for permission to quote extracts from *Siegfried Sassoon Diaries 1920–1922*; the Comtesse d'Harcourt for permission to quote letters to Robert Nichols from Enid Bagnold and reproduce drawings in them; David Higham Associates for permission to quote letters to Robert Nichols from Edith Sitwell; Edward M. Lamont for permission to quote from a letter to Robert Nichols from Flora Lamont; Gosia Lawick for sending extracts from works of reference and help in obtaining other material from the London Library; Roger Morgan Esq., CBE, for permission to quote from an essay on Robert Nichols in Charles Morgan's *Reflections in a Mirror*; The National Portrait Gallery for permission to reproduce the portrait of Robert Nichols by Augustus John; Paterson Marsh Ltd, on behalf of the Estate of Dorothy M. Richardson, for permission to quote from a letter to Robert Nichols; The Peters, Fraser and Dunlop Group Ltd, on behalf of the Estate of Mrs Claire Blunden, for permission to quote from works by Edmund Blunden; The Society of Authors as Literary Representative of the Estate of L. P. Hartley for permission to quote from a previously unpublished letter of L. P. Hartley and as Literary Representative of the Estate of St John Ervine for permission to reprint an extract from his report in *The Observer* of 30 December 1928; Trinity College, Oxford, for giving access to tutorial records of

Robert Nichols and to letters presented by him to the College; Mrs B. W. Walthew for permission to quote extracts from writings by Sheila Kaye-Smith; The Dean and Chapter of Westminster Abbey for permission to reproduce a photograph of the memorial stone to poets of the First World War in Poets' Corner.

FAMILY TREE

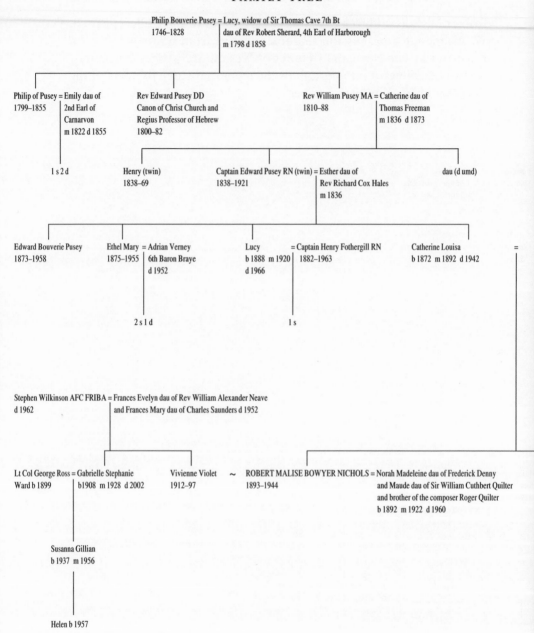

Philip Bouverie Pusey = Lucy, widow of Sir Thomas Cave 7th Bt
1746–1828   dau of Rev Robert Sherard, 4th Earl of Harborough
m 1798 d 1858

Philip of Pusey = Emily dau of
1799–1855   2nd Earl of
Carnarvon
m 1822 d 1855

Rev Edward Pusey DD
Canon of Christ Church and
Regius Professor of Hebrew
1800–82

Rev William Pusey MA = Catherine dau of
1810–88   Thomas Freeman
m 1836 d 1873

1 s 2 d

Henry (twin)
1838–69

Captain Edward Pusey RN (twin) = Esther dau of
1838–1921   Rev Richard Cox Hales
m 1836

dau (d umd)

Edward Bouverie Pusey
1873–1958

Ethel Mary = Adrian Verney
1875–1955   6th Baron Braye
d 1952

Lucy   = Captain Henry Fothergill RN
b 1888 m 1920 1882–1963
d 1966

Catherine Louisa
b 1872 m 1892 d 1942

=

2 s 1 d

1 s

Stephen Wilkinson AFC FRIBA = Frances Evelyn dau of Rev William Alexander Neave
d 1962   and Frances Mary dau of Charles Saunders d 1952

Lt Col George Ross = Gabrielle Stephanie
Ward b 1899   b1908 m 1928 d 2002

Vivienne Violet
1912–97

~

ROBERT MALISE BOWYER NICHOLS = Norah Madeleine dau of Frederick Denny
1893–1944   and Maude dau of Sir William Cuthbert Quilter
and brother of the composer Roger Quilter
b 1892 m 1922 d 1960

Susanna Gillian
b 1937 m 1956

Helen b 1957

FAMILY TREE

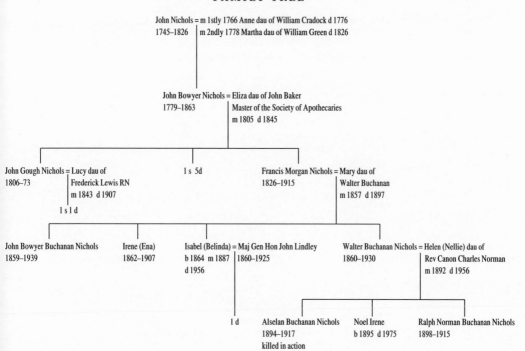

John Nichols = m 1stly 1766 Anne dau of William Cradock d 1776
1745–1826 | m 2ndly 1778 Martha dau of William Green d 1826

John Bowyer Nichols = Eliza dau of John Baker
1779–1863 | Master of the Society of Apothecaries
m 1805 d 1845

John Gough Nichols = Lucy dau of
1806–73 | Frederick Lewis RN
m 1843 d 1907

1 s 1 d

1 s 5d

Francis Morgan Nichols = Mary dau of
1826–1915 | Walter Buchanan
m 1857 d 1897

John Bowyer Buchanan Nichols
1859–1939

Irene (Ena)
1862–1907

Isabel (Belinda) = Maj Gen Hon John Lindley
b 1864 m 1887 | 1860–1925
d 1956

Walter Buchanan Nichols = Helen (Nellie) dau of
1860–1930 | Rev Canon Charles Norman
m 1892 d 1956

1 d

Alselan Buchanan Nichols
1894–1917
killed in action

Noel Irene
b 1895 d 1975

Ralph Norman Buchanan Nichols
1898–1915

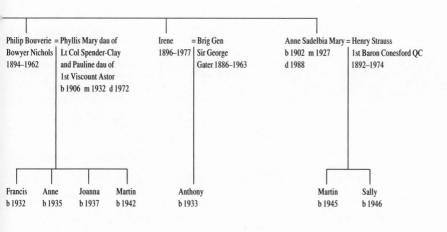

Philip Bouverie = Phyllis Mary dau of
Bowyer Nichols | Lt Col Spender-Clay
1894–1962 | and Pauline dau of
1st Viscount Astor
b 1906 m 1932 d 1972

Irene = Brig Gen
1896–1977 | Sir George
Gater 1886–1963

Anne Sadelbia Mary = Henry Strauss
b 1902 m 1927 | 1st Baron Conesford QC
d 1988 | 1892–1974

Francis
b 1932

Anne
b 1935

Joanna
b 1937

Martin
b 1942

Anthony
b 1933

Martin
b 1945

Sally
b 1946

I

Background and Childhood

Robert Nichols was the author of ten books in four genres not often attempted by one and the same writer: lyric poetry, satirical poetry, drama and imaginative fiction. Each of these books when it appeared was taken seriously by the literary establishment, and most of them were warmly applauded. This alone would justify a study of him. But he also had an interesting life. He lived and worked in several different countries, England, Japan, America and France; he volunteered in 1914 and fought in one of the bloodiest battles of the First World War; he was present in Germany when the Nazis came to power and in France when it capitulated in the Second World War; he was on terms of friendship with many of the leading writers, artists, musicians and actors of his time; and he made a fine mess of his relationships of the heart. He left behind him trunkloads of personal letters and unpublished manuscripts which have descended to the present writers; and it has seemed best to us not to attempt a critical assessment of his work, a task, in any case, for which we are unqualified, but to present the material at our disposal in such a way as to let Robert Nichols speak for himself: a man at once gifted and ill-starred, who can offer both pleasure from his writings and lessons from his life.

Nichols is chiefly known today as a poet of the First World War. When he died Reginald Snell said in the *New English Weekly*[1] 'Of the five significant poets of the last war, none went on as they had begun.' Wilfred Owen, he observes, died, Robert Graves, Edmund Blunden and Siegfried Sassoon turned to various forms of prose, and 'only Robert Nichols continued to take himself and his calling as a poet very seriously indeed.' Nichols in fact gave his whole life to poetry; he never seriously considered any career but that of poet. He did not 'go on as he had begun' chiefly in that his later reputation did not quite match his early promise. His first two volumes of poetry, *Invocation* (1915) and *Ardours and Endurances* (1917), received enormous acclaim. *The Times Literary Supplement* of 12 July 1917, said: 'Nothing can prevent poetry like this from taking its place among those permanent possessions of the race which will remain to tell the great-grandchildren of our soldiers to what pure heights of the spirit Englishmen rose out of the great war's horror of waste and ugliness, noise and pain and death!' His war poetry seemed to respond perfectly to the needs of a patriotic people in the throes of war. What was not sustained was this rapport with the public. That was not because inspiration failed him. Partly it was due to independence of mind: he always wrote what he wanted rather than what would please the critics, and his later ambitions lay in a genre for which there was little demand, large-scale poetical dramas of tragi-comic character. And partly it was due to a tragi-comic or manic-depressive cast in his own character, which caused him to swing between wild, infectious enthusiasm and abysmal, and to his friends maddening, self-pity. Condoling with his family after his death in 1944, L. P. Hartley wrote:

> His personality had genius. I never remember meeting anyone who had so much spiritual electricity – one could say to him after a few minutes' talk things one never knew one had thought of. And his work had genius too though he never managed to express a tenth of what he had in him. But he stuck to the main stream of litera-ture at a time when it was running into backwaters and shallows.
>
> I remember well how sympathetic his presence was, for though he was a great talker he was also a creative listener and drew out as much as he gave out. His impulse to share his mind with you was a most lovable trait.[2]

Intensely introspective, Robert had his own theory about his person-ality, and in 1932 expressed it in these words:

> I was born in 1893 of parents of temperaments so antithetical and complementary that I can, I believe, trace to the blended stocks every contradiction in my work and all qualities, good or bad, that it possesses. My mother is a Pusey – that is a person of a race with such gifts as enthusiasm, religious mysticism and a tendency to action. My father is a Nichols – their gifts are those of the scholar, the aesthete and the critical humanist. From my mother, then – fervour, imagination, violence; from my father the use of words, the love of art and some interest in ideas.[3]

He says a little more about his family background in a *curriculum vitae* he prepared in the 1920s for a stay in Hollywood:

> Mother is a Pusey – niece of the Oxford Movement Pusey. All that

side nearly were sailors, including some famous ones, starting with Sir Cloudesley Shovell whose monument is in Westminster Abbey and who in his youth was a sort of VC at the battle of La Hague.* Father's family were printers – the first of whom was a great friend of Dr Johnson. Later they became Government printers.

The nautical tradition of the Pusey family may go some way to explain the love of the sea which is a recurrent feature of Robert's poetry. As for the printing tradition of the Nicholses, that was so distinguished that when the firm came to an end in 1939 it received an obituary in *The Times Literary Supplement*.

There can be very few privately owned printing firms in London or elsewhere [wrote 'A Correspondent'] with activities extending from the time of Queen Anne to George VI: and none of them has such a fine and voluminous literary record as J. B. Nichols and Son of Orchard Street, Westminster. ... The outstanding figure in this long history is John Nichols (1745–1826) who with his son John Bowyer Nichols (1779–1863) and his grandson John Gough Nichols (1806–73) figure at length in the 'Dictionary of National Biography' not because they were printers but because they were authors.[4]

John Nichols wrote a *History of Leicestershire* in eight folio volumes and seventeen octavo volumes of *Literary Anecdotes* and *Illustrations of Literary History*, besides editing *The Gentleman's Magazine* for half a century. His son and grandson succeeded him in that editorship, and the firm of Nichols and Sons, which was a continuation of the business started in the seventeenth century by William Bowyer, printed the minutes of the House of Commons for 200 years and also the publications of the Royal Society and the Society of Antiquaries.

Robert Malise Bowyer Nichols – Malise Graham was an Oxford friend of his father – was born on 6 September 1893, the oldest of the family.

---

*1690. In his later years he was more of a martinet. On his last voyage he and his navigator were uncertain where they were. One of the ordinary seamen, convinced that they were more than a hundred miles from where they thought and that the ship was in imminent danger of driving onto rocks, made a protest in which it emerged that he had made his own computation of their position. This, for an ordinary seaman, amounted to mutiny and Sir Cloudesley hanged him on the spot. Unfortunately the seaman was right, and within twelve hours the ship went down, causing the deaths of Sir Cloudesley himself and all but one of his crew.

His brother Philip, usually called Phil, was born just a year later, on 7 September 1894, a sister, Irene, followed in February 1896, and a second sister, Anne, in 1902. For the first few years of his life his home was 7 Bryanston Street, London W1. Then, in 1897, his paternal grandmother died, and his grandfather handed over his house in Essex, Lawford Hall, to his elder son Bowyer, Robert's father. From then onwards the family lived partly at Lawford and partly at the house in Bryanston Street. Neither house was a happy one, though Lawford, at least, seems made for happiness. It is old and very beautiful, an Elizabethan building of timber and plaster with Georgian fronts of delicate red brick on two sides, and it looks over the valley of the Stour where Constable lived and painted. Nevertheless the gloom prevailing in both houses is a recurrent theme in Robert's letters and must have had a profound influence on his life.

For this unhappiness there was a simple and tragic explanation. From the earliest years of her marriage Robert's mother suffered from mental illness. First intermittently and then permanently she was away from home in private mental hospitals. Robert writes of Bryanston Street as follows:

There was a horribly dark despondency over Bryanston Street that all the children could feel – above all in the living room. Mother used to keep it at bay by lighting the candles on the little black upright Bechstein. After tea she would sit and play and sing: usually Schubert and Schumann. How beautiful she appeared to me then! – so beautiful I was spellbound and scarcely dared speak to her between the songs. Sometimes she cried when she was playing. And I used to look at her in silent amazement, more than a little scandalized that a grown-up could be unhappy. But when I went to her and tried to comfort her and asked her why she was crying, she answered 'Nothing – for no reason.' I understood that perfectly. One could for no reason. Just because she was sad. And why was one sad? The reason could not be put into words. It was a weight – that was all. And mother didn't even know that I understood. She didn't even begin to guess that I dimly understood things had failed her.[5]

His earliest memories were purely happy:

When Phil and I were very small she used to come and say goodnight and sit on our beds, each in turn. I can see her now – dressed for a dinner party with her beautiful haughty head held up and a great string of pearls round her neck. She had the loveliest ears and her expression was entirely contrary to the carriage of her head – for it changed every moment. She was full of sensibility and fire, you know: a rare creature like a bonfire in the snow on a black night. Her love for us quite distracted her and we both loved her fanatically. We used to get one on each side of her and put our arms round her neck and refuse to let her go. She excited a peculiar devotion in us – we would have liked to go out and kill bears for her. She was at once a sort of mascot and a princess to us.[6]

But later her love became frightening:

She used to rush up to the bedroom after dinner and clasp me in her arms because she thought the house was going to catch on fire that night. Did she do anything about that fire? I think not... And all I could do was to kiss mother till she sat there sighing over and over again. Then, quite suddenly, she would become gay and practical (as they call it) and bid me goodnight: a beautiful creature and, as I now see, a girl again.[7]

And she was unpredictable. He recalls that 'she would snatch us to her and then accuse us of "whispering against her" and we would be despatched upstairs in disgrace. So that just when one seemed closest to her one would be shocked and chilled.'[8]

Another letter gives a painful glimpse of the final breakdown, which apparently occurred at Lawford in 1909 when Robert was fifteen:

Ophelia – she was so like Ophelia to the end – there was always something virginal about her – her eyes gazed so often on what we didn't see – rose from the dining table in the room next door to where I write – took out her ear-rings, dropped them on the red carpet and turned her heel upon them. Yes, these things sink in – not *that* scene – I got over that – indeed I hardly appreciated its full significance at the time (though I was only to see her once again: in a bare room full of sunlight – without a fire though it was a coldish day – and with a nurse passing by every few moments – that same nurse who said to me in the passage – confound her! What did I care? – 'Don't let her get behind you! Don't let her get behind you!') No, what sinks in is not her but *him*.[9]

– 'him' being Robert's unhappy father, whom in this letter he compares to an aged Hamlet, 'shrunk and wizen, with a huge nose and beautiful eyes, now for the most part apathetic and expressionless'.

In 1922 when he was in Japan Robert wrote a piece for the *Japan Advertiser* which gives a picture of Bryanston Street while his mother was still living there.[10]

Bed-time was always later on Christmas Eve. One discussed endlessly with Brother Phil in the darkness as to whether Father Christmas was Daddy or not. And one never knew. How he must have yawned, poor man, sitting up till one in the morning to make sure that the little demons were asleep ere he stole in – one heard the click of the electric light in one's sleep – to tie a stocking full of good things to the bed-post. And always, sure enough, Brother Phil would drop off just when one was getting a bit weary and when whispered conversation was a real comfort in the darkness after the light disappeared from beneath the day-nursery door as Authority vanished bed-ward.

The carols were doubly welcome then: first they kept one awake and secondly they made one feel safe in that thick darkness from the Bat-headed Thing that abode, so Nurse averred, up in the left hand corner of the room, and from the crocodiles whose cold snouts protruded from beneath the ship itself in which one went sailing to the Land of Dreams. The carols were of all sorts. Sometimes there sounded a raucous and starved crying ascendant in a quavering troll from the throat of a pinched old man who, in a tail coat buttoned at the chin, wearing cuffs over his hands and a crushed bowler battened down over his ears, perambulated the streets all autumntide to croak his few stanzas and halt beside the gas-lamp to turn up a filmy eye toward half-horrified children peeping from warm nursery windows. Or maybe it would be a tipsy woman much disapproved of by Nurse, a figure of secret romance and commiseration to myself, much put [out] at not being permitted to minister to her needs. "She'll only drink it!" "Why not, Nursie, if she likes it?" For, always an anarchist, I didn't see why people shouldn't be allowed to be happy in their own way – a thing not seldom forbidden me myself.

On Christmas Eve, however, such untuneful wayfarers were few. We were visited by rival choirs and I could hear Emily above knock on Cook's bedroom wall. "Mrs Bloom, it's St Mary's come. I recognise the tenor." "All right, my girl, let me sleep in peace: you and your tenors. Who's your latest – Caruso?" "No, but – ah, there's 'Hark the Herald Angels Sing'!" Cook's window would go up with a bang. The choir would bellow, the ladies would coo and both choir and ladies would fall suddenly still as the vestryman pounded on the door and father's voice would be heard below, "Confound them! I can't go down in the cold. It'll be the death of me. They'll have to catch it from the window. Hi! You! There's half a crown. Goodnight." The coin would ring on the ground. I could hear from his voice that father hated them. So did I. They were odious – both choirs. One came and bellowed and screamed in sore-throated vociferation; the other sang neatly, elaborately, and wore surplices: both levied discreet blackmail upon respectability – for even agnostics, like my father, prefer peace to a reputation for stinginess – and both were utterly lacking, not only in reverence, but in romance. Carols and carol singing should be poetical or nothing.

One group there was, however – I would keep awake for them night after night and even on the supreme night itself they took precedence of Father Christmas. These were itinerant minstrels – a very old man with a very white beard (like God I thought him) who used to sit on a folding stool in a heavy brown Inverness cape playing a harp; another man, I took to be the first's brother, who played a harmonium with his eyes shut; a small boy; a tenor with a barrel-like chest and a knitted grey comforter cast about his throat and, last, and best, sometimes a masked woman dressed in black whose voice in retrospect has even now power to thrill, for I thought it even more beautiful than my mother's, only not so pure. Twenty years and more after, when I read Wilhelm Meister for the first time, that group flashed upon my mind.

In bed, however, on Christmas Eve I could not see them. Bitter experience in daring – despite the crocodiles and the horror of skinny-fingered capture by Nurse – had taught me that I could never get a proper view of them from the night-nursery window. I had only seen them twice, when they played three doors away to the annoyance of my parents then giving a dinner party and to my joy who, in my night-dress, was thus enabled to sneak past the busy servants, open the hall door and take a long and longing look ere I was captured and should have suffered sadly but for the intervention of a guest on my behalf. Carols! Carols! Shall I ever hear their like again? Yes, she is in my pantheon now, that masked woman. Usually she sang airs from Italian operas – not vivacious, florid airs, but airs long and sad and her voice seemed to me to have a great melancholy and loneliness in it as if she were singing at the blank faces of the houses and yearned to see some expected figure emerge onto one of the little balconies and raise a hand in greeting. But on Christmas Eve – I only heard her one Christmas Eve, one only – she sang carols and I, in my cot, lay wondering whether it might not be possible to run away with her, to become her child and make her happy.

We obtain another glimpse of Robert's early life from a piece he wrote for a Japanese tree-planting society:[11]

When I was a small boy at school my father lived in London, and so I passed my days between the school window looking out upon a windy field and the harbour of Harwich, darkened by the perpetual East coast bluster, and the day-nursery window looking out upon grimy leads where those cantankerous vulgarians, the London sparrows, were for ever fighting. I did not see the country save one day in the year. Then we small boys were driven in a brake through twisting lanes to a neighbouring estate, the property of the father of one of my schoolfellows, where we picnicked in the spinney. What a revelation to the little boy in his harsh tweed suit and stiff collar that spinney was! When we arrived we lunched. Afterward some played rounders and others went in search of wood to make a gypsy fire to boil the kettle on. But as for me, I busied myself how most rapidly I could get lost. I always wished to be lost at school, for then I should be alone – free to lie on my back and look at the great clouds swimming up the sky, free to watch the ants streaming over a bald white stone, free above all and beyond all to gaze as I gaze today at a branch silhouetted against the transparent peaceful blue of the sky, a sight in which the perfection of what is little and the perfection of what is great are beheld together and give rise to a reverie such as transcends the power of words.

Lose myself I did and made for one corner of the wood where – shall I ever forget it? – a few wild cherries were in blossom. Beautiful wands! Delicate blossoms! So white you were that, though I was only twelve years old and had never heard of Japan and still

less of her poems, I remember I thought, surely these are butter-
flies which have alighted upon those branches! I lay down in the
little winding path, getting damp and dirty I remember, and gazed
upward till my little self passed away and there seemed nothing in
the world but these ethereal blossoms poised against the translucent sky.

If, in his wife's absence, Bowyer Nichols could have closed ranks
with his children, it would, of course, have been better both for them
and for him; but that was probably a psychological impossibility. He
was educated at Winchester and Jowett's Balliol, the best preparation
for an able and conscientious public servant, but not, perhaps, for a
spontaneously affectionate parent. At any rate:

> If there's one thing that was discouraged in my youth it was any dis-
> play of affection. Really I don't know how the tradition grew up
> but Phil, Irene, Anne and I considered any such display very 'soft'.
> I think this must have been due largely to father. Later there was a
> great deal of derision at the expense of affection in such writers as
> GBS and S. Butler. But the crucial things had happened before. You
> know what father's like. One simply didn't know how to get near
> him. His irony too was devastating to youthful enthusiasms.[12]

Although Robert's father was unable either to give or to receive
warm affection, it is clear that in his youth Robert both loved him and
had boundless admiration for him. The older Nichols was a prominent
figure at Oxford in the 1880s. He figures in one of the Balliol Rhymes:

> Mark the subtle smile that trickles
> Down the Sphinx-like face of N-CH-LS.
> My hair is black, my china blue,
> My Botticellis fifty-two.*

From an early age he must have had a flair for art history and art

---

*The author of this rhyme was Nichols's lifelong friend J. W. Mackail. There is also a
slightly tarter rhyme by Spring-Rice:

> My love is redder than the rose is,
> My love is longer than my nose is,
> Love is death but what am I?
> Wan white lilies fade and die,
> Cultured roses have their prickles
> And my name, alas, is Nichols.

criticism, and for many years he was art critic for the *Westminster Gazette* and a trustee of the Wallace Collection. He was himself a talented though not a prolific artist and used to communicate with his daughter Anne, the child to whom he was probably closest, by sending her pictures portraying himself and whatever was engaging his interest at the time in the guise of the adventures of an aristocratic golliwog. And most significant for Robert, he was a poet. At Oxford he carried off the prize for poetry, the keenly contested Newdigate Prize, with a flawless Augustan composition in heroic couplets on the subject of Inez de Castro. After his death this and a collection of lyrics, epigrams and sonnets by him was published by his friend J. W. Mackail.[13] His daughter Anne used to say that it piqued him to be remembered chiefly for his epigram 'On the Toilet-Table of Queen Marie-Antoinette at South Kensington Museum' but perhaps it was revealing. It runs:

> This was her table, these her trim outspread
> Brushes and trays and porcelain cups for red;
> Here sate she, while her women tired and curled
> The most unhappy head in all the world.

Of uncles and aunts the one most interested in Robert was his father's sister Irene, known as Ena. Robert corresponded with her and found her loveable.[14] She was also inspiring. A foundation member of Lady Margaret Hall, she was therefore among the first women to enter the University of Oxford. She obtained Honours in English Literature, a special examination in that subject having been prepared to spare her sex the coarseness of Aristophanes and the unwomanliness of Natural Science. But Miss Nichols had no inclination to a conventional womanly life. She had a passion for freedom and adventure, injustice aroused in her a white heat of anger, and her sympathy with the oppressed led her to travel in Poland and Russia and learn the local languages. She also learned book-binding. She acquired the rudiments in an Italian workshop and then apprenticed herself to the great T. J. Cobden-Sanderson and became a real artist. She set up a workshop of her own in Millbank Street, but left it on the death of her mother in 1897 and went to keep house for her father in Green Street, off Park Lane. Then in 1906 she threw herself into the cause of women's suffrage. According to E. F. Matherson, from whose memoir[15] this information is taken, 'She had a strong clear intellect, imagination and an unswerving will; but above all, so true and tender a heart, that where her affections had once been given, nothing in the chances and changes of life could alter them.' Just the friend Robert needed after the disappearance of his mother. But unfortunately she caught cold at a suffragette demonstration, it turned to influenza, and she died in January 1907. Robert's father wrote to him:

> You must never forget her, for she loved you all very much, and when she was in great pain she asked me after all of you and what you had been doing – and I think it was you she cared for most of all the four and thought most of your future and your happiness. She praised you always when she could, and was concerned when you came short of what she would wish you to be; and was interested in all that happened to you. You are too young yet to understand all that she was, but you must remember that she was the best friend you have ever had. She was the kindest and the bravest and the cleverest woman I have ever known.[16]

There was another person at this time who might have been expected to play a part in the lives of the children. Their grandfather, Francis Morgan Nichols, continued to live in Green Street until 1915. Robert liked to recall 'his keen blue frosty eyes, his hawk face (preserved in a drawing by Sargent), his beard the colour of Atlantic spray flying on the gale, his strong yet delicate frame, his imperious expression'.[17] But he seems not to have seen much of this patriarch in his later years. When he was leaving for active service in August 1915 and needed £20 to settle his debts he could not get hold of his father in London. He applied to Green Street and, to quote his father's subsequent letter, 'If it hadn't been all rather sad as well as very tiresome I could have laughed to think of the dreadful time you must have had trying vainly to explain to poor dear old grandfather who you were and what you wanted and why, and then waiting in a pestilent hurry till Miss Revill came in. I'm so glad she did and that she was able to get you what you wanted ... But it's a nerve-racking affair at the best to get F. M. N. to understand the simplest things nowadays.'[18] 'F. M. N' by this time was in his ninetieth year and may have succumbed to the family deafness. But one incident in Robert's childhood made a deep impression. When he was a small boy his grandfather, then in his seventies, said to him 'Remember this, my boy, whatever happens the clouds are always beautiful.'[19] Again and again in his poetry Robert celebrates the beauty of clouds. But beyond this,

Grandfather is mysterious. There are different reports about him.

Father tried to make him out a neurasthenic valetudinarian. He told me how his mother's life was 'spoiled' by grandfather insisting on going to live in Shanklin in the Isle of Wight (where I was born) so as 'to be near a doctor who was useful to him' (There's a parallel between me and him) 'and directly she was dead – she who loathed the Isle of Wight – he left the island and never went back.' I said nothing. But it instantly flashed upon me that why he went to live near this doctor may have been because he found life with his wife more supportable when near this doctor. This, of course, is a very unorthodox view. Aunt Nellie (wife of Uncle Walter) said to Irene 'None of the Nichols men are any good.' By which she meant, I think, that they had a Hamletic strain. But the fact remains that my grandfather did extraordinary things and accomplished a very large body of work (incidentally grandfather accomplished much of his biggest – his monumental edition and translation of the *Letters of Erasmus* – when my grandmother was dead). I think he must have been rather a brittle man like myself, a man of ups and down, with a hidden tenacity when it came to writing, but for the rest a man of sudden enthusiams but not much staying power, a lack due perhaps to the play of a sceptical intellect. The point is that scepticism was likely to be his weakness, not an excess of sensibility.

As for my grandmother, I cannot remember her. All I know is that I have never looked at a photograph of that dark, plumpish, liquid-eyed woman without a feeling of repulsion. This feeling of repulsion, quite instinctive and going back as far as I can remember, is, I think Henry will agree, a very singular phenomenon. I am sure it was she who transmitted to father the disease of hyper-sensitivity. That and the scepticism from grandfather destroyed him. Fortunately I inherited a furious élan and fits of cockney pluck from mother (she was a very plucky woman, father once said) which have to some extent offset this morbid sensitivity. I imagine grandmother as tremendously the mother of a family – rather Madame Tolstoyish. My theory is furthered by an incident I think I once told you of grandfather taking me to his sister Amy and how he said to her 'Amy, I married the wrong woman', and how she got angry and said 'Nonsense, Francis, you have no right to say that – above all when she's dead. She did very well by you, etc., etc.' But I fancy Francis had been violently in love with somebody else. The more I think of old Francis the more I love him.[20]

Francis Morgan was the third son of John Gough Nichols, and took no part in the printing business. J. W. Mackail wrote of him: 'His health was delicate and his interests lay in history, literature and archaeology. He was a Fellow of Wadham College, Oxford, until he vacated his Fellowship by his marriage, in 1857, to Mary Buchanan. Soon afterwards he purchased Lawford Hall in Essex.'[21] Robert adds some more colourful details. 'He tramped Spain in the forties, fought bandits, is said to have killed his bull in the bull-ring.'[22] Besides the Lawford estate he acquired property in London and built Nichols Square, E2, not a fashionable district but for the mid-nineteenth century an enlightened piece of development. The houses were built on the same plan as a new farmhouse at Lawford, the gardens were planted with trees, and it was a great sorrow to the inhabitants when it was all swept away by the new brooms of the 1960s planners.

What, however, may have been particularly significant for Robert and his brother and sisters was what he calls his grandfather's scepticism. The eighteenth-century John Nichols had been a man of cheerful Christian faith. In his old age he celebrated each birthday by composing a hymn to God thanking him for another happy year of life. The Puseys were a devout family and Catherine's two sisters, Mrs Fothergill and Lady Braye, both became Catholics. But Bowyer Nichols inherited his father's atheism and made it the dominant ethos of the household. 'You cannot conceive what it is like', Robert wrote in 1931, 'to be brought up believing in nothing whatever, and not only have to create one's articles of faith but faith itself as one goes.'[23] Philip, Irene and Anne were content or even proud to follow in the patrilinear scepticism; Robert always chafed against it, much of his writing is strongly religious, and though he could never commit himself to joining any Christian denomination, an inability either to take Christianity or to leave it alone is a recurrent theme in his work.

2
Pre-Oxford Poetry and Schooling

The earliest of Robert's poems to survive is in a letter to his mother dated 11 June 1905, when he was eleven years old. He was not precocious and the poem is no masterpiece, but it foreshadows what was to come in several ways: Robert instinctively attempts a complicated rhyming system; he is already fascinated by matters that pertain to religion; and his view of love is shaded with ambiguity and mistrust.

Irene

I

Irene! Dear Irene!
How yet I loved thee!
But now thou art gone above;
Where everything is joy and everything is love.
But yet I'm sure you did love me,
My darling and my dove.

II

Irene! Sweet Irene!
I know you *do* love me
But after years, do you yet love me still?
And if you do, what wish can I fulfil?
So let my humble tries yet please thy will.
But yet I'm sure thou does *not* love me
Yet my love for thee can no man chill.

III

Irene! Ever sweet Irene!
To thee I bow my knee
And do thou grant for ever,
That I may rest with thee, –
And so to leave thee never
Though youth and power do flee –

> So we will love, and death can only sever
> Us two, loving yet for all eternity.

His notes on it are even more revealing than the poem itself.

> You can tear it up if you think it's rot but I would rather you did
> not as I am rather proud of it because I am a spring poet and not a
> summer one. It is nothing to do with my sister or Aunt Ena. I
> chose the name because I could rhime [*sic*] with it and because it is
> pretty. It is a kind of 'Dirge', you know. I am afraid the metre is
> wrong but it does not matter so much in a song does it?

The cavalier attitude betrayed in the last sentence remained with him
and drew a remonstration from his friend Eddie Marsh many years
later:

> The impression I get is that you put down your thoughts in the
> first words that occur to you. If the words fit the metre you are
> writing in, well and good – very often they do, and then the effect
> is fine. If they don't, you can't be bothered to mould them into
> form and pattern.[1]

Robert had been sent to school some years before this. His mother,
he recalled,

> was very upset when they packed me off to school among a lot of
> savages at the age of eight. I was, I can see now, quite unfitted for
> such treatment. If this had to be – and I was supposed to be
> becoming too rumbustious for home (what eldest small boy of 8 is
> not rumbustious?) – they might at least have given me some 'tips',
> some technique for making something of my new life. Nor is it fair
> to thrash any child of eight as I was repeatedly thrashed at that
> school. And in the case of a child so sensitive and imaginative as I
> was, it is sheer madness. Often indeed I was so unhappy that
> though I did not know what madness was I felt completely irre-
> sponsible. I was so unhappy that I was simply a bundle of anguish,
> sobs and quivering nerves and nothing else. Mother understood
> something of this. Then it was 'poor Katie' and she was kept away
> from me. This was supposed to be good for her.[2]

This was Earleywood School, Ascot, Berkshire. The beatings were
administered by

> the second in command under Miss Sandwich: a big man with a

flushed pimply face. He used to use the most awful canes that twined round one's legs. I can see his face now – and I don't think it was either a good face or what one saw in it when he was caning a small boy was good.[3]

Perhaps his father paid more attention to his sufferings than Robert realised. After a year or so he was removed to Orwell House, Felixstowe, the school from which he made the excursion described in chapter 1. There were only eighteen pupils and he had 'two good years'[4] there under a Dr Paul who set him to read Richard Walter's narrative of Anson's Voyages, a book that should, he thought, he used in preference to Ovid 'between the ages of ten and twelve to excite the heroic imagination and help in the formation of a sound prose style'.[5] It was here that he first experienced the 'impersonal tenderness' which he believed to be at the heart of his best work.

I can remember the birth of it quite clearly. It was born one night of wind and rain at my second preparatory school, Orwell House, Felixstowe. The curtains of the dining room were not drawn (I don't know why, for it was quite late). A lamp was burning on the drugget that covered the big table. The panes of the windows were quite black and golden tears seemed to be running down them. I was not ten years old. I burst into tears because of the sudden mysterious pain of love in my breast, a pain that arose at my sense of the emptiness of the room, its silence, the sound of the blustering of the wind and the sight of these so many golden tears gathering on the pane. It seemed to me that something everlasting was crying to me and that I must give myself to it. But I didn't know how. So I sat with my head on the drugget, with my wet cheek to its queer surface, pressing my kisses against it, and spreading my hands upon it and drawing them across its surface as if this drugget and the table beneath it made up between them a sort of representative of all I wanted to comfort.[6]

Here too the atmosphere permitted the germination of Christian faith:

At twelve years old I had a bout of religiosity – one could not style it religion. I considered myself lonely in the world, and Jesus Christ, who was of a somewhat tearful disposition, as my particular friend. In order to realize his pains more acutely I remember lying awake as long as I could with my arms outstretched and inserted in the iron girders of the bed until sleep supervened. This I remember as the crisis of that phase, a phase which ended abruptly when the headmaster was changed and one less kindly, less comprehending, and less, in the simplest and deepest sense, Christian, took his place.[7]

It is perhaps the abrupt end of this phase which he describes in a gloomy letter he wrote to his friend and doctor, Henry Head, in 1918. Having said: 'I'm done for. I see nothing, I feel nothing, I can record nothing. All is ashes. God has taken away the desire of life from mine eyes,' he continues:

Curious! I knew all this when I was twelve. Suddenly in the midst of a sort of meeting of all the school ... suddenly in the middle of the choral singing I knew it was all nonsense and that you couldn't keep the blackness out or forget it. And I remember I made an excuse and went out and cast myself down by the umbrella stand at the side entrance – we used to put our hockey sticks in the stand but there were none there for it was Christmas term – and cried feebly.[8]

At about this time the Nichols parents launched an in-house magazine called *The Roysterer* which contained poems, articles and pictures contributed mainly though not exclusively by the family. There is a poem by Robert dated January 1908 on the recent earthquake in Messina. He seems to have been much impressed by this calamity since he also wrote a story in which the narrator is the first mate of a ship that went to the rescue of the inhabitants. *The Roysterer*, however, ended with its third number, perhaps because of increasing absences of the editor, Mrs Nichols.[9]

In January 1908 Robert went to Winchester, 'that hellish Winchester' as he later called it.[10] He entered late because his health was poor – he may have been suffering from the start of the tuberculosis which was to be a recurrent handicap in his later life – and he initially failed the entrance examination.[11] There is a glimpse of his Wykehamist life in the sketch of his religious development already cited:

I remember no more religious or pseudo-religious emotions [after the Felixstowe episode] until at a Public School the day of Confirmation approached. Then I recollect undertaking a pretty comprehensive – an only too comprehensive – scheme of religion. I set about confessing my misdemeanours on the understanding that no action would be taken. No action was taken, and the head-master was sympathetic. He asked me what I cared about in life; I promptly replied, "poetry." Thereupon he recited "Shall I compare thee to a summer's day?" So beautifully did he recite it, and so overwhelmed was I at finding one who understood poetry in the sense that I understood it, over whose grave, benign face there ran no shadow of a smile at my enthusiasm, that I burst into tears, and I verily believe that at that moment I might have been converted to any creed whatsoever the good man had cared to propose had he understood how to take advantage of the situation. To this day I cannot think of him without devotion. But when I returned to my House it was not long before I perceived, having bared my breast of its poor misdemeanours to my House-master as I felt bound to do, by way of getting "square" as I called it on all points with life, that I was under surveillance. Today I am persuaded that the surveillance was perhaps the master's duty, for I was then extraordinarily restless and possessed of such a violent passion of hate for my school as I have since never experienced for any institution or person; and it is not altogether impossible that this restlessness and abomination of nearly everything accounted sacred in my House might have proved catching. For I was an astute little beast with my tongue. Confirmation Day came – a farce. First Communion came – another farce. On the evening of that Sunday I tore my white tie off and shred it viciously with scissors and swore undying hate to all I took it to represent. I was a humourless pup. Should I not have known that spiritual enlightenment is not a proper part of the education of English gentlemen, of those youths who are destined, particularly destined in my school, to become the consuls and pro-consuls of the widest and most varied empire, having beneath its control heaven knows how many creeds, the world has ever seen?[12]

In 1925 Winchester asked Robert to write something about 'my beloved A. E. Wilson, the most human person in the place in my time – he let me read in his own library – told me about poetry – was a light to me in dark days.' The school authorities did not like what he sent them and refused to print it, saying it would not be understood by 'the average man'.[13] These memories of kindness, however, may explain why many years later Robert was prepared to believe Winchester might suit his nephew Francis; at least he wrote to Phil with advice on how to persuade Francis to go there rather than to Eton, the earlier Francis Nichols's school.[14] Robert's own Winchester career, however, ended abruptly after only two years. He made an unauthorised trip to London and telegraphed his housemaster to say he had gone to visit his doctor. The school telegraphed back to say he need not bother to return.

The remainder of his preparation for Oxford was accomplished by crammers. In the autumn 1910 he was in Westgate, Kent. He later recalled the crammer there as a 'horrid old brute. Stupid, bigoted. And it is just this type who take on themselves to handle backward and difficult boys: hardly a boy there who wasn't a psychological "case".'[15] Nevertheless 'I have got a room', he told his mother, 'from the window of which by looking sideways I can see the sea, the great unquiet sea breaking on the cliff and tossing its spray onto the road. The sea is ever with me, wherever I go I hear its murmuring and at night in bed with half a gale blowing outside (there is always half a gale here in winter I am told) I can distinguish the cries of the gulls amid the subdued crash and roar of the water.'[16]

He loved the sea,[17] and while he was at Westgate he met Harold 'Boy' Gough who became a close friend, and who was killed early in the war. 'What are boys' friendships made of? I don't know. I remember we discussed motorcars. We pulled other people's characters to pieces, Boy and I. It was settled I should become a great writer. Boy was to live on a bog in Ireland.'[18] In later years his thought often returned to Gough. 'He, at least,' he said in a spell of loneliness and melancholy in 1927, 'would have remained on such terms as to display the sort of animal joy which is what I best understand between friends of an age. He had a wild heart too – hence his overfondness for the bottle. ... There was, thank God, nothing decorous about him.'[19]

In October 1911 Robert exchanged the disagreeable Mr Burge of Westgate for the gentler Rector of Uffington in Lincolnshire, near Stamford. Robert liked this place where he had one fellow crammee, the orphaned Count Zobrowski, and where he did eventually acquire enough Latin and Greek to get into Oxford. Throughout his cramming years, however, he gave more time to modern literature and to his own writing and than to meeting the University's entrance requirements. In August 1912 at Lawford he wrote to his mother 'I have not written anything at all lately – growing out of it perhaps',[20] but of course he never grew out of it, and this must have been just an intermission in what was on the whole a very productive time.

In spite of the feelings of revulsion that had followed his Confirmation two years later Robert decided

> I would give religion another chance. I went to Communion. One day a young Jew asserted to my face that I went because certain handsome girls knelt beside me at the rails. I knocked him down. But afterwards I recalled the beating of my heart as I approached the altar and the fact that I certainly did feel more changed in heart, crammer's dull scamp that I was, when particular girls were present. From that day to this I have never partaken of the Sacrament.[21]

Whatever motivated the temporary conversion, from 1910 onwards religious themes appear in his poetry. He may have encouraged to tackle them by Francis Thompson. In 1912 he wrote a poem entitled 'To Francis Thompson' which reads like a sincere tribute:

> As by a brook I walked – a brooding boy –
>   An iridescent thing – green, gold and blue,
> Dashed wildly past, taking my heart with joy,
>   Making me see all earth afresh; so you
> Recall that moment's trance and give me a new; –
>   The kingfisher returns – in verse of thine
> A new world opens as my eyes pursue
>   The intense speed and splendour of your line.

He acknowledged the influence of Thompson on another poem he wrote in 1912, 'Before Jerusalem', which adopts the viewpoint of the Crusaders, and which he included in his first published volume, *Invocation: War Poems and Others* in 1915.

Robert's poetry, however, was never predominantly religious. In 1911–13 he was engaged on several ambitious projects. First, there are fragments of a poetic drama on the ill-starred love of (as he chose to spell them) Tristran and Isolt. This was started in 1911. In 1912 he was at work on another drama which was to deal with Prometheus, always a figure that fascinated him; and that autumn he began a series of poems about Danaë. Winchester had failed to give him the ability to enjoy the poets of Greece and Rome in their original tongues. 'Greek and Roman literature', he says, 'had perished for us in the Public Schools which purported to teach them.'[22] He tended to approach ancient subjects through English Romantic writers like Shelley and Keats. But his treatment of the Danaë legend, at least, is quite distinctive. It consists of short lyrical bursts of direct speech, without connecting narrative, starting with the noisy building of the brazen tower in which Danaë was imprisoned, and when it was published in 1917 in *Ardours and Endurances The Times Literary Supplement*[23] and *The Athenaeum*[24] singled it out as the finest of the pre-war poems.

Another series of short poems belonging to 1912 is quite different in character. Entitled 'Tragic Rimes' it invokes a more vernacular style to deal with jealousy, betrayal and the darker side of love. These poems, which were never published, foreshadow Robert's later fascination by tragi-comedy.

It is clear from the surviving work of his pre-Oxford years not only that Robert felt a strong call to write lyric poetry, but also that he desired to stand in the tradition of the English poets. He admired the Romantics, but he took his models more from the sixteenth and seventeenth centuries. The *Tristran* fragments occasionally seem to echo Marvell. In April 1913 he wrote to Robert Ross, well known as a friend of Oscar Wilde but also a friend of Bowyer Nichols, and sent him three sonnets. 'I wish they wouldn't be so Shakespearean,' he said. 'But the first sonnets I read were Shakespeare's and I've never recovered.' The first goes:

> O love of mine, O flower that never fadest,
> Blossoming broadly in my happy heart,
> Grow yet more beautiful as time invadeth
> And withers other flowers that now have part,
> Bearing their pale foils to thy royal colour;
> For though they're sweet they do but contrast thee
> And thou shalt deepen ev'n as they grow duller
> Till with thy blossom my heart filled be!
> So richen, rose of mine, and Time confute
> By waxing till all men thy wonder see
> And they shall mind thee when my mouth is mute
> And graft thy splendour to their memory.
> > So thou shalt glow amid the gathering gloom
> > And not fall even at thy master's doom.

These were published by Margaret Ross in *Robert Ross, Friend of Friends*[25] and there are several others in his unpublished papers to show how easily the style came to him.[26]

He had the same facility for imitating Milton. The following lines

(dated 9 July 1918 and published in *The New Witness*) have the anno-
tation 'Suggested by a dream following a reading of Milton':

> Thus Satan spake 'To hell with utmost speed!'
> And at the speed th' Infernal driving down
> Shot like a fireball from the lowering Zenith
> On close-shut wings. Fiercely the cleft air blazed
> About him swooping, while upon his brow
> The sullen jewel fanned by tempest flight
> Burned furious, flashing twin wakes of fire.
> So dropped he in the flicker of an eye
> Height beyond reckoning, the while the stars
> Like cressets volleyed by him, till at last
> Ten thousand times a thousand leagues below
> Like to a pool of pitch that seething flames
> Hell's fiery nest he spied; upon spread wings
> Gyrating suddenly then stooped yet swung
> Somewhat aside, heeling a giant wing,
> Baffled and partly blinded by hell's glare,
> Though swooping yet, till in the growing roar
> Of winding flame and torrid exhalation
> Pierced by the never-ending ringing cry
> Of those who turn terribly fire-tormented,
> He vanished utterly and in the night
> The plying flames gushed up somewhat more fell.

Robert also experimented in story-writing and the young novelist
Sheila Kaye-Smith thought his prose even more promising than his
poetry. Just before he went up to Oxford he had a correspondence with
her to which she refers in *All the Books of My Life*.[27] It is interesting
both in itself and as the first of several literary friendships with women
which elicited from them outspoken and lively letters.

Sheila Kaye-Smith was only four years older than Robert but she got
off to a flying start as a novelist and had published three novels by the
age of twenty-two. Robert's attention was caught by the third of them,
Spell Land, and he initiated the correspondence by writing her a fan
letter dated 13 June 1912.[28] At this period of her life, she tells us in her
autobiography *Three Ways Home*,[29] she was liberating herself from a
strict Evangelical upbringing in the country. She put up at a boarding
house in Kensington and looked out for literary friends: 'I was grateful
for the smallest poet or novelist.'[30] A pleasant evening with a Catholic

writer, Alice Meynell, had the surprising effect of making her discard her Christian beliefs 'like unfashionable clothing'* and plunge into Nietzsche. She had found that 'one has only to want a thing badly enough for it to happen sooner or later. I had wanted literary success, and it had come to me, largely through my own efforts. I wanted love-affairs, and they came to me – I will not say largely through my own efforts, but certainly not without some enterprise on my part.'[31] A letter to Robert which lacks its first page and hence even the most imperfect indication of its date[32] contains what may have been siren singing:

> I've just come back from a walk after my own heart, which means, I'm afraid, that my clothes are ruined, as in the course of many other adventures I alighted in several feet of mud. I ought to give you a pen portrait of myself on my homeward journey – a debauched looking female, with her hair half down, her hat on one side, her skirts held up to her knees, no stockings, and shoes too deeply imbedded in filth for anyone to do more than guess their colour.

Robert must have sent her specimens of his writing since on 1 July she writes:

> My dear boy,
>   Forgive this grandmotherly form of address, but as a matter of fact you have left me rather at a loss what to call you. It can't be Mr Nichols, and the best people are never called Robert – all the Roberts I know take refuge in Robin or Bob or Bert. You aren't Bert, are you? – I could never write to Bert.
>   I have been reading your work with the greatest interest, and I am going to say exactly what I think. First, I think that for your age your powers are most unusual. ... You have thought, and you have thought originally, and my only advice on this is to go on thinking – and keep green. That is such a possible and happy combination, you know. With regard to the feeling part, I should say you had come as near real feeling as anyone can at 18 – the years between us diminish when I talk like this, don't they?

She goes on to some detailed (and very judicious) criticism of his poems:

---

*The alienation from Christianity, however, was not permanent; in 1918 she returned to the Church of England, and in 1929 she and her husband became Catholics.

'The Wife' you hardly need me to tell you is simply *soaked* in Masefield, but it is very good all the same, though here and there one wishes you had stopped to choose your words more carefully. … I like the 'Tragic Rimes', but to this again I must apply the criticism about the choice of words. You have a certain carelessness both in their choice and in their arrangement which often spoils a good phrase or a good verse. *Don't* please say "I sit the window under" or "the sadness that me throngs." These inversions can always be avoided after some thought. In 'Wedded' too, "wed-bed" is a *wicked* word. I like 'Mad Sharon' the best of these poems.

Robert did not take her advice on these points, but he dedicated the series to her.

In her next letter, dated 12 July, she selects Malise as the name by which to address Robert and urges him to persevere with a novel he had started, *Sidney Paxman*. This deals with the unpleasant experiences at school and the clumsy first attempts at courtship of a character modelled on the author. She also has some more personal advice:

Of course you pose, my dear Malise – why ever not? One would not more dream of going without a pose than without one's clothes. One's real self was never meant for the public gaze, and we can cover it either with reticence or with a pose. Reticence is a dull game, and works more harm in us, I believe, than the other. So pose. But pose *consciously*. Check all tendencies to unconscious posing, or when the great occasion comes which you must face stark, you will be unable to strip off the pose, and so will lose part of your experience.

In the next six weeks they exchanged photographs and talked about sin, religion, feminism and their emotions. Robert was 'at loggerheads with his surroundings', but eager to exchange sexual experiences. She replies:

When did I fall in love? Well, sometimes I have my doubts as to whether I've ever been in love at all. If love's an affair of the senses merely, then I have – if it's an affair of the soul, then I have too – but if it's an ideal blending of both in one glorious dream, then I haven't ever. I've often thought myself in love, I've even shivered on the brink of marriage, but nothing has ever touched my dream…

Fancy you waiting till 15 when you fell in love. I should have
expected it to take you earlier. I started at 15, but always looked
on myself as backward. No, I will not tell you the second one – it
hurt so much that later and more violent attacks have been pain-
less in comparison. I remember now that over the page I told you
I had never been in love. Well, you must reconcile the two statements – if you can.[33]

Eventually they arranged a meeting and Robert, Sheila Kaye-Smith
recalls,[34] thought that 'our meeting would be more interesting if we
were in love. This was rather more difficult to arrange at short notice,
but by no means beyond the powers of either of us.' The romance, she
says, 'lasted about a week, but my broken heart was still painful a year
afterwards.' *All the Books of My Life* contains no further details, but
Three Ways Home tells us:

> Now though I still lived at home, I was definitely leading my own
> life. I had a number of friends, male and female, whom my parents
> had never met ... It must therefore have been a tremendous shock
> to them when one of my affairs burst, as it were, all over them,
> and they were suddenly brought up against a completely
> unknown young man threatening incoherently their daughter's
> life.
> I shall never forget how splendidly they rose to the occasion; in
> fact I cannot help thinking that my father got a certain amount of
> kick out of it. We were staying in an hotel, and I can still see him
> trotting round the winter garden to arrange just where I should
> take cover if my swain should arrive blazing away with his
> revolver – which of course he never did, contenting himself with
> fuliginous letters.[35]

Robert is not mentioned by name, and there is no reason to associate
him with this episode except that a revolver features in the dénouement
of his later romantic attachment to Nancy Cunard.

In December she went to nurse a friend in Switzerland, but the correspondence seems to be resumed in April 1913 when her new novel *The
Isle of Thorns* has appeared.

Robert did not like it as much as *Spell Land* and his criticisms so
incensed her that he thought it best to send her some books and ciga-
rettes. They restored peace, but not the warmth of the previous
summer, and the lives of both correspondents entered on new phases,

Robert going up to Oxford and Sheila Kaye-Smith coming under the influence of W. L. George. They did not meet again until the 1930s when both were married and living not far apart. 'His greeting', she says, 'after twenty years sent a chill down my spine. "Hullo, Sheila! So we meet again. *I've still got all your letters.*" '[36]

3
Oxford 1913–14

Robert went up to Oxford in October 1913 when he was twenty. Unlike his younger brother Phil, who also went up that year but followed their father to Balliol, Robert went to Trinity, a college lying next to Balliol geographically but some distance away in its traditions: it was easier-going, less high-minded, a place at which the sons of squires and intending clergyman might feel at home. Ronald Knox was chaplain-fellow there when Robert entered.

Among friends he made at Oxford and retained afterwards were two other poets, T. W. Earp, son of a Yorkshire businessman, and Evan Morgan, later Lord Tredegar, and the composer Philip Heseltine, better known as Peter Warlock. After Heseltine's death his biographer Cecil Gray asked Robert to put down his recollections of Heseltine at Oxford, and they supply incidentally a picture of himself at that time.[1]

It was 'Jiggers'* – let me so style him – who first informed me of Philip Heseltine's existence. Jiggers and I were both in our first Oxford term in 1913. We had been talking motor bicycles, Jiggers's favourite and indeed sole topic, when, as he rose – some loose-limbed yards of him – to leave my gloomy digs, he said, "There's a chap in the House you ought to know. An extraordinary chap – plays the pianola, the piano and all that. In fact I think he's a what-do-you-call-it – a musician." "I'll go at once," I said, "I've been here some weeks and up to date I haven't met a soul who cares about that sort of thing." "I wouldn't," Jiggers returned, "he might not be in the mood. He's queer. I'd drop a note." "Very well, I'll take a note with me and, if he isn't in, I'll drop it." Jiggers regarded me dubiously. "I wouldn't," he said. But I was not to be dissuaded.

When I entered Mr Heseltine's room the occupier was not at first sight to be descried. He was in fact ensconced behind the sofa and his attitude betokened grief. "Go away," he cried, "I don't

*Possibly a friend from Winchester named Burton: see letter to the Heads dated 10.10.31.

want to see you. Go away." But I was not to be deterred and approached the pianola. "So you compose," I remarked. "Setting Yeats? I admire him very much. I compose poetry myself." (I was intensely proud of the fact.) "It's no good. Go away." "I'm not going away. I've been at this so-called home of learning and art for some weeks and I have yet to meet anybody of my age who practises any of the arts. I have been trying to write poetry at a couple of crammers' for four years now, and have never yet met anyone of my age who tried to create anything. Won't you play it over to me?" "Are you fond of music?" "Next to poetry I like it better than anything in the world." "Have you heard much?" "Quite a lot," (a lie but, secure in a few Queen's Hall wallowings in Tchaikowski, Dvorak and Wagner etc., on winter Sunday afternoons, I didn't know it for a lie.)

He came often to my rooms where, with a bottle of wine, or, as the shillings grew scarcer – for I shared with him the inability to sew up the pockets – bottles of beer before us, we talked on every subject under the sun save such as occupied the majority of our fellows. He had read Havelock Ellis, Carpenter and Otto Weininger. ... From Carpenter we turned to Walt Whitman, whose rhapsodies upon sexual love and nature delighted us. We agreed that the course of honest passion did not admit impediment and we castigated Christianity with a fervour only equalled by our ignorance of all but its unpleasing manifestations as seen in our Public Schools and in parochial affairs. ...

In the afternoons we sometimes took a walk. Philip was not communicative on such walks and the autumn dismalness depressed us ... I gathered that by and large he had not really detested his life and the customs and institutions of his Public School as I had detested mine. ...

January found us both again at Oxford. That term was full of trouble for me. I had got out of leading strings at last and proceeded to indulge in capers unpleasing to the Academic authorities. I did foolish, but not I think reprehensible things, and I did not know why I did them. Such capers Philip regarded with an indulgent eye, and indeed they signified no more than the ebullience of youth and the extravagance due to a passion which had created a condition of anarchy within. Philip's passion appeared to be in an elaborate decline and he sometimes busied himself holding an examination of the state of the patient.

The passions referred to were inspired by women. Robert had fallen in love with a young violinist, Daisy Kennedy, whom he had heard play in the Town Hall, Oxford. She was the first major love of his life, and he always retained a tenderness for her. Inspired by her charms he produced in 1914 a series of poems much more powerful and deeply felt than anything he had done before. But far from reciprocating she was hardly aware of his feelings at all, and his state of mind

> was weekly becoming more frantic. Here, I think, is the place to mention that he [Heseltine] then behaved in very characteristic fashion, for when I was completely out of pocket he furnished me with the wherewithal for the presentation of a luxurious bouquet to the object of my affections at a concert in town which I could not attend. But it was ever so with us throughout our friendship. Whoever happened to be in funds paid, and it did not matter in the least on what the money was to be spent so long as the recipient needed it for a specific purpose. I do not imagine Mrs Grundy would have approved some of the items of expenditure. Far from it. But the mere fact that her shadow fell athwart the scene was but an additional reason for forking out. Aesthetic fastidiousness more often, I fear, prevented us from outraging that shadow than moral scruple. When Philip's passion in due course petered out he did not take to riot as I did when mine suddenly collapsed.

Daisy Kennedy became Mrs Moiseivitsch in June, and Robert first 'felt as if someone had hit me on the head' and then 'cried for five hours without ceasing'.[2] Robert was still grieving for her in autumn 1915, and records a service Heseltine performed when

> I, lying in hospital, prostrated after service in France, was in a bad way, was in fact verging toward the condition of a borderline case. For such had been the exalted desperation of my feelings that I had at the front indulged in a piece of entirely useless bravado that should properly speaking have cost me my life. I told Philip of this when he visited my bedside and declared to him how much I desired to see the face that occasioned so much folly and could, so I fancied, by one small kindly act help deliver me of that folly's consequences. I said "I know it is all over" – indeed I had spoken to the lady less than half a dozen times – "and that she is married and happy and that from the first I have only myself to blame for my troubles, since never by word or look has she displayed any more

interest in me than any beautiful woman does in the least of her admirers. Yet for all that I think I should mend and rapidly would she but stand a moment within the door and say, 'I hope you will get well'. I do not ask her to be sorry for me – I have no right – I desire but this small evidence of goodwill and will not presume upon it, if granted, or ever ask to see her again." Philip immediately volunteered to approach her. He went home and wrote what was probably one of his most elaborate, as it must have been one of his most difficult letters, to a married woman he did not know. In it he craved an interview. The interview was granted. In vain. "I pleaded with her for over an hour," he said, "and she answered always that such a visit would do you more harm than good. I replied that I knew you very well and she hardly knew you at all. But it was all to no purpose. In the end I went down on my knees to her, literally went down on my knees. But she refused." The tears stood in his eyes as he said it. They were my only alleviation. I still believe that had he succeeded in his object the whole course of my life would probably have been different and better, for to my desperation there ensued a state of complete and blank despair in which I no longer cared what I did. Yet she is not to be blamed. She decided for what appeared to her the best course and my consolation is that this incident served to demonstrate how well Philip knew me and understood my state of mind that he should go to such lengths.

Robert's progress in his studies during his year at Oxford was undistinguished. At the end of his second term he failed* both Pass Classical Moderations and an examination known as 'Divers' (Divinity Moderations), since discontinued, which was designed to ensure that graduates of the university had some knowledge of the Christian religion. 'Term ended,' he says in his memoir of Heseltine, 'and I was not encouraged to return to the University till I had mastered the peregrinations of St Paul and could display a working knowledge of certain authors of the antique world: a sentence due, I think, largely to the unfortunate trajectory of a mangel-wurzel which, thrown by me in an undergraduate "rag" during Mr Lloyd George's visit, knocked the episcopal top-hat from the head of His Grace of Winchester.' Rusticated from Oxford he was sent to a clergyman at Warrington for cramming; but this process did not deliver the desired result; at the end of the summer term 'I came

*The tutorial record at Trinity records 'Non Satis'.

up to be "ploughed" again ... [and] I did not expect my father would allow me to return to Oxford [in the autumn] even if the authorities permitted it.'³ He failed papers in Greek Unseen Translation, Logic and Cicero, scraped through on Plato and Tacitus, but had, over the months, achieved a respectable amount of poetry.

In December 1913 he composed 175 lines of a poem on Ceijx and Halcyone, an unfortunate couple in a Greek legend who were turned into kingfishers. At Lawford for the Easter vacation he composed a series of love-lyrics under the title 'The Prince of Ormuz'. By this time Daisy Kennedy was having her effect. In the spring he began, and in July he completed, the three long religious poems entitled 'A Triptych' in *Ardours and Endurances* (1917).⁴ Her marriage in June inspired 'Elegy of Early Sorrow',⁵ a poem which appeared in *Invocation* in 1915. And at the same time he was working on an even more ambitious project, the future *A Faun's Holiday*.

Although he later expressed dissatisfaction with the 'Triptych' it is the most accomplished work of its kind that he achieved in his early years, and one of the poems in it, 'The Tower', appeared in several anthologies, including Harold Monro's *Twentieth Century Poetry* (1929). The first panel, 'The Hill', shows Mary playing on a hilltop with her child and making garlands of daisies and buttercups for him while singing of the future passion:

> When they nail thee to the wood
> Cleft from out the crooked tree.
> Can it be,
> Daisies innocent and good,
> That ye star black Calvary?

'The Tower' is the central panel. At the top of the tower the Last Supper is taking place, but the mood is sombre rather than festive,

> Because their lord, the spearless, was hedged about with spears;
> And in his face the sickness of departure had spread a gloom...

And after the meal we follow Judas as he 'wound down the turret, creeping from floor to floor' and ran out into the city praying 'to stern Jehovah lest his deed make him afraid'. Finally the third panel is called 'The Tree', but we are still following Judas, not Jesus, the tree is that on which Judas hangs himself, and it is Judas, not Jesus that we see

> with tongue-choked mouth that sought to cry
> Bitterly and beseechingly.

An unusual treatment; but the character of Judas had a special fascination for Robert; he recurs to it in later poems and in his play *Guilty Souls*.

The talent of this undergraduate did not go unrecognised. *Oxford Poetry 1914* contained his 'Prophecy', a bitter poem written before he came up (it is dated 1912) that imagines the scene of his death. Much lighter in mood is 'Man's Anacreontic', dated summer 1914 and eventually published in *Ardours and Endurances*. E. B. Osborne, reviewing in the *Morning Post*[6] remarked: 'The Elizabethan fantasy lives again in its riot of radiant images.' Its beginning is almost more Catullan than Elizabethan:

> Kiss! Kiss me and kiss again,
> Making kissing almost pain;
> Close your fingers close on mine,
> And our grappling looks entwine;
> Kiss again, and when that's done
> Blind me with each facing sun
> Of your clear and golden eyes,
> Till my spirit in me dies,
> And endures a long eclipse
> Till rekindled at your lips.

Oxford Poetry 1915 was to contain three poems of this first year, 'The Prince of Ormuz Sings to Badoura', 'The Tower' from 'The Triptych', and 'Midday'. Robert reports that Delius liked this third poem and wished to set it to music;[7] its opening shows how far he had advanced in expressing his feelings for the beauty of nature.

> The earth is still: only the white sun climbs
> Through the green silence of the branching limes,
> Whose linked flowers hanging from the still tree-top
> Distill their soundless syrup drop by drop,
> While 'twixt the starry bracket of their lips
> The black bee, drowsing, floats and drowsing, sips.
> The flimsy leaves hang on the bright, blue air,
> Calm suspended.

These lines were often quoted by his sister Anne, perhaps because the scene is not imaginary. In 1914 Lawford was approached by a magnificent double avenue of old limes which were deeply loved by all members of the Nichols family. In early summer they were thick with flowers and when the house belonged to Phil a special crop of lime honey would be taken from them. The poem continues:

> The earth sleeps. Sleeps the newly-buried clay
> Or doth divinity trouble it to live always?

and the movement of thought is suggested by the fact that the avenue ended at Lawford Church.

'Midday' was later used in *A Faun's Holiday*. This is Robert's first major work, and is dedicated to his brother Phil. It consists of twenty-one poems running in all to about 1,700 lines and forming a connected narrative. The title indicates its content. It describes one full and exhilarating day in the life of a faun, largely through the faun's eyes. Why a faun? Referring in *Seven Men*[8] to the period just before the outbreak of the 1914–18 War, Max Beerbohm observed 'Fauns still had an air of novelty about them. We had not yet tired of them and their hoofs and their slanting eyes and their way of coming suddenly out of the woods to wean quiet English villages from their respectability.' Robert Graves had 'woodland fauns with hairy haunches' in a poem written in 1911.[9] Aldous Huxley contributed 'L'Après-midi d'un Faune' to *Oxford Poetry 1917*. More generally there was current a romantic admiration for paganism. Robert later acknowledged being deeply impressed by Richard Jefferies's autobiography *Story of My Heart*[10] and he may also have been influenced by Kenneth Grahame who introduces Pan into *The Wind in the Willows* (1908) and whose earlier *The Golden Age* is full of classical allusions and starts off with children enjoying an exuberant holiday. Robert had a copy of the 1895 edition of this book. But the main sources of the poem are youthful elation and the European tradition of pastoral poetry which even in English literature goes back to the sixteenth century. *A Faun's Holiday* was published in 1917 as the central section of *Ardours and Endurances* but it was begun in 1914 or even earlier. A prefatory note to it says: 'Roughly planned in Spring, 1914, at Oxford. "Midday in Arcadia" composed July, 1914; "Catch for Spring" adapted from a version of 1912 during the same month: both at Grayshott. Taken up again in February, 1916, continued at the Hut, Bray,* and, after being frequently interrupted, finished on February 18, 1917, at Ilsington.'

The opening poems show the faun waking at sunrise on a mountain,

---

*Frank Schuster's country house. See p. 64.

meeting a vigorous young centaur, and challenging him to a race down the mountainside. By the time the centaur overtakes him the faun is among Arcadian downs, peopled with melodious shepherds. Descending a little further he listens to a young girl singing a song to a pigeon, and then plays Puck-like tricks on the neighbouring villagers. It is their children who sing the 'Catch for Spring'. Next the faun passes through forests to the sea and stampedes a herd of sea-horses. Resting in a wood he listens to a soliloquising philosopher and scares him away by pretending to be a snake. By now it is the heat of the day, and the faun is attracted to a spring from which rises sad music made by naiads:

> Come, ye sorrowful, and steep
> Your tired brows in a nectarous sleep:
> For our kisses lightlier run
> Than the traceries of the sun
> By the lolling water cast
> Up grey precipices vast
> Lifting smooth and warm and steep
> Out of the palely shimmering deep.

Twenty-five years later Robert included this poem in his retrospective book *Such Was My Singing* and in 1917 a reviewer turned to it for an illustration of 'passages of sheer lyrical beauty whose music is not the least of their charms'.[11] It was set to music by Arthur Bliss.

The naiads are answered by a young shepherd-poet with the 'Midday' poem. There follows a riotous feast with satyrs and a dithyramb to Dionysus. Later in the afternoon the faun dances with nymphs to piping by Pan, but then his mood becomes pensive and he remembers a prophecy that the rule of the Olympian gods is coming to an end. This idea is anticipated by Richard Garnett in *The Twilight of the Gods* (1888), a brilliant work of which Robert possessed a first edition; but in his development of it here he departs from the intellectual fashion of the day (though not from the spirit of Virgil's Eclogues) by introducing a mention of

> a new world no more forlorn
> Sith unto it a Babe is born,
> That in a propped, thatched stable lies …

The afternoon closes with the faun listening to a fountain that tells the story of Narcissus. Then the sun sets, a nightingale recalls the gruesome legend of Philomel, a shepherd addresses a hymn to the night, and writer ends on a down beat, laying aside his carefree faun's persona and returning to the duties and sorrows of his poetic calling:

> I wander on, I fade in mist,
> O peopled World, and dost thou list?
> Pipe on, difficult pipes of mine;
> There is something in me divine,
> And it must out.

A Faun's Holiday had a mixed reception from the reviewers of *Ardours and Endurances*. Cecil Roberts in *The Poetry Review* calls it the worst poem in the book and speaks of the author's 'appalling facility in rhyming'. *The Times Literary Supplement* pronounced it 'long and too ambitious'.[12] Edward Shanks, in contrast, said it was 'the most interesting part of the book'[13] and Herbert Read 'the most important'.[14] Charles Scott Moncrieff went further. It is 'a complete Pastoral, untrammelled by any of the associations that have hidden the purity of its predecessors ... I confidently foresee that, in schools that are as yet unfounded, the dim-eyed, ill-walking eugenicised scholars will date this epoch – as I use Morte d'Arthur or Gray's Elegy – with the names of Robert Nichols and "A Faun's Holiday".' Robert recalled this praise with gratitude when Moncrieff died in 1930.[15] The poem found friends also in America, and Gordon Ray Young wrote in the *Los Angeles Times* that it 'will never be forgotten by any lover of poetry, and particularly by anyone who has no aversion to the older poetic ideals, to rhyme, rhythm, quick flashed imagery, pagan gods, nymphs and woodlands'.

These were published comments; Laurence Binyon wrote privately:

> I hope the immediate interest of the war poems won't divert people from the Faun's Holiday, which has entrancing things in it, and is kept up at a glowing pitch all through. It is full of glorious youth: and I think the scheme of it is very happy. If criticising, I should perhaps think the Faun spoke sometimes out of character: but it is a kind of super-Faun you have conceived. And I don't want to criticise. I have enjoyed it all too much.[16]

Binyon was a friend of Robert's father. Robert later spoke of him as having an appearance of 'scared friendliness. He's an odd creature. He has a way of looking at a person before he speaks exactly as if he were doing a sum in mental arithmetic.'[17]

If the slightly sombre reflectiveness of the closing sections of the work seems not quite in keeping with the spontaneous elation with which it opens, that is a consequence of the time over which it was composed and the change brought about in the author by the coming of the war and his war experience. The convalescent Gunner officer of 1917 could not be expected to recapture the joy in his youth and strength of the first year undergraduate of 1914.

4
The Earlier War Poems

In the spring of 1914, Robert says in his memoir of Heseltine, 'I discussed with a New College man, one Roper, destined to fall in battle, the possibility of a visit to Germany the following summer with a view to gaining some insight into the latest developments of the German stage. (In those days the possibility of a National Theatre was seriously considered in the country of Shakespeare.)'* Robert may have been interested in Germany not only for its theatre but because he had fallen under the spell of Nietzsche. In June (when pining for Daisy Kennedy) he composed a long brooding meditation on human suffering, part of which, 'Chant Predictive of Tomorrow's Burden', appears in *Invocation* (1915). It mixed Christian themes with pagan themes which betray a Nietzschean origin. There are references to 'The Delphian' and Dionysus and the poem has a note 'I had intended to proceed to a glorification of Fortitude attained through pain.'

But the visit did not take place. Robert met Heseltine in Oxford in June when he came up for his unsuccessful second attempt at his examinations, and says:

> Our spirits were low. We walked out to a neighbouring hill and
> leaned upon a gate. We could not know how few of the under-
> graduates then in residence would ever return to Oxford, but we
> certainly felt that this was the end of an interlude for us since he
> was due to stay up and I was only too probably to be sent to
> France for an unknown period in order to acquire the language.
> We did not talk much but watched the light lessening upon the
> fields. At length he spoke of art and nature as perpetual refuges ...
> During the summer vacation we kept in touch and the outbreak
> of war occasioned an exchange of violently phrased epistles, I
> being indignant at this barbarous break-up of a so-called Christ-
> ian Europe and he furious at the public prints which, then as now,
> grotesquely ignorant on the subject of Nietzsche's personal history

*Robert was still trying to collect support for a national theatre in 1942 (see chapter 19).

and published works, ascribed to the German-Pole the philosophic responsibility for the conflict.*

The flaring up of the European war out of nothing filled everyone
who read the newspapers with appalled incredulity, but Robert's reference to a Christian Europe may seem surprising in view of his recent
conversion to paganism. What he felt, however, can be gathered from a
frantic apostrophe to Europe he wrote after the war to explain the
origin of *Guilty Souls*: 'O Europe, Europe, who didst know Greece; for
whom the death of an Eastern beggar engendered awhile the greatest
moral force in history, binding the nations together so that they formed
one vast cathedral, each class in its place in the mass of living stone, lift-
ing its pinnacles like hands outstretched from darkness towards God
…'[1] The custom Robert's father and grandfather had of spending long
periods in Italy, and his own confidence he would feel at home in
France and Germany, must also have contributed to his conception of
pre-war Europe as a fundamentally united Christendom.

That summer, he recalled, 'I, who had never been good at sports,
learned to ride and satisfied the R.A. Major (retired) at Grayshott with
[whom] I was then staying as Paying Guest. … It was, I remember, a
very hot summer. The Major was friends with a horse dealer. I ended
by taking his biggest horse over quite respectable jumps.'[2]

The memoir of Heseltine continues:

Toward the end of September Philip and I met again. We stood,
I remember, awhile on Westminster Bridge, just below Big Ben,
to gaze up-river at a quince-coloured moon, slightly veiled by a
tawny skein of vapour, sinking its round head in deeps of fulig-
inous cloud. A curious calm overhung us. I had applied for a
commission and, having a far sharper imaginative notion of
what modern war was like than most of my contemporaries, did
not expect to survive and had already accomplished one half of
that act of renunciation which was to be completed, in so far as
in me lay, almost exactly a year later … Nothing for me, as for
myriads of others, has ever been quite the same since that
autumn.

He volunteered in September among the First Hundred Thousand –

*Robert may have shared Heseltine's opinion in 1914; in 1922 he was less under the spell
of Nietzsche and did assign to him part of the blame for the growth of Prussianism (article
of 13.12.22 in the *Japan Advertiser*).

conscription was not introduced until 1916. He listed his reasons as follows:

1 Honour as regards Belgium (this was the biggest influence).
2 We were all guilty but Germany was guiltiest.
3 Even, say England were wrong, ... still there was the general idea of England and what she stood for. You see I clearly envisaged, which I don't think my contemporaries faced or face even now, the possibility of England's heavy defeat. Germans in England! Germans in Westminster dictating to us. Immense indemnities beside which that of France in '70 would be nothing. An enslaved generation.[3]

He had some difficulty in being passed as fit. His major thought he would not be up to marching, but helped him to obtain a commission as a Horse Gunner. He remained in England training throughout his first year of service. Letters show him at Grayshott, near Haslemere, and later at Christchurch in Hampshire. His men were mostly articulate cockneys.[4] In his Preface to *Guilty Souls* he says:

That year of training is the happiest I have so far experienced. I had everything (save one) the heart could possibly desire – the sky over me, beautiful horses, loyal companions in the men, an officer whom I intensely admired as my major, a definite and, in its way, noble creed – for I never thought of killing: if ever I thought of the future I was merely certain that I should be killed.[5]

Invocation contains a sonnet which, though there is no precise date for it, perhaps shows his state of mind in the first autumn:

I have no strength now save in my new will: –
    Having sought Love whom Chance bade me desert;
    Too false for Love, Passion pursued until
    My heart was soiled and sickened by mere dirt;
Too stale for Passion, Fame I sought and found
    Poor Notoriety, more fool than knave,
    Liberty next, but left lest I were bound
    To prove for Her that I too dared be slave.
Lost to Love, Fame, Passion, Liberty,
    Afraid to face their debts I have incurred,
    Alone I go, resolved to render Thee,
    England, such due as one who ever erred

Toward thy dispraise dare pay silently:
A life unworthy and a fame deferred.

It is difficult to be sure of what led to all the elements in this complex of feelings, but the memoir of Heseltine lets us see him in pursuit of passion. The 'he' is Heseltine and the time September or October 1914:

> Later that night, or some night closely consequent, he and I and my friend Harold Gough (afterward killed in action before Ypres) and a blonde girl, a rather pretty street-walker picked up in a Greek Street night club, boarded a taxi and set out for my father's country house in Essex. We drove through the small hours, I on the roof and the others within. Why we took the girl I cannot imagine. But the whole affair was a somewhat desperate and forlorn lark. Toward six o'clock we arrived at the top of the double avenue of elms* that lead to the old house. We were then in a quandary, for the girl's profession was unmistakable, the Rectory windows all too close, and uncertainty prevailed as to quite who was at home at the further end of the avenue. Philip was left with the girl while Gough and I went in and breakfasted, to emerge in due course with food for the stranded pair. We then drove back to London; a drowsy Philip and a somewhat fractious girl being dropped at Colchester Railway Station on the way.

Robert's application for a commission and training did not interfere with his poetry. The greater part of his first published volume, *Invocation*, was written in the year from September 1914 to September 1915. Those poems show him preoccupied with the war, with the fate of dead friends and compatriots and with dangers he himself would face. Of the 'Five Sonnets upon Imminent Departure', the fourth is an elegy for Rupert Brooke who died in Greece on 23 April 1915:

> Begin, O guns, your giant requiem
> Over my lovely friend the Fiend has slain,
> From whom Death has not snatched the diadem
> Promised by Poetry.

The reviewer for *The Times Literary Supplement* (30 December 1915) quotes this sonnet and says of the author: 'His verse falters not in weakness but in endeavour, not because it has too little to say, but too much. It is a broken but often vivid reflection of all that direct experience of

---

*This must be a slip. The trees were in fact limes.

the war means to a mind that, casting aside the past, has submitted itself by sheer force of will to its test and is keeping saneness and control, as a sword must keep its edge.' This comment particularly fits the poem 'Invocation' from which the book takes its title:

> Courage born of Fire and Steel,
>   Thee I invoke, thee I desire
> Who constant holdst the hearts that reel
>   Beneath the steel, beneath the fire.
>
> Though in my mind no torment is,
>   Yet in my being's hazard mesh
> There run such threads of cowardice
>   That I must dread my untrue flesh.
>
> Therefore possess me and so dower
>   The sword's weak spot that the true blade
> May not in least nor direst hour
>   Betray the spirit unafraid.

This poem appeared in the *War Poems Supplement* to *The Times* on 9 August 1915; the feelings it expresses must have been very widely shared in England in the first year of the war.

Robert's thoughts, however, were not taken up with the war exclusively. He continued to work on *A Faun's Holiday*. This eventually formed the central section of his second book, *Ardours and Endurances* (1917). There are many unpublished love poems and poems relating to nature dated 1914. A fragment on Orpheus and the loss of Eurydice is dated 20 February 1915. And between 1914 and 1916 he put a lot of work into a poetical 'Drama in the Elizabethan Manner' on the subject of Orestes. Two fragments of this appear in *Ardours*, a magnificent description of an exotic feast that ends in carnage, and an outburst by Orestes at the sight of the Furies. But these are only a sample. In Aeschylus Kassandra, as Robert chooses to spell her, is murdered at the same time as Agamemnon; in Robert's version she seems to be still at Mycenae years later after Orestes' murder of Clytemnestra. In Aeschylus she has visions of Agamemnon's death and her own, but Robert gives her visions not only of death but of the deity, and characteristically mingles Apollo and Zeus with Christ:

> KASSANDRA I saw the image of my death last night
>   Still and tall and red and white;

He was still and like a God.
Red was his robe. His feet gold-shod.
Within his hands lay scourge and cord
And across his knees an icy sword.
There were fires in his eyes and He
Turned them slowly upon me.
CHORUS Unbelievable words dost thou relate.
Has thou seen God? Or held traffic with fate?
KASSANDRA Formless and black the waters meet
In a silent maelstrom about His feet.
The blind he makes to see, the dumb to speak –
In the fields of death –
CHORUS   Drown with your shriek
The impious lips that are turning pale
Lest the Winnower of Truth wield thrice His flail.
KASSANDRA God would look on me as a bride in the night.
I am a vessel in his sight.
He would pour himself in me.
I am stamped with His stamp …
Apollo has put a live coal to my lips…

The fact is that the urgencies of war could not impede Robert's quest
for the meaning of human life, and he was constantly feeling his way
towards a kind of lyrical philosophy which in the following years he
hoped might take the form of a volume to be entitled *The Living Dust*.

Robert set off for active service in August 1915. Before departing he
went with Boy Gough to say goodbye to his inamorata Daisy Kennedy.
Gough

> waited in the taxi outside. I thought I should be killed. But when I
> settled rather shakily down beside him the tears ran down his
> cheeks, not mine. He was a very sensitive chap. A moment or two
> later he bucked up in his professional 'Let's be done with this
> damnonsense' way and proposed drinks, a Turkish bath, a grand
> dinner and 'forget all this'. And he was killed, not I.

Robert's expectation of being killed was, he thought, widely shared
among his generation. In 1940, trying to explain to a later generation
the spirit in which they volunteered, he says 'What we felt was
exaltation. Beyond that there was a blank. How can a boy consider
what he can't imagine? And the only alternative to the unimaginable

was something decisive, – an event resembling the descent of a great beam of light ... And the name of that resplendence was death.' In his *Anthology of War Poetry 1914–1918*, from which these words are taken,[6] he illustrates them with poems by Rupert Brooke, William Hodgson and Francis Brett Young; but he could have used the last of his own 'Five Sonnets upon Imminent Departure':

> If it should hap, I being summoned hence
>   To an unknown and all too hazardous bourne,
> One should bring news charged with this heavy sense: –
>   *He has gone further and cannot return ...*

A poem published in *Ardours* shows him on a knoll at Lawford saying 'Farewell to a Place of Comfort':

> The bell is sounding down in Dedham Vale:
> Be still, O bell! too often standing here
> When all the air was tremulous, fine and pale,
> Thy golden note so calm, so still, so clear,
> Out of my stony heart has struck a tear.

Robert's unit was D Battery, 104th Brigade RFA. On 25 August they started in the small hours and sailed at 4 p.m. They arrived in France on the 27th and proceeded towards the front via St Omer and Hazebrouck at a leisurely pace. For the first few days he kept a journal. On the 30th he had letters from his father, his mother and his father's sister Isabel. On the 31st he heard that Elkin Matthews would publish his first volume of poetry, and wished that his brother Phil, Philip Heseltine or Cristina was there to share the good news. This Cristina, her surname perhaps Bernard, was apparently a friend who was helping him to get his poems published but whom he did not love in the way he loved Daisy Kennedy.[7] By 2 September – 'or is it the 3rd? I am beginning not to notice – so are we all and we ask each other the day of the week' – he is becoming impatient: 'God send us action soon – more especially, that I may do something and that, though it seems useless, I may be revenged.' He had just heard of the death of 'another Trinity man, Mosely... Our college has suffered severely in this war', and reading *The Times* at headquarters: 'Two more gone – a friend of Phil's and one of mine, Winkworth and Peto. W. died of wounds – damnable, and he was always fragile.' The last entry, which is for 6 September, runs 'Birthday weather' (he was twenty-two) – clear, all gold and blue. Corn in stacks all the way in our trek. Long trek and terribly hot sun.

However feel quite happy. Men and teams going a little better. Anxious to get letter off to Phil – but no opportunity.'

The journal ends here. The Western Front itself has been described by many of those who experienced its trenches, including Robert's fellow poets Sassoon and Graves. The German advance through Belgium into France had been brought to a halt in autumn 1914, and for a nearly a year both sides had been digging themselves into lines of trenches separated by up to a mile of no-man's-land, rendered impassable by barbed wire and swept by artillery and small arms fire. Robert never pretended to a prolonged experience of the Front – 'the truth is,' he says, 'I had very little war.'[8] But the picture he gives in the preface to his *Anthology* is as haunting as any:

The first fact which struck us – and struck us none the less shrewdly for striking so quietly – was our isolation. There were some hundreds of yards of front-line trench with support and communication trenches behind – the whole an ignominious rabbit-warren to the eye and sewage-farm to the nose. Behind this warren a stagnant and dispirited landscape, peopled with unseen batteries and dotted with sparse billets, faded away into a psychological void. Beyond that void and at an enormous distance lay an intangible England whence issued newspapers (the tone of which exasperated us) and letters sprinkled with news of familiar things now so diminished as to resemble the puzzling alphabet one sees from the further end of an oculist's consulting-room. To the left and right of us the warren, strung on the front line, extended into two *terrae incognitae* habited by a couple of units, the names of which we knew, and, beyond them, by other units whose names we didn't know. Before us was a third void, different from its neighbours. Entrance to it was barred by wire thickets, sunk amid which two or three moppets could be descried reclining in attitudes of extravagant fatigue. From out this void beyond the thicket enmity in various abrupt and peremptory forms proceeded, these outbreaks being acccompanied by inappropriate sounds: the crackle of a boy's stick drawn along galvanised iron palings; odd chirrups, whirs and whinings; the stately passage overhead of a ghostly excursion train, and occasional calamitous fallings of a mountain of crockery somewhere behind a dreary horizon. Some seventy yards beyond the wire and half-screened by irrelevant friths of marguerites and poppies, a long, low protuberance could be discerned, the boundary of another warren, seemingly totally deserted. An air of frowsy dereliction and weariness overhung the precincts – such an air as invests the deserted refuse-dumps beyond the last broken lamp-post and unfinished road on the outskirts of an industrial city And not without reason – for evidence of man's industry, now rusty or in rags, peered from the grasses and a sour-sweet odour, varied by whiffs so fulsome as to produce retching, seemed to taint the air with an unwholesome clamminess.⁹

Letters from Robert at the Front give us some personal details. On 11 September he heard that his brother was nearby with the West Suffolks; went over and had lunch with him.¹⁰ He greeted him with: 'Brother meets brother in the face of the enemy.' Phil was embarrassed by this theatrical speech, though bullets were in fact flying about them, but Robert could never resist dramatising. On the 20th he wrote to his thirteen-year-old sister Anne in a way which anticipates the playwright he would become. He was sitting in a field, he said, having his hair cut, and the Germans

were dropping high explosives about 300 yards away. This is the sort of thing:

R.M.B.N. Not too short over the ears.

Soldier Barber: No, sir. Curious the way these Germans turn onto that field of beets every evening, ain't it, sir? Satisfies 'em, I spose, seein' them beets fly.

R.M.B.N.: Yes, not bad for line if there was anything there. You seem to know how to cut hair well.

S.B.: Yes, I used to cut it in Bayswater, sir, before this 'ere strafe-ing began, sir.

[Conversation about London, interrupted by shout of 'Coming over!' and phew, phew, phew, bong! of shell.]

R.M.B.N. [nervously]: Where was that?

S.B. [snipping away]: Be'ind us, sir, and a bit nearer.

R.M.B.N.: Hope we shan't have to move. Steady with those clippers.

S.B.: Finish your 'air first, sir, before *I* moves, sir.

R.M.B.N. [dryly]: Perhaps.

S.B.: Post in, sir?

R.M.B.N.: Yes. Nice letter from sister here.

S.B. [sympathetically]: Yes, sir. [Conversation on sisters, punc-tuated by pauses in the middle of sentences, as we listen to shells.]

> *S.B.*: Pretty quiet, sir, nowadays. When are they going to *begin*
> I wonder, sir. 'Ave you any idea, sir?
> [A loud phew, phew, bong!]
> *R.M.B.N.*: Now, I think! Come on!
> *S.B.* [packing up]: In a minute, sir. You left your 'air brush, sir.
> *R.M.B.N.*: Well my hair's finished anyway just in time.
> *S.B.*: Lor, bless you, sir, it weren't within an 'undred yards.
> *R.M.B.N.* [sententiously]: High explosive of that size fre-
> quently has an area of 200 yards.
> *S.B.* Yes, sir, just as well not to stop a bit of it, sir. [Exeunt
> severally.]

Robert was right that this artillery fire was the beginning of the
action at Loos. Two days later he wrote to his father: 'As Phil said to
me, we live only for the moment – the past is cut off, or rather
connected only by the slender thread of letters etc., that we receive now
less regularly than a few days ago since this battle on one of our flanks
has begun raging.'

We get a more retrospective glimpse of the Front from a letter written in Vienna in 1933 when he is reflecting on the obstinacy of Englishmen generally and senior Gunner officers in particular.

> They required us to place an eighteen pounder about 100 yards in
> the rear of our support trenches – the idea was to cut the wire and
> generally strafe the German front line and above all to give it to
> the Jerry if he came over. Sheer foolery. In the first place it was
> doubtful if the trajectory would clear our front line; second,
> owing to the 'flash' we should have been spotted after a couple of
> rounds; third, shrapnel is little use for cutting wire (and the H.E.
> was untrustworthy and an order came out forbidding us to use it);
> fourth, had Jerry come over we'd have lost that gun in five
> minutes without being able to use it properly for fear of doing in
> the King's Own Yorkshire Light Infantry in front of us. Net result
> – we reduced the gun-power of our battery, which was not at all
> badly placed and shooting quite nicely, by one gun. I wasn't at this
> gun, but while in the O-Pip with my O.C., Major Richards, never
> heard him give it any orders.[11]

But the fullest account of Robert's active service is in his poetry.

The first part of *Ardours and Endurances* is a series of consecutive
war poems. It starts with a summons to arms and the 'Farewell' to

Lawford just quoted. There are then three poems on the approach to the battlefield which take us along the same road as the journal, 'Halt by the Roadside', 'The Day's March' and 'Nearer'. In the preface to his *Anthology* he says: 'I remember the first day my brigade of field artillery took the road with its guns. By heaven, I wouldn't have changed my position on a tall horse with two eighteen-pounders and my drivers and gunners beside me for a seat on the Front Bench.' In 'The Day's March' this becomes:

> The battery grides and jingles,
> Mile succeeds to mile;
> Shaking the noonday sunshine,
> The guns lunge out awhile,
> And then are still awhile.
>
> We amble along the highway;
> The reeking, powdery dust
> Ascends and cakes our faces
> With a striped, sweaty crust...

They passed through Steenwerk and settled at last on the front near Lille at Armentières la Chapelle.

The war poetry of *Ardours* is the product of reflection. But *Invocation* contains one poem which must have brought to the printer raw the feelings that inspired it. This, in his own copy of the book, carries the note 'written in a Belgian cottage while the rain rang on the roof all night and the guns thudded – the guns I was to face two days later for the first time'. That makes it contemporary with the last entries in his journal. It begins 'Now that I feel the hand of Death draw near ...' and ends with his thoughts going back to Lawford:

> Back to the quiet house upon the hill
> Where shine – alas! more than sea-separate –
> Those human hearts I loved ...

Ardours covers battle itself in eleven poems, of which all must be based on his experience that September, though the experience has been distilled or transformed. Robert starts with a glimpse of a deep trench at noon:

> Where forty standing men
> Endure the sweat and grit and stench
> Like cattle in a pen.

Next there is a night scene, first with 'no sound but the wind and the rain, and trample of horses' and the wind 'searching for the forgotten dead, hidden in the hedges or trodden into muck under the trenches'; but then 'with a terrible delight' he hears 'far guns low like oxen in the night' and his own guns are called into action. 'Sharply I pass the terse orders down', and he sees shells 'burst a cloud of rose over German trenches'.

Robert's unit had been brought over as part of the preparations for a major offensive. In the spring an unsuccessful attempt had been made to break through the German line at Ypres. Now the French and English planned a fresh combined effort at Loos, near Lille a little way south of Ypres. Armentières la Chapelle where D Battery was in action from 9 to 22 September is some five miles from Loos, and Robert will have had a chance to see the horrible carnage when the British infantry advanced into no-man's-land as if they were doing foot drill on a parade ground and were mown down by German machine-guns. It is said that the Germans were at first incredulous at the folly of the British tactics, and then so sickened by the carnage that they stopped firing as soon as the British, halted by the barbed wire, turned back.

Robert's third poem describes an officer wounded in no-man's-land and crawling back to die among his men. In this and poems VI, VIII and IX ,'The Barn, Twilight', 'Eve of Assault' and 'Assault', he tries to reproduce the uneducated voices of the troops but it is a misdirected attempt at realism as he later came to appreciate. His copy of *Ardours* contains pencilled instructions to 'cut' and he did not reproduce these poems in *Such Was My Singing*. A reviewer accused him of forgetting, in 'Assault', 'that fact does not become poetry, any more than marble becomes sculpture, till it has been worked on'[12] and the ending certainly has a rough-hewn character:

> Men, crumpled, going down …
> Go on. Go.
> Deafness. Numbness. The loudening tornado.
> Bullets. Mud. Stumbling and skating.
> My voice's strangled shout:
> *'Steady pace, boys!'*
> The still light: gladness.
> *'Look, sir. Look out!'*
> Ha! ha! Bunched figures waiting.
> Revolver levelled quick!

Flick! Flick!
Red as blood.
Germans. Germans.
Good! O Good!
Cool madness.

Perhaps, however, its very roughness gives a message to later genera-
tions. Tom Lanoye made this poem the centrepiece of his anthology
Niemands Land in 2002.[13]

Writing in 1921, when his experience at the Front was less fresh in
his mind, Robert says:

> I didn't hate the Germans. They thought a civilization could be
> imposed. We, the older peoples, considered it could only be
> induced. We were fighting for toleration, and in that sense were
> fighting and dying for men, and in that sense could be called
> Christians. (This last idea I endeavoured to enshrine in a poem
> called *Battery Moving Up from Rest Camp*.)

In this, the seventh poem of the battle series, fact has been 'worked on'.
The steamy heat of September is replaced by winter and Robert's
battery is moving through a village in the darkness before the frozen
dawn:

Not a sign of life we rouse
In any square close-shuttered house
That flanks the road we amble down
Toward far trenches through the town.

The dark, snow-slushy empty street …
Tingle of frost in brow and feet …
Horse-breath goes dimly up like smoke.
No sound but the smacking stroke

Of a sergeant flings each arm
Out and across to keep him warm,
And the sudden splashing crack
Of ice-pools broken by our track.

More dark houses, yet no sign
Of life … And axle's creak and whine …
The splash of hooves, the strain of trace …
Clatter: we cross the market place.

Deep quiet again, and on we lurch
Under the shadow of a church:
Its tower ascends, fog-wreathed and grim;
Within its aisles a light burns dim ...

When marvellous! from overhead
Like abrupt speech of one deemed dead,
Speech-moved by some Superior Will,
A bell tolls thrice and then is still.

And suddenly I know that now
The priest within, to lifted brow
Exalts the small round of the Host ...

O people who bow down to see
The Miracle of Calvary,
The bitter and the glorious,
Bow down, bow down and pray for us ...

Who scarce have time for prayer indeed
Who only march and die and bleed.

The battle series concludes with two reflective poems, one, 'The Last
Morning', invoking death and eternity, and the other, 'Fulfilment', in
which youthful love is forgotten in comradeship in arms. *Ardours*
continues with four poems to 'The Dead' and eight headed 'The After-
math'. These last include a final elegy to the fallen, but otherwise show
the poet returning to nature, and particularly to the sea. Insofar as they
can be dated, they were written after his active service had come to an
early end, and his attitude, like that of other poets of the 1914–18 War,
can be seen to change after the autumn of 1915.

5
The Later War Poems

On 25 September, just three days after the letter quoted on page 46, Robert wrote to his father:

I'm in hospital for a few days – after a rather thick time. They found me done up utterly in a road after looking for a place and I still feel rather done in – having been knocked down twice, once by the blast of a gun and once by a spent bullet.

Although my nerves have played me false [he added on the 27th], do not think that I disgraced myself – as a matter of fact I think I did all right in that way. But the strain tells on you and saps your strength – for where I was although we were marvellously lucky any moment might have been one's last – for we were close up and had whizz-bangs, heavy guns, rifles and machine guns against us – I mean where we, the officers, were observing.

This was confirmed by his commanding officer, Captain J. Richards, writing from France in reply to an inquiry about him at the end of October:

He left here about five weeks ago suffering from a slight nervous breakdown ... We did some very hard fighting during his stay in the Battery which he did not mind a bit, also whatever duty he had to perform in action or out he did splendidly and again [I] must say how sorry I was to lose him. So blessed hard for a fellow to be full of fight but his health fails him.[1]

To Robert himself he wrote at about the same time:

We had a rough time here and most trying, a terrible strain to the strongest and at the time you wasn't one of the strongest, so you must get thoroughly well this time. I felt awfully sorry for you, poor kid, you did me so well, it's one thing, although your nerves had gone there wasn't anything you would not do let it be never so dangerous, and you must admit things were very hot. I reported to the colonel your heart was as big as a lion's but no one can go against bad health which means rotten bad luck.

Captain Richards says his wife would like to visit Robert and hear 'all about myself and Battery' and ends 'I should love to have you again with me if it's possible.'

Robert left the firing line, it appears from his record, on 26 September, the second day of the main infantry battle. He reached England early in October and spent two weeks at a military hospital in Lincoln followed by two months at hospitals in London. A medical board on 12 January 1916 gave him a further three months' sick leave. Hospitality was arranged for him at Staplefield Place in Sussex, but he made no progress and in February was sent to Torquay to be under medical supervision there. On 11 April another medical board passed him as fit for light duty at home and he rejoined his depot but had to stop after two days and in May was given another two months' leave. Finally a medical board on 8 August pronounced him permanently unfit and he was invalided out of the Army, relinquishing his commission in September.

During most of this time, and for much of the following year, he was based in Devon near Torquay, though he was able to visit Lawford, London and other places from time to time. His going to that part of England may have been connected with the fact that his grandfather, Captain Edward Pusey, RN, was living in Torquay. On 3 March Captain Pusey wrote to Mrs Nichols: 'Robert was here this week and is looking very well. I am told that Dr and Mrs Cumming [Robert was under Dr Cumming's care] are nice people and their house is in one of the best situations in Torquay ... I think there is another invalid officer there too so Robert will not be dull. He is of course still lame from the chimney falling on him, but is getting stronger.' A letter from Laurence Binyon, dated 8 January 1916, implies that he and Robert had recently met, apparently at a social event in London. Poems which have notes of when and where they were written show him at Lawford in April, 'early summer' and September, when he invited Aldous Huxley to stay.[2] His poem 'In the Cotswolds' is dated 27 December 1916. But on 22 December he wrote to his mother from Ilsington, near Bovey Tracey, South Devon as though he had recently arrived there, and this was his most permanent base.

It is a pleasant house [he told her]: high up on the hills. Dartmoor is outside the porch, so to speak. I've only to go a couple of hundred yards up the road and I have – on a clear day – an hundred square miles fanshape under my eye. Where I stand up in the hills – nigh 1,000 feet up – is the handle of the opened fan, the fan's flukes are the great hills tumbling irregularly about like dogs till they subside downward and downward into the great misty plain which is the painted flat of the fan and which is bordered by the faint fringe of the sea ... No end of a place! And a most friendly person in charge – an architect – a very good one. We squabble over Life and Art and Happiness and all the other capitals to our hearts' content.

Middlecot, the house to which he refers, served as a place of retreat to Anglicans from the universities. The Cambridge architect Henry T. Lyon was the 'person in charge', and Ronald Knox in his Trinity days had held Oxford reading parties there. Such an establishment may seem a strange choice for one who was supposed to have turned away from Christian belief, but within a couple of years Robert was to experience a religious revival, and he never averted his thoughts from Christianity for long.

In London that autumn Robert was attracted by the artwork of Jean Milne that was being exhibited at Burlington House, and began a correspondence and acquaintance which lasted from October 1916 to June 1917. After his death she wrote about him:

He was then ill, and his condition gave me anxiety. At that time I, nearly twenty years older than he was, was working at a Military Hospital ... I had one or two others like him, shell-shocked, among my massage patients at the hospital. I don't think I was even a flesh-and-blood person to him, only a sympathetic entity to whom he could pour himself out, a vital necessity to him in that condition ... Each time when he left me I took him to bus or taxi, as I felt so troubled about him in that state.[3]

A medical report on him in 1926 reveals that shell shock was not his only trouble: in 1916 he discovered he had syphilis and was treated for two and a half years.[4] Robert Graves was amused to find him receiving treatment for this in January 1917[5] and later said that it was the consequence of sleeping with seventeen prostitutes in three weeks.[6] But Graves is not a reliable informant, and such a feat would probably have been beyond Robert's delicate physique. Although he admitted to having recourse to prostitutes after his active service, the source that should be best informed says he caught the disease from a French prostitute at an embarkation party before going to the Front.[7]

Ill health, in either case, did not prevent him from writing, and the months of his recovery and convalescence were abundantly fruitful. Two poems in *Ardours*, 'Plaint of Friendship by Death Broken' and 'Comrades', are subscribed 'Autumn 1915, in Hospital'. The short lyric 'Song of the Princess beside the Fountain' (*Ardours*) was written in hospital in January 1916, and in February, when he left London for Devon, he not only resumed work on *A Faun's Holiday* but started sketching a poetic treatment of a subject always dear to him, the life and duties of a poet. The last section of *Ardours*, which is entitled 'Poems and Phantasies' contains eight poems dated 1916 on the themes of love, nature and the sea.

The war poems in *Ardours* also belong mostly to 1916. The battle poems preserve the will to fight which appears in his journal; the feelings of 'terrible joy' and 'cool madness'. These feelings were fuelled by grief for friends who had been killed. Siegfried Sassoon, whom Robert was to come to know in 1917, had felt something similar. He says in his diaries for March 1916: 'I used to say I couldn't kill anyone in this war; but since they shot Tommy I would gladly stick a bayonet into a German by daylight. Someone told me a year ago that love, sorrow and hate were things I had never known ... Now I've known love for Bobbie and Tommy, and grief for Hamo and Tommy, and hate has come also, and the lust to kill.'[8] But as Robert explains at some length in the preface to his 1943 *Anthology of War Poetry, 1914–1918*, the spirit which filled the first volunteers changed as the war proceeded. The costly and fruitless offensive of Loos in 1915 was followed by that of the Somme in 1916. The original spirit had been 'a valour of ardour rather than endurance' (p. 50). That ardour had been reinforced by comradeship in arms, 'a fellowship that came to sovereign and most characteristic flower in the infantry battalions of an old regiment conscious of its tradition' (p. 39). Officers and men would have trained together, often known each other from childhood. The continuity of this fellowship was destroyed by the huge casualties and the drafting in of new replacements. Then those who went home on leave or to recover from wounds found a world that had no comprehension of their life at the Front. And the scale and prolongation of the slaughter raised questions in the most stolid about the leadership which demanded it. Some people lost faith in the cause for which they were fighting altogether. Some, like Sassoon, 'came to believe that the war was being "deliberately prolonged" by those who had the power to end it, that it had ceased to be a war of "defence and liberation" and had become a war of "aggression and conquest"' (p. 69). For Sassoon and Owen solidarity with those who suffered became in some measure a substitute for belief in the cause. That was not Robert's position: 'I ended the war only confirmed in the faith that was mine at the beginning' (p. 79). But from the summer of 1916 onwards his ardour gives way to grief for the dead, and compassion for those who endure.

The war poems in *Ardours* are dedicated to Harold Gough and Richard Pinsent. Gough was killed at Ypres in June 1916. In September Robert wrote two poems to him, 'The Burial in Flanders' and 'Boy', which begin the section 'The Dead' in *Ardours*. Pinsent was killed at Loos in September 1915. In one of his most beautiful poems Robert looks back to their time together at Oxford:

> I mind now how we sat one winter night
> While past his open window raced the bright
> Snow-torrent golden in the hot firelight ...
>   I see him smiling at the streamered air.
>
> I watched him to the open window go
> And lean long smiling, whispering to the snow,
> Play with his hands amid the fiery flow
>   And when he turned it flamed amid his hair.
>
> Without arose a sudden bell's huge clang
> Until a thousand bells in answer rang
> And midnight Oxford hummed and reeled and sang
>   Under the whitening fury of the air.[9]

Other deaths, of course, were to follow, including Alselan Nichols, his last male Nichols cousin, killed in action at Arras in 1917. Of this young man, a year his junior, Robert wrote that he was 'ugly, strong, thirsty for life, with an irregular, stifled sensibility. I liked him.'[10]

The last war poem in *Ardours* is a solemn sonnet to the fallen:

> They have not gone from us. O no! they are
> The inmost essence of each thing that is
> Perfect for us; they flame in every star;
> The trees are emerald with their presences.
> They are not gone from us; they do not roam
> The flaw and turmoil of the lower deep,
> But have now made the whole wide world their home,
> And in its loveliness themselves they steep.

> They fail not ever; theirs is the diurn
> Splendour of sunny hill and forest grave;
> In every rainbow's glittering drop they burn;
> They dazzle in the massed clouds' architrave;
> They chant on every wind, and they return
> In the long roll of any deep blue wave.

The knowledge that others were suffering while he was in England made him feel a betrayer. His contribution to *Oxford Poetry 1917* begins:

> O had I died when over the black plain
> The harsh light drifted and the roaring guns
> Lifted their voices summoning amain
> Youth from its joy in storms and flying suns
> And happy comradeship of weathered men,
> All had been as in purpose due and well,
> Honourable my service had then been
> And honoured the blank spot on which I fell.

Among the last war poems Robert wrote before the Armistice are the three he published in *Aurelia*, his third volume of poetry. The first, 'Casualty', is dedicated to Siegfried Sassoon, and shares that passionate feeling for the suffering of those at the Front which comes across so vividly in Sassoon's poetry. This poem is undated but was probably written in 1918. 'Dawn on the Somme' and 'Burial Party at Paschaendael' are dated late spring and summer of that year, though the battles to which they refer were fought in 1916 and 1917. Robert had evidently been meditating on these catastrophes. 'Dawn on the Somme', recalls the mood of the sonnet at the end of the war cycle in *Ardours*. The sun is shown rising glorious after a night of rain, and the dead are seen resurrecting as heroes in the morning mist. This is the poem that gave Arthur Bliss the title for his work *Morning Heroes*. The last poem, however, 'Burial Party at Paschaendael', perhaps captures more faithfully Robert's view of the war at the time. It describes the filling of

> Twelve graves brutishly scraped among the slime

while

>   flight upon flight
> Of hurrying bullets scythe the lower air.

The poet speaks, not of the heroism of the dead and their achievements, but of the ugliness of the scene, and looks back to their infancy,

When rosy, bubbled mouths opened to crow
A world-engendered mirth and baby-joy,

and he advises their mothers:

Let not their mothers till long aftertime
Come to this hill – when, maybe, 'twill be green,
When harebells shake or when the furry rime
Hides the gorged craters that they be not seen.

Robert had friends – the Morrells at Garsington, Cambridge intellectuals like Lytton Strachey and Bertrand Russell – who were pacifists opposed to the war absolutely. By 1917 there were many other people who were far from being pacifists but who believed that the war was being prolonged unnecessarily. There had, after all, been no real reason for it. By the end of 1915 it should have been clear that victory was out of reach of either side for the foreseeable future and that offensives against an entrenched army could result only in horrible and useless slaughter; but so much suffering had been caused already that the politicians on both sides seem to have been unable to admit that it had been to no purpose by working for an armistice and a return to pre-war conditions. Robert's artist friends Paul Nash and Richard Nevinson were among those who wanted to end the war in 1918 before the Allies had obtained a clear victory. Robert disagreed. He would make no compromise with German militarism, and there are historians who hold that if the Allies had fought on until the whole of Germany had recognised its bankruptcy the Second World War might have been prevented. In 1918 he applied to reinlist but was judged medically unfit.[11] He did nevertheless do propaganda work for the Government in the last year of the war[12], and in January 1918 the Foreign Office sent him briefly to GHQ, France, to collect material for a propaganda book on the Sappers.[13]

'This Sapper work', he told his father,[14] 'is the biggest organisation I've ever seen and extends from railway contracting to wireless. In short it is a whacking big job they have sent me on.' He was interested in the technical side of propaganda, but he was unable to complete the Sapper book[15] – as in the Second World War he was unable to complete a book the Government wanted on the Pathfinders – perhaps because he could not bring himself to a simplistic exaltation of militarism. In 1919 he issued a bitter indictment of the complacency of victory. His first book of poems, *Invocation*, had begun with a poem called 'Invocation,' the innocent sabre-rattling composition quoted above:

> Courage born of Fire and Steel,
>> Thee I invoke, thee I desire, etc.

He now published a pamphlet entitled *Peace Celebration, Invocation and Hymn*. Readers who had been enthusiastic about the first 'Invocation' may have found the second bewildering:

> Praise ye the Lord! – peace has descended,
> Those who made money now can spend it,
> And others find some fool to lend it ...
>
> First – fittest! let loud guns salute
> The pure peace, that their mouths refute,
> And all the dead – whose mouths are mute.
>
> Then dance! – since many cannot walk;
> Shoot fireworks! – for the blind won't mock;
> Sing! – since the fighters will not talk;
>
> Spend – where the pension's come or – spent;
> Join hands! – in civil discontent;
> Parade! th' occasion's innocent;
>
> Wave flags – for which most have not bled;
> Feast – since so many have no bread;
> Peal merry bells – for all the dead;
>
> *'Hip, Hip, Hurrah!'* and if you please
> Once more: *'Hip! Hip!'* What days are these
> *For Peace is dead! Long live the Peace!*

6

New Friends

When Robert was in hospital in Palace Green, London, in the autumn of 1915 he heard of the death of his Oxford friend Dick Pinsent. This later inspired the poem quoted in chapter 5, but the immediate effect of the news was to precipitate a crisis:

Either that night or the next the collapse began. First I saw him standing in the darkness of the corner with the bayonet wounds in his tunic. But I simply said 'Oh, that's you Dick' and presently got off to sleep (I think they gave me something). But next evening my heart began to go and I felt I was climbing up a slope and slipping down and a captain from next door came in and took my hands over the end of the bed and hauled me up the cliff while I blubbered and got hysterical.[1]

Next day his father's friend Violet Dickinson[2] came and, having inspected him, persuaded the neurologist Henry Head to take the case. Nine years later he recalled:

The most important event in my life to date was the occasion on which Dr Henry Head, F. R. S., a plump, bland, slightly Mephistophilean figure, pushed open the door in the hospital cell and sat down and asked me if I liked Conrad – the first sensible and honest question that had been put to me since I came out of France. You know, Henry, I took to you from the very moment you sat down. It was your way of putting your bag on the ground and settling into your seat. You set down that bag with such care – evidently you were 'on the job': I spotted the craftsman. You settled yourself down with such an air of relish and of not being hurried – of guarding against any possibility of being rushed – for all the world as if you desired something in me and felt I might be worth, not a cure, but a chat.[3]

From being a patient Robert became a close personal friend of both Head and his wife Ruth. When Head died in 1940 he contributed the following coda to his obituary:

May I as one who was for 25 years the friend of Sir Henry Head,
F. R. S., and who was, like so many others, helped back from the
'borderline' by him in the last War, add a few words as a non-
medical man to your obituary? Sir Henry possessed the fullest as
well as the wisest mind I have ever known. It was no unusual thing
to hear him in the course of one evening discourse on topics so
various as: the influence of reasoning upon Goethe and Mozart,
types of apprehension in listeners to symphonic music, sensations
while looping the loop (he was over 60 when he did so), the painting of Guardi, "coordination" in a star golfer, Ninon de Lenclos,
Conrad as narrator (Sir Henry was far the ablest literary critic I
have ever known), religious ecstasy, the relation of art and science,
the social customs of Melanesia. On each of these topics he not
only appeared to have more information than anybody in the
room but spoke after a more illuminating fashion, for, like
Leonardo (on whom he was an authority), he had a supreme eye
for the significant.

   Nor did he resemble Leonardo in mind only. He had Leonardo's
lofty compassion, humility, patience, and profound serenity of
spirit. No stupidity or even downright wickedness could ruffle
him, who, an imaginative scientific genius, looked on man but as
part of nature, the supreme and unfathomable artist. Such stupidity and cruelty he would try to thwart, but always without rage as
became the man he was. Truly a noble spirit, just as wise and calm
as kind; a sort of Quaker Prospero. In remembering him his friends
can have but one regret – namely, that in his later years of retire-
ment the disease, which he bore with such extraordinary fortitude,
did not suffer him to place on paper that mass of varied reflections
which rose in his being when he contemplated other works of
nature and of man than those particular studies to which he con-
secrated a life as fruitful as it was beautiful.[4]

In 1926 Head had fallen victim to Parkinson's Disease and become
unable to write. He and his wife left London to live a retired life in the
country, and for the next twelve years Robert wrote a long letter to
them every week which she read aloud to cheer him up. Head may have
felt a special interest in Robert partly because he was himself the author
of some war poems, *Destroyers and Other Verses*, published by the
Oxford University Press in 1919. His first non-medical service to
Robert, at least, was to recommend his poetry to Chatto and Windus. 'I

am very much in debt to you,' Robert wrote in November 1916, 'for your kindness in getting me a publisher. Chatto and Windus are of course first rate.'⁵

While Robert was in hospital in the autumn of 1915, Philip Heseltine brought D. H. Lawrence to see him and, says Robert in his memoir, 'a certain degree of acquaintance was established between Lawrence and me.'⁶ He goes on:

> That acquaintance was renewed about a year before Lawrence died. It was my ill fortune that these two periods should both have been periods when Lawrence was ill. In my opinion, during the first period, Lawrence was not only suffering from a "bad patch" of the tuberculosis which eventually killed him, but from a nervous condition which did not permit him to display that balanced and good-humoured sense which Mr Aldous Huxley and Mr Koteliansky assure me strongly characterised the other phases of his life ...
>
> Both D. H. Lawrence and his wife then harboured – I know not why – a singular bee in their bonnets, namely that both Philip and I should each of us get married, and that quickly. The Lawrences had even been so benevolent as to select the girl – a very nice girl I may say – suitable to one if not the other of us. Thence ensued a comedy. We were each in turn asked up to Hampstead to meet the lady and in my case a pretty palpable hint was dropped as to the hopes entertained. I avoided this meeting. Philip, I believe, avoided his. Later we compared experiences and both met the lady, whom Philip had encountered somewhere else than in Hampstead, one late afternoon near the Embankment. She, too, had somehow discerned what was in the wind, and the meeting of the three parties most concerned dissolved in inextinguishable laughter. I do not say that either Lawrence or his wife took the project very seriously, did in fact do more than toy with it as a warm, pleasing project, but that he should have troubled with it at all, when neither Philip nor I nor, as it appeared, the lady had displayed the slightest inclination towards matrimony, bears witness, I think, to his peculiar state of mind.
>
> Some months later I had other occasion to mark another and more serious phase of his condition. The Lawrences asked me to spend an evening with them in, I think, Mecklenburg Square. The inevitable topic of the war arose, and, the discussion waxing

somewhat intense, Lawrence declared that he was being "shad-
owed" and requested me to fling the door open and discover the
two men who had dogged his steps, so he asserted, during the
latter half of the afternoon. I obeyed, little inclined to believe him,
but in a mood entirely sympathetic to Lawrence that bade me
demand these men's names and their business should they exist.
There was no one on the landing.[7]

Whatever may have been the case on this occasion, Lawrence's anxiety had more excuse than Robert's words suggest. According to Hugh
Kingsmill, the Lawrences were much harassed in Cornwall by people
suspecting them of being spies, a suspicion based on nothing more than
his wife's being German and his wearing a beard.[8]

The Lawrences' matchmaking for Robert and Heseltine must have
occurred at about the time when Heseltine became involved with the
celebrated artist's model known as Puma. Robert described the
involvement in graphic language to the Heads:

She told Phil a hard luck story one evening in the Café Royal.
Starving. No place to go etc. Phil, Dostoievskian by nature and
having lately been reading Dostoievsky, took her off to his studio
across the river opposite Chelsea. This was a studio with an inner
balcony on which he slept. He was sorry for her. She should be
treated as a sister. He slept downstairs on a sofa-settee. She used
his bed. After a few days she did him down. She had no attraction
for me sexually but I can see she would have had for some people
– a sort of Egyptian wild-cat with long legs and I suppose very
passionate. Anyway she couldn't leave Phil alone and I suppose
she thought him an easy mark. He had an allowance (small) and
'people'. After a while she announced herself pregnant and said he
was the father. Which I am told from those who have seen the boy
that he undoubtedly was. But the very same people say it might
well have been another for she was a loose sort of animal. (Animal
certainly – much admired by D. H. L. who in his letters (see one of
15 Feb 1916) obliges with a lot of bilge about her and 'the blood
connection, the dark sensuous relation' etc., etc.) Then Philip gets
in a state, short of money. Has to tell his mother. Mother gibbers –
she's a damn fool and mean anyway – and talks Christianity one
moment and outraged Kensingtonese the next. Finally Kensingtonese wins (in which she showed a temporary gleam of sense.)
Out with a baggage, etc. This is too much for Dostoievskian Philip

– and they call themselves Christians? Almost he begins to believe in Christianity. D. H. L. horns in. Is mystical and confused like the celebrated curate. Has messages straight from Priapus and the First Family Man via the bloodstream, the unconscious flow from aboriginal darkness and other divine channels. Talks his head off, being half dotty – poor chap – already as result of hard treatment (that *Rainbow* business was a dirty shame), the war and Prussian Frieda his hard-soft great female egg of a wife. What with echoes of infant choirings of English village Christianity, voodoo hocus-pocus of Prophet Lawrence and general worry and money anxiety and wonder about the child (quite probably his but possibly not) Philip suddenly ups and marries the animal. And never gets straight again.[9]

'I always disliked Puma,' Robert later wrote to Heseltine's mother, 'and she always disliked me, but as we didn't understand each other, that was perhaps inevitable.'[10] In these circumstances Heseltine's marriage to Puma perhaps inevitably interrupted his friendship with Robert, but not before he had introduced Robert into the musical world. Among composers he met then were Bernard van Dieren, a picturesque figure in the habit of pretending to be a blind fiddler in order to collect money in East End pubs,[11] and probably Delius, a friend of Heseltine since 1911; Elgar he met a year or two later.[12]

Jean Milne speaks of Robert as a sick man between autumn 1916 and June 1917. Even in July 1917 he still weighed only 9 st 1 lb, as compared with 11 st 4 lb when he went to France,[13] but he was ready to pull out of Ilsington and it was time for him to re-enter ordinary life. On 25 July his father wrote to Head: 'If Gilbert Murray could find him a job which he could cope with it would be very gratifying, and I think much better for him, but it would never do for him to be in London, and I think he quite realises this himself.'

London was unsuitable not only because it put a strain on his health. He had been in London earlier in the month, and had to explain to a friend that he had not seen him because he was chasing a woman. 'I drew all the money I had from the bank and overdrew and with some seventy odd pounds in my pocket followed her like a pilgrim or beggar only wishing to spend the money on such pleasures as she should choose and scarcely hoping for any reward.'[14] £70 was more than a quarter of the annual allowance his father was now making him. Robert was not, therefore, encouraged to make his home in London.

But he travelled up frequently, in October he was doing some work for the Ministry of Labour in Harley Street,[15] and by the end of the year was leading a full social life.

In May 1917 he was staying at a country house in Berkshire belonging to Frank Schuster, The Hut, Bray,[16] and this became an increasingly favoured place of retreat for him – he later rented a couple of rooms in an outbuilding.[17] Robert loved the garden, which went down to the river, and put it into his poetry.[18] Frank Schuster ('Frankie' he was usually called) was a man of means and a devotee of music; he played the part of Maecenas to many composers, gave brilliant parties at his house in London, and placed his country house ('The Hut' was a nickname; the formal name was 'The Long White Cloud', the Maori name for New Zealand) at the disposal of many people who like Robert were recovering from their experiences on the Western Front. In September 1917, besides Robert, it was accommodating two New Zealand volunteers and an officer of the Rifle Brigade. Robert's father was afraid he was imposing himself, but Robert wrote to Head:

He [Schuster] loves to have youth about him especially if they've done something for their country. There's no doubt about it – and it sometimes makes me quite ashamed – to see how this dear elderly man* reveres us just because we went straight off and did our manifest duty. And in my own particular case I specially appeal to him because somehow we see the same things in the war and we have each lost close friends in it. You've no idea how good F.S. has been to me. He encourages me in my work. He believes in me. If I could see you – the great believer – oftener I should not need him, save that he is lonely and *au fond* sad enough. He's not a conventional man – he don't care a damn for the usual things and the fashionable world of which he has had so much fatigues him. As he said to me one day, 'You know, Poet, I've got my few old friends and as they pass day by day I am extraordinarily lucky still to contrive to make friends and keep them among those who would be younger than my son if I had one. They're my comfort and the hobby of my old age.' Father doesn't know Schuster – doesn't realise that young men can be anything but mere bores to men of a certain age. I *know* F.S. likes to have me there or he'd never put up angelically with my moods. F.S. too likes I think to

*Schuster was born in 1840, a Christian of German-Jewish descent and remained active and hospitable until his death in 1927.

have me to make intervals in the boisterousness – though I always have a great flow of spirits there.[19]

Schuster first met Robert in Torquay in February 1916; Robert was then reading poems to Schuster's sister Adela, a lady who had contributed £1,000 to the cost of Oscar Wilde's defence at his Old Bailey trial.[20] Robert Ross was a common friend, and music a common interest. Robert's love of music had drawn him to Heseltine at Oxford; and by the end of 1916 he was working on the libretto of Bernard van Dieren's opera *The Tailor*. Robert says of this in his memoir of Heseltine:

When he urged on me that I should write librettos for [Kaikhosru] Sorabji and Bernard van Dieren, each of whom happened to need a libretto in a hurry, he seemed to think that this hurry was of no account whatever, whereas to extract the full significance from a series of situations (not to speak of making up the myth to start with!) always requires, in my experience, considerable time. My librettos for *The Rider by Night* and *The Tailor* were (in Hollywood studio-slang) "so gosh-awful they was jus' t'rrible". There was, I hold, a genuine idea in each, but Philip, in tyrannic mood, only allowed me about a week (if that) for the first and something less than a fortnight for the second. Nonetheless he appeared satisfied with them, nor, when I ran through them with him pointing out what damage this haste had done and how particularly it had impoverished the strictly dramatic interest, did he seem to care a rap.[21]

One poem at least from *The Tailor* pleased Robert enough for him to include it in *Ardours*: the 'Girl's Song' that begins:

O silver bird, fly down, fly down,
Bring thy fair gifts to him and me,
A purse contains a minted crown,
A golden ring for me.

Robert's meeting with Robert Graves in January 1917 followed a letter which he had written to him, probably in December, asking if he might dedicate the third part of *Ardours and Endurances* to him.* Graves was two years younger than he, and had been prevented by the

---

* In *Broken Images*, p. 61. Graves later wrote to Marsh: 'The last part of the book was dedicated to me until the last minute when one of Bob's lost loves consented to accept it' – p. 74. This part is now dedicated to Mr and Mrs Moiseivitsch.

war from going up to Oxford in 1914. Like Nichols he had had a
passionate desire to write poetry from an early age, and had failed to
enjoy his time at an eminent public school (Charterhouse). Each liked
the other's work, and for a while they were on very cordial terms. In
February 1917 Nichols asked Graves to help him with the finishing
touches to *The Faun's Holiday*, and received from the Front the charming plea to be excused:

> Here by a snow-bound river
> In scrapen holes we shiver,
> And like old bitterns we
> Boom to you plaintively.
> Robert, how can I rhyme
> Verses at your desire –
> Sleek fauns and cherry time?[22]

In 1918 Graves invited Robert to contribute to the publication he was
starting with William Nicholson, *The Owl*. The letters from Graves,
however, published in Paul O'Prey's *In Broken Images*, raise a doubt
whether Graves really took to Robert personally. Certainly they later
became estranged, and in 1931, referring to the war years, Robert
wrote to the Heads 'I thought I was friends with Graves but it appears I
was mistaken.'[23]

On 16 June 1917 Bowyer Nichols wrote to Robert Ross:

> My dear Robby, I'm not sure I quite caught the import of what
> you were telling me about the 'apotheosis' which Robert's friends
> are preparing for him, – I hope nothing serious but I can't help
> feeling a little anxious. His vainglory is so obvious and pathetic
> that I wish people would leave it alone, for they don't know how
> much harm may conceivably be done: and the very people who
> think it amusing to play on a weakness might with equal cruelty
> trample on it presently.[24]

Many years later Robert said :

> Father has always filled me with perturbation. It is sad to think
> that all my youth when he was lonely and unhappy we might have
> been friends and useful to one another, but for the most part
> inclined to be foes – or rather I inclined to find a foe in him. ... I
> try not to be [hard on him] but he wounded me so. I know now
> that he usually didn't mean to – but there you are: it's done.[25]

Perhaps Bowyer's letter to Ross was written in good faith, but if his son had seen it he might have found it wounding. It did not, however, check the rise in his celebrity.

The same June, Robert sent a copy of *Ardours* to Edward Marsh. They had corresponded in December 1916 about Rupert Brooke, and Marsh had expressed interest in Robert's 'publishing plans'.[26] Marsh was enthusiastic and invited Robert to meet him.[27] In the words of Marsh's biographer Christopher Hassall, 'Quite suddenly Nichols leaps into the small circle of Marsh's close friends with a fervent, occasionally tiresome, but obviously quite irresistible charm'[28]; and thereby began a friendship next in importance to that with Head. Marsh (born 18 November 1872) is perhaps best known as the friend and secretary of Winston Churchill. But he was also a scholar and man of letters, who edited the five volumes of *Georgian Poetry* that appeared between 1912 and 1922 and in these years was a figure of enormous authority in the literary world of London. Robert contributed to the two *Georgian Poetry* collections of 1916–17 and 1918–19 and when Marsh sent him his share of the takings for the first of these, was unwilling to accept it on the ground that 'You invented us and gave us a status.'[29] Marsh became a *confidante* second only to Henry Head, and nearly 200 letters to him from Robert survive.

In 1926 Robert wrote about Marsh:

I have had some very sensible and one or two more than sensible, wise and finely *corrective* letters from him. He is frivolous and worldly and sentimental and too accommodating to the world's foibles and his own pet little vices (we are all rather that last way) but you see, dear Sig, there is much that is very absurd and callow and, above all, doctrinaire about me and it sometimes does me good and anyway provides me with food for thought to be answered sometimes with the wisdom of this world especially when there is an occasional astringency of wit in that answer. One must remember that Eddie lives in three worlds (a) in connection with literature (b) as a Social Parasite who is under the delusion that some of the disgraceful wasters he frivols with are other than singularly disgusting prostitutes of all kinds, liars, pandars, backbiters, smart-alecks, womanisers, dinner table riff-raff and deplorable personages (c) as a lesser member of the indubitably great world of affairs. His Social Parasite side deserves everything you say and more. But I think

you forget the Great World a little. A man of some sensibility
and intellect even if his integrity as a person is a little too easily
suborned cannot move for years in the Great World of the highest politics and at the centre of great events without acquiring
certain kinds of knowledge and intuitions scarcely to be acquired
elsewhere.[30]

If Robert was glad to receive encouragement he was also ready to
offer it. In the summer or autumn of 1917 he wrote to Dorothy M.
Richardson. Her novels, which are now considered pioneering and
have been reissued by Virago, were then little known. Robert seems
to have been directed to them by Henry Head. She wrote thanking
him warmly for his 'most kind expression of sympathy and understanding', and said it gave her 'just the sort of encouragement I
needed'. There followed an exchange of letters that continued until he
went to America the following year and it is clear that like other
women with whom he corresponded, she found he put her on her
mettle. In one of her letters[31] she develops, in a heady fashion that
must have appealed to him, the theme 'that you are real and that the
famous figments art and love and God are expressions of the reality
within'. She winds up:

> But I know you know all this and probably much better than I, for
> I think you have had much more actual experience. On the other
> hand a certain kind of certainty is perhaps easier for me because I
> have not had a shaped education and ordered life to get rid of,
> having lived in a various jumbled haphazard way, stumbling on
> things I wanted. The light of reason I have always suspected and
> only now very late begin to see its place and respect it.

While Marsh was bringing out biennial volumes of *Georgian Poetry*,
the Sitwells were issuing annual volumes of *Wheels*. Robert did not
contribute, but in October 1917 Edith Sitwell invited him to visit her in
her Bayswater flat, and there began a friendship and correspondence
that lasted until November 1919.

The Sitwells were close in age to Robert, Edith being six years older,
Sacherevell four years younger and Osbert almost an exact contemporary; and there was further common ground in that their mother, like
his, was a source of anxiety – in 1915 she disappeared, not indeed into
medical care, but (by what now seems a miscarriage of justice) into
Holloway Prison. It is not surprising that Edith took to Robert, and her

letters, besides being in very clear and attractive handwriting, were in content well calculated to raise a moody poet's spirits. She flatters graciously: 'Why do you say you will "only attempt side glances"? The only Prometheus we have got, pretending he is frightened of fire.'[32] She gives good advice: 'Your letter made me very unhappy, though, in some ways. You mustn't get to love pain; it is such a danger for anyone like you. One thinks "as long as I can feel pain, I am alive", but I don't believe that is true, really, though I thought it was once.'[33] And she writes amusingly about herself: 'God, I am so bored with nearly everything; have had a horrible week, pursued by virtuous female cousins like very large empty omnibuses on very small wheels, who live in drawing rooms like railway carriages – only one never gets anywhere, even to a terminus.'[34]

A figure in the literary scene older than Marsh and the Sitwells and perhaps even more eminent was Edmund Gosse (1849–1928). H. G. Wells called him 'the official British man of letters' and T. S. Eliot said 'The place that Sir Edmund Gosse filled in the literary and social life of London is one that no one will ever fill again, because it is, so to speak, an office that has been abolished.'[35] Marsh had been a friend of Gosse for many years – they met in 1894[36] – and intended to introduce Robert to him, but Robert anticipated the introduction by writing to Gosse in October 1917. Gosse said 'Why wait for Eddie Marsh? When the trouble you speak of has passed away (and all cloud-shadows do pass in time) write and tell me, and I will propose a meeting.'[37] They met, probably in November, and according to Gosse's biographer Ann Thwaite, 'Like Graves and perhaps for the same reasons, Gosse was bowled over by Robert Nichols.'[38] What reasons? Perhaps that 'He behaved the way Gosse had always expected poets to behave',[39] but Gosse's being a friend of Robert's father[40] probably helped.

Gosse's critical eminence and Robert's belief in his own poetic star sometimes chafed against each other. Robert was wounded in 1919 when he sent Gosse a poem and Gosse replied: 'These verses are execrable, and I am shocked that you seem unable to perceive it ... I am afraid that flattery and excitement and the silly criticism of a circle of adoring admirers have completely turned you, for the time being, out of the true path.'[41] Gosse, for his part, remarked of a letter Robert sent him in 1923 along with his new book *Fantastica*: 'Really, it is as though Shakespeare were writing to an insect.'[42] Among Robert's unpublished poems is the following sonnet to Edmund Gosse (dated 5.12.19):

How difficult an art this friendship is
To know when least to give, when most to take
Of its inevitable contraries;
For the strong comfort of sweet friendship's sake
Sometimes too clearly burns the destructive mind
In a discussion born of single trust
And corporate interest, sometimes too blind
Against an argument in construction thrust.

Again, though not in traffic of mind's use,
The current of amity blows hot or cold
Whence rebuff must be suffered or abuse
With such skilled patience as true love may hold.
          Yet if man master this most difficult art
          He builds the mightiest citadel for his heart.

November 1917 was the beginning of another important friendship.
Siegfried Sassoon, having decided in July to protest against the contin-
uation of the war by refusing to perform any further military duties (a
protest that could not be misconstrued because he had already won the
MC for conspicuous bravery), had been persuaded by friends to appear
before a medical board. The board, deeply embarrassed, sent him to
Craiglockhart, near Edinburgh, the hospital for shell-shock sufferers
run by W. H. R. Rivers – the implication being that he was off his head.
Visiting London in November he was invited to dinner with Robert by
Robert Ross. He describes the evening in a letter to Lady Ottoline
Morrell:

> I met R. Nichols in town; and liked him. (Probably because he
> behaved so charmingly to me.) R. Ross gave us dinner, and we went
> on to see some people called Colefax, and I found it was a small at-
> home and that I was expected to read poems! Pretty thick, I
> thought; they might have given me *some* warning. However I slung
> a few ugly things at them – 'The Bishop tells us', and so on. Nichols
> read in a curious chanting manner which made me uncomfortable.
> But his things are very fine, when one reads them in the right mood.
> He is *the* poet for people emotionally wallowing in the blues.[43]

Uncomfortable feelings notwithstanding, Sassoon invited Robert to
Weirleigh, his parents' house in the country, at the beginning of December, and told Robert Graves that he 'was charming. He is quite different
when in town among a lot of people.'[44] Unlike some others that Robert

met at this time when *Ardours and Endurances* was bringing him fame, Sassoon was an extremely loyal, wise and unjudgmental friend whose patience and devotion never faltered.

The Colefaxes in whose drawing room Sassoon and Robert read were Arthur Colefax, a lawyer and Member of Parliament, and his wife Sibyl, founder of the decorating business. They were friends of Bowyer Nichols,[45] and entertained frequently on a large scale. The reading in November was followed by a more important one on 12 December. The poets on display included Edith and Osbert Sitwell, Aldous Huxley and T. S. Eliot; Sassoon and Graves were to have come too but did not show up. Gosse presided at what seems to have been a slightly sticky occasion. Huxley described 'the Shufflebottoms' (he meant the Sitwells) as nervous and Gosse as 'the bloodiest little old man I have ever seen'; as for Robert, Huxley said 'he raved and screamed and hooted his filthy war poems like a Lyceum villain who hasn't learned how to act.'[46] A letter to Robert from Edith Sitwell gives a lively vignette of the Colefaxes:

> Mrs Colefax dined with Osbert last night, looking more like a wrought-iron railing than ever. We had a lovely symbolic interlude. She arrived saying she had something in her eye … we all hunted – quite in vain. Eventually she and her husband paid a visit to the doctor next door, and emerged triumphant, Mr. C. saying proudly "It was a piece of iron-filing, and the doctor says we should *never* have found it; it was practically indistinguishable from the eye! I can't think how it got there, my dear." "Oh," said Mrs C. "I bumped into the railings in the dark. That is how it must have happened." – Diamond cut diamond, I presume.*

Aldous Huxley's description of Robert's reading to his brother Julian might suggest that the Huxleys did not much like him. In fact their father, Leonard Huxley, had been a friend of Bowyer Nichols at Oxford, Aldous was at Balliol with Philip Nichols when Robert was at Trinity; and the Huxleys and the Nicholses remained friends throughout their lives. But affection, especially in Bloomsbury, can cohabit with some acerbity.

---

*Letter dated 16.1.18, but 1918 could be a mistake for 1919. Robert was in America in January 1919, and she writes as if he were a long way off: 'We all miss you so much; and the parties are no longer the same; they haven't the same vitality. But all that must seem so microscopic to you now. I try to imagine how you must regard our life and us, from out there. Have we lost all separate personality for you? Do we differ from each other only in physical detail?' In January 1918 Robert was in France, but only at GHQ and briefly.

On 26 February 1918 Enid Bagnold wrote to Robert: 'I expect we shall meet – and when we do – well, I've met you already, as a matter of fact, at Mrs Colefax's Poetry Recitation. I was sitting in the distinguished crowd among the gold lace hats, listening.'

Enid Bagnold was four years older than Robert and belonged to much the same social and literary world. She had attended the select school in which Mrs Huxley, the mother of Aldous and Julian, had educated twelve privileged girls. She had then studied art under Walter Sickert with Gosse's daughter Sylvia, and she knew many people who either already were or were to become friends of Robert, such people as Desmond MacCarthy, Lady Ottoline Morrell, W. H. Davies, Ralph Hodgson and Max Beerbohm. In 1914 she trained as a nurse and worked at the Herbert Hospital. Apparently Robert had written to her about her book *A Diary without Dates* which gives a vivid and powerful picture of her work there. Its publication had resulted in her being sacked on the spot, and she was grateful for Robert's sympathy.

> I wrote my book [she said] for the patients. Absolutely and single-heartedly for the patients. During all the year I was writing it I would go down to the hospital each day, leaving my scrap of writing behind, tucked into a book, and ready for me to add to, and at the hospital I would fight and fight with myself to see nothing but the men, never to be disturbed by those other mentalities, all the women running about their tasks, and obeying each other. In the end I daresay I became impossible: – I didn't rush about enough, I would forget things. They were glad to get rid of me, perhaps, and now they are very bitter... [When she met women from the hospital in the buses they would cut her.] It's not that I mind their opinion, only of course they won't let me go back, and without the men I drop like a lump of lead to the old levels. Perhaps I shan't ever be able to write another book,* – perhaps it was only the men who wrote it through me. You are the only person in the world who said in words ... (oh, not only in your letter ... I gathered it at Mrs Colefax's) ... that the relation between one's men and oneself is something that makes all other relationships trite and pale. I say "my men" because in the ward they are under one's orders, and come a little bit into line with the position which they take with

---

*She went on, of course, to write several, including *National Velvet* and – in a different vein – the anonymously published *Serena Blandish*.

their officers. ... Your letter has given me, I think, the most happiness since I published the book. Because apart from being a poet, which hasn't in this special case got anything to do with it, you are a man from over *there*, you are one of those whom I know to have that strange freemasonry, you are the new soul that is being born of I. You are a patient, really.

Some more sprightly communications followed. She sent him an ink and wash drawing of himself in a bath with a cloud of steam, thoughts and poems rising out of it. This must have elicited a serious reply, since on 3 March she wrote (in pencil at 11.30 p.m.):

Dear Mr Nichols,

I've just this second got your letter, and my *spontaneous* answer is: – Lord how seriously you are taking me.

I'm not accustomed to it. – You see, people used to take me on my *own* merits and not on my book's (because there wasn't any book) – and I'm not a serious person.

Please don't tell me to be simple and sincere. You might as well tell a poor man to be God. He would if he could; but pity him in silence if he can't!

I'm *not* simple. It's better to be complex than to be mock-simple.

No, I'm not dealing blows, only laughing. I'll write tomorrow.

Goodnight.

The letter ends with a drawing of Robert asleep in a bed with large brass knobs.

What may be the promised letter of the next day – it is undated – runs:

Dear Mr Nichols,

Alright - *All* the letters "supposed a washout" if you please. Now let's start again; - and be

simple
sincere

If we could be that, on top of our other gifts, we shouldn't be writing letters at all, but

Plutarch
Balzac
Shakespere
Bible.

Do you know, I really understood about one in every four sentences in your last letter.

My fault, sure to be, but what is:

"not in essence physical, but rather a philosophical dead end, which harder, much harder" mean?

It stands by itself, without explanation.

Oh – I see you say I must be "gentle" whereas you say I'm being rough.

But not really. It's only my "exclamatory method".

Is it any good wanting to have "things in common" – wanting to be understood? Nobody *understands* anybody.

What I *meant* about love was (I know I didn't say it) –

What a woman does for you when she is in love with you amounts to nothing – and vice versa.

Because it's only indulging her to let her do it!

  Yours, EB.

PS *Don't tell me to work*. I can't stand it. Not from a new friend.*

It's bad enough when the old ones groan about it.

No, don't *ever* tell me to work again. It makes me feel ill.

Now, let's pretend I've been gentle and charming, instead of being prickly.

Anyway – what a long letter you're reading.

The postscript ends with a picture of him reading to the light of a drooping candle, with the words 'Even the candle is tired of my letter.'

On 26 June Robert wrote to Head: 'Enid Bagnold (she's a real help to me) says I ought to be married.' It is not clear whether she meant to herself. In her autobiography she says that in 1917 she was starting to get engaged.[47] She also admits to a poor memory of such matters. She can no longer remember the name of her first fiancé,[48] and looking through old letters she is surprised to find she was once close to W. H. Davies: 'How could I forget a warm friendship with a poet? But I have.'[49] At any rate, she married Sir Roderick Jones, head of Reuter's, and Robert's name does not appear in her autobiography though he and the Joneses remained on friendly terms at least until 1930.[50]

Edith Sitwell was a more faithful correspondent. Early in August 1918 she wrote from Renishaw, the Sitwells' house in Derbyshire, to Robert at Lawford:

---

*She is being a little unreasonable. In her letter of 26 February she had said 'Can you work? I can't, except under pressure, and scourgings from my friends.'

Dear Robert,

I take it that both you and I have by now been gathered to our forefathers, so do let's exchange experiences. I arrived here to find my Father, my Mother, and my Duty, in residence, – rather an uncomfortable ménage à trois.

How *did* one's parents produce one? I stare at them admiringly; they don't know why...

There is nothing to eat, and I sustain a nymph-like existence by splashing among the muddy streams of watered coffee which flow at breakfast time. My mother has a pony which thinks it is a Pekinese and tries to sit on one's lap; it has a glassy eye, and I am absolutely terrified of it; and, though no athlete, fly for miles, pursued by its affections and cries of "Your grandfather was such a *sportsman*! I can't imagine what makes you like this."[51]

Robert replied and she wrote back:

Dear Robert,

Thank you ever so much for your letter and the most wonderful poem, which I treasure. I always tell Osbert that whenever I see you, I feel like pinching you to see if you are real. It is incredible. I do hope you are better; Aldous described your sufferings. My own sufferings are pretty acute, but they are of a purely mental nature, however they are so intense that I feel they may corrode the body at any time. – In this district, a year or two ago, a living toad was discovered in a coal-mine, walled up in a seam of coal; he had been there for from two to three million years, – since the coal changed from trees into its present state – with nothing to look at and nobody to talk to. As Sachie remarks, the first million years must have seemed a bit long. Well, only that toad could even attempt to enter into my agonies, though with only partial success, as at least he had silence. With his advantage in that direction, I should have written better poems.

Ginger [her father; worse-tempered than Robert's and equally unappreciative of his offspring's poetic achievements] is too marvellously fantastic, so Italian Comedy, I expect him to break into tail-feathers at any moment. Whenever he looks at me, he bursts into floods of melodious tears, – my personal appearance having not come up to his expectations. At one moment I used to play the piano, but had to give it up as jellified females would melt over me; Ginger weeps over this: "Oh, my darling, every girl should have *some* talent or other!" This is a very pleasing device, as it swipes my poetry one in the eye without the possibility of a retaliation on my part. – He too has a fine library [Robert had perhaps written about the library at Lawford, which absorbed most of his father's time and which, thanks to Francis Morgan Nichols, was rich in works of learning]: a tract on fishing; Annals of the History of Eckington; "The Cloister and the Hearth"; "How to Propose", and a book he once tried to palm off on me, but didn't quite dare: "How to be Pleasing, though Plain." His courage suddenly failed him.[52]

Back in October Edith wrote asking if she might include Robert among the patrons of a concert she and her friend Helen Rootham were giving in aid of the Serbian Red Cross. This was to include works by Robert's friend Bernard van Dieren, 'so you will see', she says, 'that for once the good are not being rude to the clever, but are popping their heads confidingly into the mouths of the latter. The millennium must certainly be at hand (I can hear you say.)' She adds:

> Osbert is standing as Independent Liberal candidate for Scarborough. We are all a bit vague about our principles, but *ever* so staunch, which is the great thing. Osbert will have to preach and prance to country gentlemen gaping like fish with red and yellow waistcoats, red gills and no chins. Ugh! It is so dreadful to have to pretend that they are alive! Such a mockery![53]

To support Osbert's candidature the Sitwells went down from London to Scarborough (they had a house there, Wood End) and Edith sent Robert an account of their efforts:

> Ginger has been put to bed by mother, who has told him that he has gastric influenza. (In reality, he has put too much energy into his sole war work – that of nourishing himself: "keeping in good condition for whatever may turn up.")...
>
> The most awful woman on God's wide earth has just been staying here – Elizabeth Asquith. Her sandy desert of a mind has been poured out like the conventional dust and ashes on our afflicted heads. I like Lady Diana [Manners]'s epigraph for Asquith: "He was the father of Elizabeth Asquith, *but* he was Prime Minister of England."[54]

The Sitwells stayed at Scarborough over Christmas, and on Boxing Day Edith wrote:

Dear Robert,

In the midst of this bloody festival I like to remember that poetry exists, so as a matter of course I write to you. Do come back to England soon; surely your time is nearly up in the New Jerusalem [i.e. America], and, as the recruiting songs would say – "England needs you." Do you suppose Milton wrote the Hymn on the Nativity on Christmas Day? ... I guess not! How *did* the Plebs succeed in turning a thing of beauty into this festival of Moloch-Mammon?

She tells Robert she has been discussing religion with the mother of their artist friend Richard Nevinson, and remarks 'It makes me feel more and more as though one day I shall become a Roman Catholic. (It is the only creed for someone like myself, I do feel that more and more.)' This was a piece of advanced prescience, since though she actually did become a Catholic, it was not until August 1955, thirty-six years later.

This series of letters ends here; it is rather sad, after the friendliness which animates them, that the next exchange of letters between Robert and Edith Sitwell which has been preserved was in the columns of *Time and Tide*[55] and marked by considerable acrimony. Edith Sitwell retains her wit, but uses it against Robert with gracefully lethal effect; Robert, now bitterly at feud with her brother Osbert, is reduced to undignified bluster.

By the middle of 1918 Robert had come to know a good many writers and artists to be met in London. To those mentioned one might add J. M. Barrie, Walter de la Mare, Augustus John, John Masefield, Paul[56] and John Nash, William Nicholson, William Rothenstein, W. J. Turner and H. G. Wells; also Nancy Cunard, later to have a strong influence on both his life and his work. Bowyer Nichols, besides having a wide acquaintance among the men of letters of his generation, was close to the Pre-Raphaelites, and Robert could be said to have inherited, without seeking it, an accepted place in the creative social world. An article he wrote some years later helps us to imagine his life at this time:

'Listen to him' said Arnold Bennett, waving a hand at Swinnerton as we sat in the Reform Club discussing the merits of Tchekov and Maupassant, 'listen to him – did you ever observe anybody with so enormously serene and clear and arid a vision in your life.'

'Not arid,' returned Swinnerton, smiling his sad remote faun-ish smile, 'only dispassionate, purely dispassionate!'

'How he coos,' said Bennett, 'the very softness of his voice gives one an impression of distance, of remoteness!'

Sassoon suggested that Swinnerton was Destiny itself embod-ied – sitting in its superterrestrial club, stroking its pointed beard with a slightly humorous expression about the lips and a slightly sad expression about the eyes and remarking in a soft voice that looking out of the window on the world it could only see things as they were and might feel capable of pity or laughter if it could only observe a little more or a little less intelligence in the world. Privately I said to myself it isn't Destiny and a club window; it's only an absolutely first class social bacteriologist elucidating the nature of the infusoriae in a pint of drinking water from Highgate.[57]

Robert enjoyed doing verbal portraits like this one of Swinnerton. He admired E. M. Forster – he had a particularly high opinion of *Howards End* – and described an encounter with him at a Prom:

I think he's rather like a thrush – he has the same bright, enquiring nervous eye. He has an air of regarding me as a dangerous acquaintance – a sort of human containing a bomb – he wants to be nice to the human and he even dares to like it for a few minutes – but there's that accursed bomb – so he puts his head on one side and listens intently for a moment as though he was rather inclined to wonder whether he didn't hear it tick, becomes extremely shy and embarrassed at the problem of how to dismiss R.N. and himself, drops a 'g-goodnight. Nice to have seen you' and hops away, disappearing as effectively, none knows whither, as the thrush that leaves the garden path. He is more acutely shy than almost anyone I ever met. He is also extremely guarded. I do my best, but it is rather a nuisance never to be able to be direct but to have to approach every topic on tiptoe. One carries even the merest commonplace to him as if it were a piece of fragile glass or the thrush suddenly shakes himself till he is all feathers (you should see the motion of his mackintosh – he always seems enveloped in mackintosh) gives a faint embarrassed scream and flees away.[58]

A description of a weekend with J. M. Barrie shows Robert at the receiving end of an unnerving effect:

I don't think Sir James cottoned to me and though I did my best and he was certainly very kind I couldn't cotton to him. He makes everyone uneasy. Silence falls when he comes into the room. Even the children's laughter with him is rather hysterical. He is excessively odd in his gestures; his small dark eyes have something very unpleasant in their scrutiny and this oddness etc., is not lessened by his tiny gestures and little hands etc. He has the elusiveness of a fairy and I cannot persuade myself that this fairy is altogether a good fairy. Everybody was very busy being simple and self consciously unselfconscious ... J. M. B. is in his obscure elusive way a tyrant – it sounds strange but there's something cruel about him and his resolution to be wayward beyond what is natural and to pretend that all life is a child's game.[59]

7
New Poems

One of the things that attracted people to Robert was his total absorption in writing. At about this time he recorded the following 'Table of Intentions':

1. *The Book of Plaints*, in two parts: I Plaints various
   II Plaints of the Book of Love
2. *The Living Dust*: I The Return (poems to do with my war emotions since my return from the front)
   II Love Poems including the Elizabeth Cycle and the Sea Cycle
   III The coming of the unanimist idea: that is, after proving in I and II my ordinary emotions I come on to this change which has come over me. 'I know not how the spell came on me.' Then the poems of strangeness, or vague unrest. Then 'The Stranger' and other poems akin.
3. *Polyphemus*: blank verse interspersed with opera bouffe. Some pagan poems added at the end.

Polyphemus was begun in July 1917 at Joey's Temperance Hotel, Lamorna, Cornwall. All that Robert composed was a dialogue between a shepherd and a country girl which is supposed to take place after Galataea has gone off with Acis and when Polyphemus, the gigantic Cyclops blinded by Odysseus in the *Odyssey*, is mourning her departure. He entitled it: 'Closing lines from "Polyphemus, his Passion: a Pastoral"' and it is in blank verse without any interspersions. There is a suggestion, however, of opera bouffe in the shepherd's description of Polyphemus on his rocky headland.

> Long time disconsolate
> Bowed he his massy head, quite dumb with grief.
> But, at the last, confusedly arousing
> His sluggish hands, groped for and found his pipes,
> Twin, dry, boughless trunks of beech fire-hollowed
> And with huge cinder slotted. These he set
> To cave-like mouth, then, pursing hairy lips,

Vented, with monster fingers laid on stops,
His heart's deep sorrow: 'twas a wounding sound.

'Polyphemus' is dedicated to Tommy Earp. It appeared (along with a poem by Earp himself) in *Oxford Poetry 1918* and subsequently in *Aurelia*, so Robert seems to have been satisfied with it as a complete work. It belongs, in fact, to the same genre as his 'plaints'. He compares Polyphemus's lament to

> the mournful blowing of the waves,
> Which in the pyloned gloom of norward cave
> Nightly with flood soon-swallowed and discharge
> Of pouring foam, deep tide, and troubled ebb,
> Makes profound plaint and dreary melody
> To lightless waste, huge night and solemn stars.

And he was slightly piqued to discover, after he had finished it, that Leconte de Lisle had already written some *plaintes du cyclope*.[1]

Between 1916 and 1918 Robert composed at least sixteen poems that he called 'plaints'. At least three made their way into print. Although his chronic tendency to self-pity was always liable to impart a plaintive tone to his writing, the idea of a plaint is in fact rooted in the pastoral tradition and does not exclude grotesque or even comic effects. Robert's plaints vary considerably in subject and character. He projected several that he seems never to have begun, for example a plaint of dogs to the Dog Star, a plaint of the Man in the Moon, and he never divided those he did write into separate categories of 'plaints of love' and 'plaints various'. His poem 'The Pilgrim', which is not really a plaint at all but a religious poem, and which appeared in *Georgian Poetry 1918–19*, was originally destined for the *Book of Love*.[2] On the other hand 'Plaint of a Simple Simon', which was projected as a 'plaint universal', is straightforwardly lovelorn.

Ardours contains 'Plaint of a Pierrot Ill-Used', dated November 1916. This looks like an allegorical account of Robert's own life: born with moonshine in his head, loving Columbine but going away to college, overspending and coming back to find her faithless and departed. 'Plaint of a Simple Simon' and the slighter and more satirical 'Plaint of Love's Martyrdom' are of the same date. In *Aurelia* there is the quite different 'Plaint of a Humble Servant', dated April 1918 and dedicated to the composer Elgar. The humble servant is a donkey, and the burden of which he complains is not just his uncouth appearance but his inability to join in creation's praise of the Creator. A similar mood is expressed in the unpublished 'Plaint of a Baboon' which begins:

> I am not nice: I know it.
>   But why take me to task?
>   My way is nasty but I did not ask
> That you should cage me here to show it.

and in 'Plaint of a Leper' which has the refrain 'Unclean! Unclean!'

The Living Dust was apparently to be a volume of lyrics in several parts, but what Robert says about it in the 'Table of Intentions' is more programmatic than clear. The 'poems to do with my war emotions since my return from the front' may include the war poems printed in *Aurelia* and discussed above. He was writing both love poems and poems to do with the sea in 1916–18 when he was spending much of his time on the Devon and Cornwall coasts, and loved a girl called Elizabeth[3] Birchenogh (later Dodds),[4] the subject of 'November' in *Aurelia*. By 'the Sea Cycle', however, as distinct from 'the Elizabeth cycle', he may mean the sequence of poems entitled 'The Flower of Flame' in *Aurelia* (in which case the 'Table' would have to be as late as 1919). As for 'the coming of the unanimist idea', that phrase is opaque. In a letter to Head dated 13 April 1918 he says: 'I am more and more struck by the unanimity of the greatest minds – on certain points – or by the unanimity of approach. Look at the tolerant atmosphere of Rabelais, Aristophanes, Shakespeare, Leonardo, Goethe.' That is a list that comprehends, one might have thought, a considerable variety of minds and approaches. But 'I know not how the spell came on me' is a quotation from a poem intended to be introductory to *The Living Dust* in which he describes a sense of alienation not only from his surroundings but from himself: 'Self from myself felt strange defection.'

The phrase 'the living dust' is intended to signify humanity. 'Dust' is the word used in the King James version of Genesis for the substance out of which God made Adam. 'Before th' Eternal spoke its word,' Robert says,

> I lay or lifted, streamed or stirred,
> Dust of the lifeless dust;

but then 'a drift of white power stooped', and:

> The dead dust quaked and stood upright,
> And that live dust was I.[5]

Robert's womanising during his convalescence, mentioned in chapters 5 and 6, seems to have aroused feelings of revulsion from the bodily. In a sonnet which probably dates from this time he asks:

> O to what end did Beauty body fashion,
> That with its gusts it ruins so my being? ...
> O to what end? If end not this in smother
> Of dust in act with sense-befuddled dust?

But his own adventures were not the only factor. 'I had bought', he says, 'a copy of the *Confessions of St Augustine*, induced to do so solely by the fact that Edward Pusey, who had based this translation on a version of Watts, was related to my mother's family.'[6] Opening it idly in a train at chapter 27 of book 10, he was struck even more forcibly than Augustine had been struck by Cicero's *Hortensius*. He graduated to Pascal and Thomas à Kempis and for a while even 'to reading regular prayers, to bodily penalties and mental mortifications'. 'The Pilgrim' is not the only religious poem of this period. In the summer of 1917, perhaps just after the July episode, he wrote a poem echoing Francis Thompson. It begins:

> Long have I fought thee. Here the end is found.
> In hills first sought I to evade thy face:
> There the rain met me and in that profound
> Grief I perceived thee and received thy grace.

Another poem preserved among the plaints has echoes of Thomas Campion:

> Why so anguished wretched soul
>   Is there nothing will content thee?
> That to self-contempt and dole
>   Thou thy force spendest and hast spent thee?
> Wildly, bitterly thou plainest
> But His peace, certain peace, with ire, with grief, with
>   shame disdainest.

The culmination is a sequence of highly devout poems, dated to May 1918, in which he invokes the Saviour, meditates on Christ's Passion and seems to feel guilty about the pleasure he has been accustomed to take in the senses. 'Saviour,' he says, 'I love the pleasure of the eye', but:

> I wish not anywhere to rest my eyes
> Save where the light of Thy loved face yet lies.

Robert's exploration of religious themes was not confined to poetry. On 11 May 1918 he paid Head the compliment of sending him no less than sixteen questions about the existence and nature of God, and added artlessly a couple of days later that Head's equation of God with the laws of nature 'seems rather remote'.[7] Like Aldous Huxley he wanted to 'attain the Olympian balance, tolerance and intelligence of Landor in his "Pericles and Aspasia"', but unfortunately 'I am cursedly crossed by a severe strain of mysticism of a purely religious sort – an inheritance from the Puseys. I cannot – it seems – be satisfied with the great calm mysticism of Goethe's aphorisms on Nature (which I take him really to mean Law). I want something personal, so personal.'[8] His dilemma is put more succinctly in a letter to Marsh: 'There is now nothing I seem to care for except the idea of a Personal God and he does not seem to exist.'[9]

Apart from this doubt about the fundamental article of Christian belief, Robert was troubled by rather a one-sided view of the general character of Christianity. His poems are apt to equate it with grim asceticism. 'The Christians have harmony,' he conceded to Marsh, ' – yes, but by a dire subtraction of every Promethean and Apollonian quality – for them intellectual pride must be sacrificed and intellectual poise – for them the soul is not in a state of grace (happiness) save it cease to aspire for knowledge and can learn only a state-of-sickness in which it is too feeble to rise from its knees.'[10] Whether for these or for other reasons, *The Living Dust* was to contain the following lines, perhaps as its final statement on the subject:

> O thou the Power of Powers, that dost exult
> The clay which Thou has moulded to insult
> With the sad gift of life, which is the power
> To suffer and wish suffering every hour,
> Receive the vengeance of the dusts which live:
> We endure, we defy Thee, we at length forgive!

8

First Visit to America

In June 1917[1] Robert told Head he would like to go to America and lecture on modern English literature; the idea came from his Middlecot friend Henry Lyon who had a visit planned and wished Robert to accompany him. A week later he had second thoughts. He was afraid of being sunk by a German submarine: in early 1917 the Germans had started attacking merchant shipping without, as international law required, giving the people on board an opportunity of taking to their boats. He also thought he would 'cordially dislike America'.[2] But once conceived, the idea would not go away. 'The Foreign Office wants me to go to America,' he told Head in February 1918. 'I don't want to go. Everything unites to make me dislike it.'[3] In June his boss G. H. Mair put forward a 'pressing proposal':

> It is to be a sort of visit of honour [he told his father]. I shall not have to tub-thump. Apparently the book (*Ardours and Endurances*) is making quite a place for itself over there and the Propaganda people of the British Mission seem to think that if I appeared in person it would do good. I am to tour the principal universities – including Harvard and Yale. I shall not have to speechify though I have offered to give one or two addresses on modern English poetry etc., if it would help. (Partly because I'd like to help my friends – Sassoon, Huxley, Graves etc.) All I have to do is to talk about the war and to try and show that we appreciate the American effort, also to get in touch with American writers and the American intelligentsia.[4]

Finally in mid September his destiny overtook him and after some doctoring up at a London nursing home he sailed from Liverpool in a convoy of five liners escorted by destroyers.

Despite this escort 'the Hun attempted to torpedo the ship behind us', and 'the great ships began a complicated saraband.'[5] That and the heavy sea gave Robert some qualms, but he always found the sea inspiring and composed an ecstatic 'Ballad of Mid-Atlantic' in which Venus appears to him out of the foam of the ship's wake. He also recorded a real incident that was hardly less bizarre:

At night when in the creaking ship
Huddled I lay and vainly sought
To sleep but lay afar from sleep
Meshed in a dumb distress of thought

Suddenly sounded – and so near! –
A single, gasping, hellish laugh
That shook my very strings with fear
And cut my latest breath in half.

It is the madman whom they lead
Hid from the decent daylight's view,
Tramping the dark deck overhead
'Outcast, unseen, and drenched with dew.'

Robert was officially attached to the New York office of the Ministry of Information. This organised propaganda against Germany – very effectively, he claimed in retrospect.[6] His first engagement, he told Marsh, was 'to do with a picture-show of Orpen, Kennington, Bone, Nevinson, Nash etc.' This was an exhibition of British war paintings. He had a lecture on English poets of the last twenty years, which puts his own contemporaries into relation with the poets of the Nineties. This was illustrated by readings from Graves, Sassoon, and above all Charles Sorley, whom he had not known personally but only glimpsed asleep in a dugout a month before his death in October 1915. He seems to have admired his poetry more than that of any other of the early Georgians. While in New York he also lectured on shell shock,[7] placed a wreath on the catafalque of Joyce Kilmer, the first American poet to be killed in the war, and with John Galsworthy attended the centenary celebrations for James Russell Lowell. Frank Harris was in New York at that time and 'tried to be matey, which wouldn't do at all as I was on the Mission and he was due to appear before the U.S. Senate on a charge of treason. He tried to nobble me at the opera and later wrote to me he was in New York as Jesus Christ was on Golgotha. Whereupon I replied I couldn't see him and that the similitude in his comparison seemed to me exaggerated.'[8] Robert did not like Harris.

Neither, as he had apprehended, did he much like America. In a letter to Marsh of 26 December he says 'Nearly everything is like the Blue Point Oyster – very large and very insipid.' He speaks of 'the cold, clear, uninteresting bleakness of the New England landscape'. He was particularly disappointed by the women: 'They are like icebergs and not nearly so beautiful though their beauty has something of the same *impersonality* about it.' He did, however, see the point of American architecture which he found 'amazingly young, good and fresh. They have in New York some of the most beautiful buildings on earth – for instance one called the Bush Terminal which is more beautiful than almost any cathedral in England.' And in January he was able to report one exception to the general frigidity of American womanhood:

This is just a line to say that my delightful friend Mrs Lamont, to whom I was sent by Masefield,* is coming to England, and I have asked her to come and see you as she is a lovely person and really loves and understands the things we love and understand. Her husband is a junior partner in Morgan's and a man I very much respect. Both have treated me with the utmost kindness since I landed here – in fact Mrs Lamont is my greatest friend in America. She is a person of character – she has the brain of a philosopher (she is a friend of Bergson), the courage of a lion and the heart of an angelic child. She wishes very much I think to meet Siegfried if she can – d'you think you could manage it?[9]

In the event Mrs Lamont made friends with Bowyer Nichols – she saw him on visits to Europe in the 1925 and 1927 – and to Robert himself she became a fairy godmother. Her faith in him was unfaltering, in bad times she gave him encouragement, and in lean times financial support. A later letter of hers to Robert conveys the flavour of her personality:

After Christmas, which really was unusually gay because Austin [her son] came home for it, we had the great fun of a visit from General Smuts. Do you know anything about him? He came over for the tenth anniversary of the League of Nations celebration. He is one of the two or three really great men whom I have ever met. Woodrow Wilson was one. I cannot think of a third. I fell head over heels in love with him. He is a philosopher, a real professional one, as well as a statesman and is a great charmer. ...

I had a very gay month of January. It is the gay month of New York life. It ended for me February 6, by a hideous dinner at the White House. Tom [her husband] the Bluebeard dragged me down by the hair of my head to Washington to the President's

*The Lamonts had met Masefield in England in 1917. (So Edward Lamont, *The Ambassador from Wall Street*, Maryland, 1994, p. 97.)

dinner. We left N.Y. at noon, reached Washington in time for dinner, and came back on the 1.35 a.m. train – pretty strenuous. The dinner was too dreary for words – the most solemn affair I have ever attended. Funerals are frivolous in comparison to the gloom of the Hoovers in the White House. When we went in to dinner I found myself sitting between two New York bankers, whom I had been trying to avoid all winter. I suppose that I must have looked pretty desperate because Tom advanced to me in a menacing sort of way and hissed in my ear "Play the game." After the dreary dinner was over, and the men joined the ladies, my heart leaped when Hoover came in to the room, for I thought he was coming to talk to me. I had figured out that of the 20 women there I was the third most attractive (this isn't as conceited as it sounds, you should see the women!) and so there was a 33⅓% chance of his coming to talk to me. But alas, each man went up to the woman he had taken out to dinner and offered her his arm and escorted her to the big East room to a concert. So the same man and woman sat together the entire evening. The concert consisted of a revolting little Latin rolling his eyes and shrieking in a high tenor voice. At the end, the Hoovers arose and arm in arm, solemnly stalked out of the room.[10]

The Lamonts were not the only American friends Robert made. On a Sunday evening in January he passed an open church and, going in, heard Vachel Lindsay reciting his poem 'Abraham Lincoln Walks at Midnight'. Lindsay was, as Robert put it, 'something of a character, had been an itinerant preacher, an art student, a fire-eater, a rabid Middle Westerner'. Robert conceived a high opinion of his poetry and helped him to obtain recognition not only in England but also in New York where Middle Westerners were not immediately welcomed by the literary establishment. When Lindsay came to England with his mother in 1920 he visited Robert, Robert returned the visit when he was back in America in 1924–6, and on Lindsay's death in 1931 in Springfield, Illinois, Robert sent his condolences to the Mayor of Springfield on the loss of 'a man whose distinction in the field of letters would confer honour on any city in the world'. The letter was published in the *Illinois State Register* of 22 December.

Another American friend Robert made at this time was John Jay Chapman.[11] Some thirty years Robert's senior, Chapman was a writer of eccentric personality and violent views. At the age of twenty-five, having assaulted a friend in a fit of jealousy, he put his left hand in the fire and kept it there until the flesh was burnt off the fingers and knuckles. The hand had to be amputated. Later, in 1900, he had a breakdown and went to bed for a year. Initially he was a fierce opponent of American involvement in the 1914–18 War. His son Victor, against his wishes, joined the Foreign Legion and was killed in 1916. This made him as passionately in favour of fighting as he had been against it, and may have been what first drew him to Robert; but they soon found other common ground: a romantic feeling for Prometheus, a hatred of industrial capitalism, a desire for a Christianity that would cut out ecclesiastical authorities and dogmas and embrace all mankind.

In the letter in which he commends Mrs Lamont to Marsh, Robert says he is about to go on a lecture tour, and he lectured at the universities of Yale, Vassar, Cornell and Chicago.[12] His contract with the British Government ended on 31 December, but in a letter to his father of 26 December he says he has been offered $2,000-3,000 for ten weeks' lecturing. Other cities he visited included Nashville, Tennessee (where he addressed the Centennial Club), Pittsburgh, Pennsylvania, and he even got to Toronto where he stood in for John Galsworthy.[13] His main theme was the British war poets, and his warmest praise was for Sassoon, Graves and Charles Sorley. During his stay in New York he was roused by the January weather to compose a short verse dialogue in which he and Graves compare their ideals of winter and Sassoon refuses to adjudicate between them – this appears in *Aurelia*. He particularly impressed the Nashville audience when he was explaining the change which came over Sassoon's poetry in the course of the war:

In a shaking voice and with outstretched, nervous hands he said passionately:
'There are no spiritual properties to war; I do not think being shot at improves a man's temper or his moral fibre. War is what one of your American generals called it – "hell", and it is a suffering and defilement. Any man who justifies it, except in the cause of defending national honour, is a liar and criminal, and ought to be crucified. The love of officers and men is the one beautiful thing which developed, and these will disqualify them for civil life. The mere capacity to suffer in company does not help anything. And the awful suffering did not help at the time, or now. You may learn more about life. A soldier simply has to stick it. War makes no man finer. It is a process of defilement, a time when you wait

and lurk to kill your neighbour, as he is waiting and lurking to kill you. To say that such as that makes a soul better is blather.'[14]

In Chicago Robert met the poet Conrad Aiken, who was to become a lifelong friend in spite of the fact that, thinking Robert too hard on American poets, he wrote a lampoon 'Verbum Saphead' which was printed in the *Chicago Tribune*.[15] At this stage of his tour Robert was suffering from home-sickness induced by absence of spring flowers,[16] but Chicago raised his spirits. According to a newpaper report he said:

> New York is a beautiful hell. Boston is a plaster cast of Athens. But Chicago – Chicago is a real city. It has, if you don't mind bad language, what we call in England guts.
>
> I love Chicago. I love the power of it, the drive, the great gehenna on the edge of the frozen sea as one comes into it. There is more material for the poet under one's eyes in Chicago than anywhere I have been in America. It is inherently American.
>
> It may sound queer to you, but it is really much more like an English city than either New York or Boston. There is something Parisian about New York, its hectic gaiety, its sensualism, and yet it is a much wickeder city than Paris because Paris at least has emotions. New York is neither hot nor cold, but always luring for the game of luring. It is the most calculating city I was ever in in my life.
>
> Boston still lives in the days of a unitarian form of ancient Greece. Instead of building itself a great temple of living marble it lives inside a plaster case of the Acropolis. But Chicago! There is something honest and forcefully potent about its very dirt and smoke.

That Robert was not merely being diplomatic (seldom a weakness of his) may be inferred from a poem he sent Marsh on 5 March:

> *Hobbledehoy's April Impromptu*
> Don't your quick feet feel like dancing
> In this foolish April weather,
> When the Sun himself advancing
> Ducks and dips amid white weather
> When the willows by the river
> Rattle, sprinkle, shine and shiver,
> When the goose-flock waddles clacking,
> When the washing hangs asmacking...

But his mood did not survive arrival in Pittsburgh later in the month. On 30 March he wrote a long letter to Marsh from which it is worthwhile to quote at some length because it reveals the beginning of thoughts that were to shape his main prose writings in the next few years.

I have attempted to approach the saloon [of the Pitt Hotel where he was staying] to write to you. But no. I couldn't face it. Picture it – a pseudo marble tank with a low roof peopled by, O, hundreds of leather and oak armchairs (of the most dispiriting and uncomfortable variety) and by acres of little crotchety writing tables and dozens of brass spittoons. Sitting in these chairs, exhaling a stale cigar miasma, using with a remarkable fecundity of tobacco-juice these spittoons, butt-end of rank weed in mouth, crushed hat or bowler on back of head, sits the average man: the plague of civilization and the detested of the Gods. He will not die young. No: he is in all shapes and sizes: uncouth as a seal on dry land and not nearly so much of an amusing gentleman. I hate him! My God, how I hate him. The aroma of his mediocrity is a worse savour than the vapours which rose from Sodom and Gomorrha. He is complacent. Yesterday he made $20 more than his record. By the faint glimmer that passes on his vacuous eyes enquiring of the jejune goddess Fortune – naked nearly and obviously emanating from local vaudeville – I see that he guesses tomorrow he may top that record and make it $25. God damn and blast him! The future of civilization, I am informed, is in his hands – in the hands of that thing: that air of shoddy-fine boots, that sack overcoat, that bowler, that cigar-butt! ...

So I seek refuge in my dingy bedroom which is at least lifted above the quotidian horror of that grubby mediocrity against which, it being one of humanity's conditions, I should not inveigh were it not quite possible for most of this to be mended and rendered if not beautiful, at least sane. But even here is no refuge. A ghastly Gibson woman arches her hips at me from the picture on the wall and in my bathroom a plumber is grubbing and whistling the while a devastating tune. I did think that plunging – before I wrote – into a white porcelain bath and towelling with rough towels smelling like new baked bread, I could escape, and in my mind as I stood refreshed stand tasting with some feeling of reality those lovely lines

Oh, take me to the mountain! Oh,
Past the great pines and through the wood,
Up where the lean hounds softly go
A-whine for wild things' blood (what a line!)
Where frantic flies the dappled doe. *

But I see my Grecians are dead in Pittsberg [*sic*]. Not that Pittsberg isn't fine in its way. So is Hell in its. Which brings me after two devious and excoriated pages to the purpose of my letter. Eddie, I'm stuck: one side of my mind and two thirds of my spirit simply long to begin making anew the Greek world of the Romantics – casting perhaps a little strange light on it by the queer illumination garnered from *The Golden Bough* etc.: a Cretan and Cyprian Greece rather than an Athenian. The other third is bothered about those clothed insects in that padded limbo of a saloon: what they are: whether they are as mechanical as ants and *au fond* as infecund (they secrete only tobacco juice, it seems, though on a heroic scale) or whether some dim and gigantic idea informs this chaos they are making – for Pittsberg is theirs – the cinder heaps, the blasted trees, the rusty old iron, the fume-laden air. Somehow I find it hard to think what they are up to – I deem it more likely that they are in the clutches of the thing. For nowhere over the whole earth do I see anywhere an attempt to adumbrate quite what the Monster is after –

'They heap up wealth but cannot tell who shall gather it!'

I see no directing spirit anywhere.

It is not enough to increase the wealth of the world – it is but to transmute what was powerless for evil when hidden in the womb of nature to an abortion. The beauty that is made for the rich is only the heart's luxury, an outward thing which at its worst does but corrupt the soul by turning it to perversity and at the best merely refines it to delight rather in material than in idea. For the Highest Beauty is in Idea: it is this lack that makes Herculaneum so inferior (the coarse grain of it is unhideable) to Athens. And towards Herculaneum rather than Athens the world is turning. There is however a third path – that is it seems to me toward what I can only call Gothic strength: I see it in these factories. How much diabolism rests in the admired gothic none have computed.

---

*He was reading Euripides' *Hippolytus* in Gilbert Murray's translation, but here quotes from memory.

A cathedral, says Claudel, is either a Pit (i.e. Pittsberg) or a Flame. The same spirit of melancholy and majestic will that jointed the towering arches of Notre Dame, most sinister of cathedrals, rejoices today in the more Satanic resources of steel, glass and ferro-concrete. The Flame is no more – for the spirit of Chartres, rushing upward in lyric appreciation, is dead. The Renaissance provided the coffin, the black spirit of the Pit that one may designate as Intellectual Pride (Chartres is Intellectual Humility) drove in the nails with the pistons of the first steam engine as hammer. But the insects under bowlers in the hall understand neither Greece (which is Harmony) nor the Modern World which is prompted (though not guided) by Intellectual Pride. They are blind to the light of the one and deaf to the might of the other. Between these two I, by virtue of fortune, stand. Do I have time to interpret – in however ephemeral and unsatisfactory a way – both?

Robert was to make the attempt in his play *Guilty Souls* and his novel *Golgotha*. It would be difficult because he combined the intellectual arrogance of the Bloomsbury and Cambridge intelligentsia (betrayed in his embarrassing description of the men in bowler hats) with a mistrust of the optimistic liberal economic theory which alone could put a plausible face on it. But at least Pittsburgh (which he never took to the trouble to spell correctly) seems to have opened his eyes. The industrial city he saw has now disappeared but the gothic spirit he discerned still prevails in the gothic skyscraper of the university.

9
Aurelia

L et me that pure delight declare
      Her body to my senses yields
When nakedness makes doubly fair
      Her beauty, – as the still clear air
      Does the flame-roseate, noble, bare
Moon risen on frosty autumn fields.[1]

Whether or not this particular poem is founded on an actual episode, much of Robert's early love poetry reads more like an expression of fantasy than a distillation of experience. But his best work sprang from a relationship with a real person.

Nancy Cunard, the daughter of Sir Bache Cunard of the shipping line, was two or three years younger than Robert but an early developer. At the age of sixteen she was sent to Munich to study music and improve her German; at eighteen she was taking a place in the literary and artistic world of London; and at nineteen she made an unhappy marriage. She contributed the opening poem to the first number of *Wheels* in 1916. Robert could have met her in 1917, when her marriage was coming to an end, or earlier; they had a number of friends in common. He was certainly sighing after her in 1919. He had returned from America in May and after spending most of the summer in the vicinity of London,* in October took lodgings in Brecon to write and save money. His income, he calculated, was £200 a year,[2] and he could live in Brecon for 55/- a week.[3] On 1 November a letter from Nancy Cunard to this retreat carried him up into a state of wild euphoria.[4] Shortly afterwards he went to London at the invitation of Frank Schuster[5] and there followed some kind of love affair in which he wrote the poems to Aurelia which appear in *Aurelia* and other works which remain unpublished.

The affair cannot have been of long duration, since it appears from a letter to Marsh dated 26 April 1920 that by then it was completely over, and Nancy Cunard moved to Paris on 7 January, though not in a way

---

*His letters of this period are written from Lawford, London and Schuster's house, The Hut, but he also visited Harlech, presumably to see Robert Graves and the Nicholsons.

that excluded being back in London from time to time. She herself was inclined to play it down. The *Aurelia* poems, she complained, 'tell of every kind of lurid occasion that never arose at all between us – poetic licence, if ever there was.'[6] In fact, while the poems do imply that she and Robert slept together, she prided herself on being sexually emancipated and there are no details of lurid occasions. Her diary for the period contains entries that are not at all flattering to Robert. 'Lord had I but known what I was starting, when I got hold of that young man ... He is mad, no doubt of it, and very, very common, but thinks he is a genius instead of which he is really a shocking poet.'[7] But although she never managed to spell his name correctly she remained friends with him. Tommy Earp was a bond between them; and his letters were among those she lamented losing when her cottage in France was looted at the end of the Second World War. In April 1921 she wrote a long letter asking to hear from him, and in May sent him a copy of her first volume of poetry, *Outlaws*. By this time he was in Japan. What prompted her to describe him as 'very, very common' is unclear; certainly the Nicholses were a match for the Cunards in birth. Perhaps she detected in him vestiges of bourgeois morality, distasteful to one so scornful as her of tradition and convention.

Robert's side of the story is given in a letter to Marsh in April, when he was awaiting the publication of *Aurelia*:

I saw Nancy in London. We are I think friends. She spoke very gently to me, heaven bless her. She was looking rather tired, poor darling. It became more than ever evident to me that she had never loved me – she told me so, you know, a number of times but then her acts belied her words. I think she has a totally different idea of what love is to what I have – hers is the 'intrigue' conception – a sort of battle of wits with a certain witty refined exquisiteness of interchange on the way and a consummation which is given with a sort of shrug between grief, pride and ironic satisfaction at such an end. An eighteenth century conception - there have been great lovers in this sort, I suppose, but I am not one of them. For me love has quite a different and a more fatal meaning. Yet it is curious: no book in the world almost fascinates her as much as *Wuthering Heights* in which love is a sort of heavenly and hellish *possession* as if by a rebel angel, which it is to me. She knows what it is to have the *other* present in the room when the corporeal presence is many miles away.

Under it all I suppose I bored and frightened her – I was something with which she could not deal and she isn't equal really to
dealing with most things – that is what makes her so frenetic:
playing harder like a gambler when chance is going against him,
one who hopes to retrieve himself before ruin and who at the
same time says 'What matter? Ruin must come – let it be greatly,
then.' But alas, it isn't her own soul only she gambles with. But I
forgive her, poor darling suffering thing. There is no more love in
me now – only gentleness and care and concern for her. I have
come back to what I started from, before she diverted me (and
yes, I suppose I in some part diverted myself) from my purpose; I
feel as if in the trough of this life-sea I wished to support her in
my arms to the last and that without a cry, without asking anything of her or even letting her know who is trying to hold her up.
She is no more woman to me now, she is a child – but I don't pity
her – she scorns pity and in a way is too strong, too imperious in
spirit to need it – however much she wrongs herself – and she has
wronged herself much. She has sinned against herself more than
against any other – no, I don't pity her, I feel a gentleness toward
her that has nothing superior or condescending about it. We are
both weak, and the 'wrong is mixed'. At one time I wished her
dead to relieve me of my torment and that she might find peace
which she will scarcely find elsewhere. But now her death would
be a catastrophe and the last unfairness of a Fortune which has
played us so many tricks.[8]

At the height of the affair it was in fact himself rather than her that
he wished dead. Daphne Fielding in her book *Emerald and Nancy* says
that one day Robert

produced a Colt revolver and threw it at her feet, imploring her to
prevent him from blowing out his brains. She calmly picked it up
and put it away, but could not think what to do with it afterwards
or how to get rid of it. Eventually she smuggled it across the Channel on a journey to France with G. M. [George Moore], who
fortunately did not enquire into the nature of the bulge in the
pocket of her leopard-skin coat.

Aurelia was not what admirers of *Ardours and Endurances*
expected. Laurence Binyon, who had been so enthusiastic about *The
Faun's Holiday*, wrote a rather muted review in the *Observer*: the

author 'has plenty of faults entwined with his strong qualities' and 'if
this volume does not mark a great advance in Mr. Nichols' art, it shows
him expanded and growing.'[9] *The Times Literary Supplement*, though
it gave it a full column, was unrelievedly negative.[10] But although
Robert was disappointed by its reception, there were also encouraging
voices. Francis Brett Young told Marsh 'I'm absolutely out of agree-
ment with his reviewers, and think *A*. admirable of its kind, and full of
a far greater promise.'[11] The *Morning Post* reviewer wrote 'It is impossible to doubt, unless you are obsessed by some clique-spirit, that Mr.
Nichols is the greatest of the "Georgian" poets ... In his new volume
his star shines steady, and he comes closer yet to the fulfilment of our
hope, expressed long ago, that he was destined to become the Keats of
a new century.'[12] After his death critics recognised the book as his greatest poetic achievement. Its centrepiece is a sequence of twenty-seven
sonnets to 'Aurelia'. Reginald Snell, in the *New English Weekly*,[13] calls
these 'the finest of his poems' and says it 'shewed him in full grasp of his
powers'. Norman Mawdsley in *The Poetry Review*[14] says they revealed
'a poet of a power that seems unlimited'. Charles Morgan, writing as
'Menander' in *The Times Literary Supplement*,[15] describes the whole
book as being 'as substantial as *Ardours and Endurances*, containing
as well as the bitter and impassioned sonnet-sequence which gave it its
name, idylls as enchanted as "The Sprig of Lime" and the lovely group
of poems called "The Flower of Flame".' Morgan appreciated the
Shakespearean quality of the sonnets: 'For his forms he went back to
the masters, for his sonnets to Shakespeare himself.' In a personal letter
to his widow, he urged her to write his life because 'His work needs a
personal background if it is to be seen rightly by posterity, particularly
the sonnets'[16] – rather a lot to ask of someone to whom Nancy Cunard
had been a successful rival. Nancy Cunard, when Robert sent her the
sonnets as they fell from his pen, complained that they 'don't scan'.[17]
Charles Morgan puts the record straight about this:

> His aim was always so to develop the classical forms that they
> would accept the rhythm of his ideas and the flow of his 'atten-
> tion-stresses'. For this reason he was among the subtlest of
> modern prosodists, though, because he had a natural ear, his
> subtlety was so little conspicuous that it often passed unobserved.

The Aurelia sonnets, in Laurence Binyon's words, 'make their
impression as a whole'; but a few samples may give some intimation of
what these readers saw in them. The series starts:

Aurelia, when our bodies shall be rotten,*
    Our holy rites and our unsanctioned revel
Alike of this inquisitive world forgotten,
    Which watches me and you, my angel-devil,
Still shall the World-to-come our love review,
    Dissect my pain and analyse your pride,
Dispute our deeds and their complexion's hue,
    And over our right and wrong wrongly divide.

For as in love not any rest I have
    Save in the course of love truly recorded,
So the late world shall rest not by our grave
    From ever revaluing the love I worded;
    But we who our love's qualities best know
    Shall then enlighten it no more than now.

There are good times to begin with.

'Lover,' you say; 'how beautiful that is,
    That little word!' and still you sigh it over
Till the twin syllables become a kiss
    Against the brow your lips' slight whisperings cover. [IV]

Robert is under no illusions about his beloved's reputation:

Though to your life apparent stain attach,
    Yet to my eyes more fair shines its hid fame;
Though tongues repeat what deceived eyes may catch,
    Yet to my ears your praise grows, not your blame. [V]

But he is taken aback when 'seeing you in your sleep so rosily lie' and reflecting 'how brief the hours for knowledge ere we die',

                I stooped a kiss,
        Challenging Time that moment's bond to sever,
        When, deep sunk yet, you made a tender sign
        And tenderly sighed a name. It was not mine. [VII]

Reproaches mount as the sequence proceeds:

Sometimes I think you know not what love is
    But only pang of amorous delight. [XIII]

---

*The *TLS* reviewer singled this line out for particularly severe reprobation: 'Are we to believe that the author who begins with this assault has really aimed at pleasing us?'

Excruciate me then, if dealing pain
    Can to your hapless heart bring any pleasure
Make writhe my pride with frivolous disdain
    Mock my heart's fullness with your own short measure ... [XXI]

Corrupt, corrupt! the mildness of your eyes
    Your patience dangerous bids me beware
In every look some miracle of lies,
    In every gesture foulness aping fair. [XXII]

Finally, in a sonnet which Robert reprinted in *Such Was My Singing*, the series closes with a romantically ghostly vision of Aurelia in bed at midnight:

How white, how still you lay, though shuddering yet
    In the last luxury of oblivion,
    As if of Death you had taken love long denied,
    With on your face the bliss of suicide. [XXVII]

There are some unpublished writings which provide a little of what Morgan called 'the personal background'. In *Aurelia* besides the sonnets there is a short lyric to Aurelia:

When within my arms I hold you
Motionless in long surrender,
Then what love-words can I summon,
Tender as my heart is tender?

When within your arms you hold me,
And kisses speak your love unspoken,
Then my eyes with tears run over,
And my very heart is broken.

Charming; but Robert also wrote:

When upon your golden bosom
My storm-wearied head I lay,
Forthwith seem I safely cradled
In some Hesperidean bay;

And there would I rock for ever
Did not suddenly I start
To hear so close the rising dudgeon
Of your guardian dragon heart.

This prose fragment is revealing:

She sat down composedly. Not a hint betrayed that she was sensible of any tumult within him, and indeed, if she was dimly aware of some disharmony between their states the manner of her pulling up her chair and placing her bag on the table sufficiently hinted that for her any positive eruption would be indeed out of place when she had merely glided, so to speak, not only into her usual chair at the usual time but into the accustomed ritual of her afternoon pleasure as well.

The past apparently had not been ... Was he to accept this? a most extraordinary convention ... and yet?

There she sat and slightly moving her shoulders as she often did when she appeared to feel his eyes upon her, now stretched hands to the sempiternal bag as if in search of the invariable powder puff.

His arm shot out: 'No.' (How curious the detachment of his voice!)

'No?' Small eyebrows were raised: humouring of the bear.

It was on the tip of his tongue to risk a decided 'Well?' that should provoke he knew not what save that it should inevitably precipitate them into the deeps. But this was not easy when he could not take his eyes off her.

There she sat – and in the twilight of the afternoon café it was as if some exotic, but to him not wholly unfamiliar flower now sedately displayed itself, and took a faint pleasure in the greeting of its own image reflected in the shadowy glasses upon the walls.* How still she was! He inspected her, letting her physical closeness become a luxury to him.

She was gazing at herself and the greeting of her own image in the shadowy glass upon the wall appeared to afford her a novel pleasure. At least she honoured the spectre opposite with a slight smile. Or was the smile almost unconsciously directed against him, as much as to say 'Well, here I am. I've come somewhat perhaps against my will but it is not in my nature wholly to disoblige sometimes.'

'Aurelia, for God's sake say something.'

---

*This may have been an idiosyncrasy of Nancy Cunard's. Anne Chisholm's biography contains a photograph of her (taken in about 1927) staring at herself in a mirror much as Robert describes.

But the disregard continued, broken only by a slight expansion of the smile, which then abruptly vanished. The camellia fell out of her button hole and was negligently replaced.

This little action serving to display as it did the single ruby with its chaplet of startling diamonds upon her forefinger upset his thought which subsided into merely emotional pleasure at her presence. She might not have come! This satisfaction was to be tasted.

How, he reflected, he would have liked to be in any way sure that the new dress she had donned had been donned for him, not as a palliative for his inevitable smarts of which she seemed so startlingly unaware but simply for his pleasure, out of her knowledge that he took a delight in the richness, the variety and the originality of the ensemble. For this 'get up' as she would lightly phrase it was – not his eye but his intellect told him – a, for her, more than customary triumph. Upon her head was squashed a little hat composed apparently of a bunch of parma violets. The severe coat of her dove grey gown was closely buttoned with three monstrous military plaques, and the military appearance of these completely contradicted the creamy silk ruffles of her blouse, the collar of which nestled over the coat. Her whole person exhaled a cool scent as if she had just stepped from rolling among dew-drenched lilies of the valley. He peeped beneath the table to see what sort of shoes she was wearing. They were grey kid with large silk bows. Something prim in their provoking nattiness struck him as witty and he glanced at her hoping she would catch his laugh.

His gaiety vanished instantly for he was suddenly and overwhelmingly aware that for her he did not at that moment exist ...

She was leaning on her hands and her eyes, searching the depths of the dusky glass opposite seemed, so vacuous were they to him, intent upon other worlds. Was she thinking of Mars? In what reverie was her soul sunk that no spark of any significance for him illumined those pupils which all at once appeared to contain a certain dreariness of expression?

There came into his head the fancy to try to arouse her by *will*. Let him gaze at her while willing that she should turn her head and occupy himself with him. Concentration was achieved with a humorous sidelong glance at the absurdity of the proceeding when he had only to open his mouth! But she did not turn and he felt as if the very least twirl of her hair upon the cheek in front of the ear was being printed for ever on his brain.

He relapsed at last into a sort of trance of gazing ... First she grew so enormously large as to interpose her spectral presence between him and the whole world, then shrank to such a diminished figure that she seemed but a white speck descried down an immense corridor ...

'Well,' broke in on him suddenly as she turned her head, 'to business.'

So she had been aware!

'Business? What do you want to discuss?' (Now for the plunge.)

'Discuss? No. What have you ordered?'

Now while she sat opposite him he could but wonder at his rage.

Robert and Nancy Cunard were perhaps both more or less unconsciously playing the part of people having a love affair for the benefit of themselves as audience. What makes the affair even more unreal is that in the spring of 1918 Robert had published a small book of poems, *The Budded Branch*, beautifully printed at the Beaumont Press and bound by Sangorski and Sutcliffe, dedicated to the woman who would soon afterwards become his wife, Norah Denny.

10
Marriage

In the two or three years leading up to the publication of *Aurelia* Robert's lyrical powers were at their height, and the period was the most prolific of his life. Besides the Aurelia poems themselves, *Aurelia* contains some of his pleasantest lyrics, the sequence about lovers and the sea-shore entitled 'The Flower of Flame'. These were originally intended as new art form, 'a cycle suitable for an, if possible, continuous musical setting',[1] but read very easily without the music. Two of them are reprinted in *Such Was My Singing*, the first, which begins 'As round the cliff I came alone', and number 10:

> I love a flower which has no lover,
>   The yellow sea-poppy is its name;
> Spined leaves its glaucous green stem cover,
>   Its flower is a yellow fitful flame...

This was probably suggested by the Suffolk coast north of Lawford.

Also in *Aurelia* are a number of longer poems. 'The Sprig of Lime', a mysterious and allusive piece in which a daughter lays a sprig of lime on her dying father's chest, is inscribed 'For Edward Marsh'. Robert called it 'a poem dealing with pure thought... Both my characters discover the transitoriness of human existence, but one discovers it in associations of joy and the other of sorrow.'[2] It has been often reprinted, and many people, Robert himself included, thought it one of the best things he ever wrote. Herbert Asquith (not the Prime Minister but his barrister son; he and his wife Lady Cynthia were friends of long standing) told Robert in 1943: 'In those few beautiful lines it seems to hold and exhale the tragic essence of life. I have read it in many moods and each reading has confirmed my first impression that it is one of the finest works of our time.'[3] It is inspired by the limes of Lawford, and seems to touch near the end on his parents' brief happiness:

> Breathe silent, lofty lime,
> Your curfew secrets out in fervid scent
> To the attendant shadows! Tinge the air

Of the midsummer night that now begins,
At an owl's oaring flight from dusk to dusk,
And downward caper of the giddy bat
Hawking against the lustre of bare skies,
With something of th' unfathomable bliss
He, who lies dying there, knew once of old
In the serene trance of a summer night,
When with th' abundance of his young bride's hair
Loosened on his breast he lay and dared not sleep,
Listening for the scarce motion of your boughs,
Which sighed with bliss as she with blissful sleep,
And drinking desperately each honied wave
Of perfume wafted past the ghostly blind,
First knew th' implacable and bitter sense
Of Time that hastes and Death who need not haste.
Shed your last sweetness, limes!

Other poems are dedicated to other people for whom Robert cared. 'Seventeen' is for his younger sister, Anne; in the motherless household all three men, Robert, his father and his brother Phil were slightly in love with her. 'Night Rhapsody' is for Florence Lamont. And there are also poems for Max Beerbohm, Aldous Huxley, Tommy Earp, Robert Graves and Philip Heseltine.

All these belong to 1919. Among those that represent earlier years are two from *The Budded Branch*. This small book – it runs to forty pages and contains a short pastoral verse play and fifteen lyrics – has the following preface:

The majority of the poems here printed will not be reprinted. They are gathered together for two reasons:

Because the book affords an opportunity to record appeals which are – save in one or two cases – to scarcely tangible emotions: those emotions which float across the mind like Coleridge's cloud

'Thin and pale and very high'

and are of import to the very few.

And because these poems form some slight memorial of an intimacy with Nature which War has destroyed since I now see Nature as the Great Indifferent.

The poems do indeed look back to Robert's pre-war poetry about

nature and contain little about love and none of the worldly bitterness
of the Aurelia sonnets. The Norah Denny to whom they are all dedicated was herself a poetess; in 1911 she had published a volume of
verse translations from Heine;[4] but she was far removed in personality
not only from Nancy Cunard but from other women writers who were
Robert's friends like Enid Bagnold and Edith Sitwell. She was quiet and
retiring, and those of her poems which survive from 1917 and 1918
look as if they were influenced by Robert without catching his fire. He
must have known her well to dedicate *The Budded Branch* to her. He
may have known her for some time. Staplefield, where he went in 1916,
belonged to a Mrs Denny, and he could have met her through Philip
Heseltine or some other of his musical friends, for she had a keen interest in music and was the niece of Roger Quilter. She was born in June
1892.[5] By the beginning of 1918 she was almost certainly in love with
Robert. She continued to love him through infidelities and marital
breakdown. They always remained friends, he calling her 'Nornie' and
she using the private affectionate names they gave each other, 'Took-
san' (he) and 'Ginksan' (she). And after his death she was the faithful
guardian of his memory and his work. Nevertheless there is no mention
of her in his surviving correspondence before 1920.[6]

After the drama of Aurelia Robert did not return to Brecon or his
earlier haunts in Devon and Cornwall. Round about this time he went
on an official visit to Prague for festivities connected with the setting up
of the new Czechoslovak state. Other members of the party were Lord
Dunsany, H. G. Wells, Sir Henry Wood and Richard Nevinson. This
visit, however, was only for a week.[7] Robert would have liked to lodge
at Lawford and offered to pay a weekly sum for his keep. His correspondence with his mother, which they had sustained over the last ten
years in spite of her being constantly moved from one address to
another, now seems to have come to an end – the last mention in his
surviving papers of letters between them is at Easter 1920[8] – and he
may have wanted to be closer to his remaining parent. But Mr Nichols
'was plainly surprised and didn't consider it for a minute. No, that was
one of his great selfishnesses, and there's no getting around it. He just
refused to entertain the thought.'[9] So Robert rented a cottage called
Rose (or Red) Copse near John Masefield's house on Boar's Hill,
Oxford. It was not comfortable, but it was the best he could afford on
his allowance.

In Oxford at the same time were Edmund Blunden and Robert
Graves, both taking the course in English Literature. This may have

been an inducement to Robert. He had done his best to make Graves's work known in America and contributed in 1919 to Graves's journal *The Owl*. In an article he wrote to commend Blunden to the Japanese when Blunden was about to take up the chair of English in Tokyo, Robert says that he often in the evening would walk up to Blunden's cottage

> to sit with Bobby Graves, 'Caesar' Blunden and his wife, while the candle shone upon the remains of cottage tea and on manuscripts written in a hand only less beautiful than that of Robert Bridges. It was the only time in my life in which I experienced, so it seemed to me, some of the romance that must have been felt in the circles that issued the celebrated magazine, 'The Germ', of the Pre-Raphaelites, or that Leigh Hunt and his friends must have known when Keats was at Hampstead.[10]

Blunden also, though he modestly calls them 'small things,' had good memories of this period.

> At that time R. Graves and his wife Nancy Nicholson lived on Boar's Hill and I had a small cottage near them; they were kind, and if sometimes dullness was about they said, Wait until Robert Nichols comes, and he will change it. How? By his "faith and fire"; Bob believes in poetry. He came, tall and thin and quick – for a time he did rain influence, and I think his principal theme was, "there is too much *niggling* on this hill." He alarmed me by his reading Goethe's prose works, and "others similar", but what he said about niggling (poetically) was quite in harmony with those deep enquiries. He also said, to me, that Oxford was full of *little* writers, and he said they were "all right", but we should go other roads. At last one day he came into my cottage, as handsome as usual, and requested to see my MSS. (That was like him; most writers do not take *that* line.) Then he sat down, and knocked a few poems about with a blue pencil. I dare say he was right, but I felt down about it, and my wife was cross: the story is not over. He returned later and gave me a ring of his with an opal in it (a fire-opal?) with this dramatic utterance, that it had been his one poetic talisman and now it would be mine. Naturally my wife got it before long. – These small things include his wearing a Murrey-coloured suit, red squirrel that is, and his romantic recitations, any time, – his excitement over Vachel Lindsay's 'Congo'

and 'General Booth', his variations of countenance, now the low comedian and now the ideal young Bard.[11]

Graves in his autobiography wrote of this period more briefly: 'Another poet on Boar's Hill was Robert Nichols, still another neurasthenic ex-soldier, with his flame-opal ring, his wide-brimmed hat, his flapping arms and "mournful grandeur" (the phrase is from a review by Sir Edmund Gosse).'[12] Robert gave Graves's book a long, laudatory review in *The Listener* and wrote handsomely about it to the Heads:

Poor Bobbie has certainly been in hell at school (as I was) at the war (which I wasn't – his experiences would have sent me daft and not even H.H. could have saved me) and since (I've had a taste of that). You must get it and read it. It's a brave book and written in good downright prose. He mentions you (with favour). He remembers me. He recalls my opal ring – given to Blunden and given by him to Mrs Blunden and retained by her. He's had so much trouble since he's forgotten the rest. I remember the times he had before the arrival of baby No 2. I actually had him in charge on the morning of the accouchement. He kept clutching his head and crying 'Sometimes they go mad! If Nancy should go mad!' and looking about him wildly. We walked it off. Please don't think I reproach him with not remembering or not counting me among his friends – he merely states I was one of the poets on Boar's Hill – I merely mention it to point out that I was his friend and that we were, I like to think, on closer terms than this book gives out. Poor Bobbie – he's had the hell of a time but now I hope he is in sight of peace. There is however one piece of real injustice in the book. He states that all his 'friends have either deserted in alarm or died.' This isn't true. Eddie Marsh, as E. M. himself told me only a few weeks ago, fixed it with the authorities over L. R.'s [Laura Riding's] attempted suicide. So that's one friend anyway and though it isn't important I'm probably among the friends he says he's 'dismissed'. I did in point of fact ring him up when I heard of his troubles and saying only 'I'd heard he was up against it' I offered him money and shelter for him and her. Not that it matters. But he shouldn't have treated E. M. so.

Never mind. He's an excellent poet and a fine man – absolutely honest and straight and if some of his views don't commend them-

selves to many, well, he has a perfect right to them for he is a rigor-
ous thinker and he has suffered for them and they aren't assumed
to cover any particular situation but are what they were when I
first knew him. I'm sorry though he's broken with S.S. S.S. was the
best friend he ever had.[13]

Blunden remained a friend but from 1920 on Graves's references to
Nichols in his correspondence become increasingly hostile. No reason
for this emerges, but it is conceivable that Graves felt Nichols viewed
him *de haut en bas*. When Robert was about to have an operation for
appendicitis in 1924 he asked his father, in the event of his death, to
transfer part of his allowance to Graves in order that Graves, who was
hard up at that time, should have more leisure to write poetry.

In July 1920 Robert arranged to make a stay at Quarr Abbey on the
Isle of Wight. Perhaps he was attracted by the community's Gregorian
chant, which at that time must have been the best in Britain, or perhaps
he was collecting material for his play *Guilty Souls*. At any rate in
August he wrote to Marsh:

> The monkery here is great fun – religious crows and eagles who
> chirrup like finches when once or so a day they get out of the cage.
> What a study they are, a sort of mixture of prattling child,
> monster and angel. Sometimes they intrigue me, sometimes
> disgust and often delight – but never, never are they dull or is the
> spectacle of their strange life dull. The fact of their being dedicated
> creatures appeals to me – I like to see soldiers and priests for theirs
> is a community life apart and not a mere welter – this directive
> purpose in their lives at once deepens and narrows both the solder
> and the priest: it concentrates the individual will into something
> sharp and like a sword at once beautiful and in its cruelty ugly,
> while at the same time strictly circumscribing the area in which
> that will can operate.[14]

In the same letter Robert says he has written a short story 'about a
devil trying to learn Gregorian' and goes over his literary plans, which
contain not much new poetry, apart from some more plaints of the
'naive and humorous' kind, but a 'strong' play and a book of philosophic '*contes*'.

'Of the Devil Who Would Learn Gregorian' was published in the
August number of *The Sackbut*, a journal edited by Philip Heseltine 'for
the free and unhampered discussion of all matters relating, directly or

indirectly, to music'. It was not Robert's first story. As his correspondence with Sheila Kaye-Smith shows, he was writing fiction before he
went to Oxford, and he wrote several short stories of a patriotic character in the first year of the war. In 1919 he was working on a story
about a mother who went out to the battlefields to find the unmarked
grave of her dead son, and thought that it might be 'one of the most
moving ever written in our tongue'.[15] But 'The Devil Who Would Learn
Gregorian' seems to have been the first of his stories to be published,
and it is an accomplished and amusing *jeu d'esprit*, a little in the
manner of Richard Garnett's 'The Demon Pope'. Although the devil in
it fails to make the grade as a Gregorian cantor, it shows that Robert
had learnt something about the chant at Quarr.

Later in 1920 Robert published two other stories. 'Harry', which
appeared in *The Athenaeum* in December, is a very short but moving
account of the last hours of a badly wounded soldier. 'The Smile of the
Sphinx' is the first of his philosophic *contes*. It was written in the
summer of 1919 and published by itself in a limited edition at the Beaumont Press in November 1920.

This edition has an Introductory Essay which begins: 'Of all kinds of
short stories – and the short story is the most difficult form in letters –
that which offers the greatest difficulty to the author is the philosophic
conte.' If a philosophic *conte* is a story in which a fanciful narrative
embodies ideas that appeal primarily to the intellect and could have
been treated philosophically, it need not be short. The term is applicable
to Voltaire's novellas or to Butler's *Erewhon* novels, and Robert's own
Golgotha and Co is the length of a full novel. But the examples most
typical of the genre, or at least most fascinating to Robert, are relatively
short. Models he knew were Richard Garnett's *The Twilight of the
Gods*, commended in the Introductory Essay to *The Smile* p. 16,
Maurice de Guérin's *The Centaur* and *The Bacchante* – he acquired the
Vale Press translation in 1916 and it is probably safe to add Violet
Paget's *Pope Jacynth and Other Fantastic Tales*.* One might have
suspected the influence of Disraeli, but Robert discovered Disraeli (and
found him highly congenial) only in 1932.[16]

'The Devil Who Would Learn Gregorian' does not aspire to being a
philosophic *conte*; it is a simple tale. 'The Smile of the Sphinx' is aimed
at the centre of the target. The secret of the smile, which its protagonist

---

* Written under the name 'Vernon Lee'. Robert certainly had a copy of her *Euphorion*,
and as an Englishwoman living in Italy she may have been known to the Nichols family,
since Robert's father and grandfather regularly wintered there.

spends his life trying to learn, is the secret of life itself, and Robert believed he had hit upon it. We grasp it (to put roughly what he wants to say) if we accept it as it is, beautiful and incomprehensible: 'In the Sphinx, with her ravaged countenance and mutilated smile, I behold Life itself – Life in mysterious might, ignorant of its own origin, conscious only of its own beauty, couchant amid the wilderness of space and eternity.'

This revelation came to Robert in the summer of 1919. In June 1920 he started a second, longer *conte*, 'Sir Perseus and the Fair Andromeda', but work had not, it seems, proceeded very far before it was interrupted and for the rest of the year Robert was writing his 'strong play' *Guilty Souls*. He was encouraged in this chiefly by Arnold Bennett, though he read drafts of it and discussed it with Sassoon, Marsh, Graves and John Masefield.

Meanwhile a job in Japan was looming up. Robert at this time seems to have been almost wholly dependent on an allowance of £240 a year from his father. A letter he had written to Head in July 1919 makes it clear that there was no chance of its being increased:

> We're people who have all the appearance of possessing a competent middle-small income (say at the outside (£4,000) - actually we're as poor as rats. Mother takes £1,000 a year (or nearly). It is a point of honour to Father that she shall have no less; though latterly I believe it's gone to £800, for that's what her father (Captain Pusey) gave her mother (who was also a complete neurasthenic). Phil in the Diplomatic will cost £400 per annum. I don't know what Irene costs. She lives at home. Anne is at school – at least £300, I think.

There was no question, of course, of not keeping up both the large house in London and Lawford, and far from contributing to the upkeep of the house at Lawford, the farm lost money consistently throughout the lifetimes of Robert, his father and his brother Phil.

£240 in 1919 had hardly more purchasing power than £7,000 in the year 2000: not enough to live on as a fashionably clad bachelor, which perhaps partly explains Robert's eccentric attire, much less sufficient to maintain a household for two. It was just as well, therefore, that when Lafcadio Hearn vacated the Chair of English Literature at Imperial College, Tokyo, Charles Whibley, who seems to have had the appointment in his gift, recommended Robert to succeed him. Robert agreed to this in October 1920.[17] The salary was about £96 a month, a considerable advance on £20. No sooner had he signed the contract in December than he told Marsh he did not want to go.[18] But in the same letter he referred to 'the girl I have grown to love and who's loved me so long'. He and Norah Denny had at last 'come', as it used to be said, 'to an understanding'. This (though Robert had difficulty in facing the fact)[19] really made taking the Japanese job a necessity.

Among the last things Robert did before departing were to write a generous review of the posthumous *Poems* of Wilfred Owen (whom he had not known personally) for the *Observer*, and a notice of a production of Hardy's *Dynasts* in Oxford. Robert thought Hardy the greatest of modern English authors, and it must have been a pleasure for him to attend this performance, the first by OUDS since the war, and their first ever of a play not by Shakespeare, and to see Hardy himself enjoying the applause at the end. This was in December. On 19 January 1921 Siegfried Sassoon recorded in his diary:

> Arnold Bennett gave a farewell party at the Reform for Bob Nichols ... Henry Head, Aldous Huxley, Frank Swinnerton, T. W. Earp, Philip Heseltine and Roderick [Meiklejohn] were there. The dinner was superb, and the conversation pleasant and vigorous. We sat at a round table for three hours, under the Thackeray portrait. Bob was at his best, quite reticent and self-effacing – for him.

Two days later Sassoon and Head saw Robert off at St Pancras for Tilbury and the SS *Kitanu Maru*. That was the last he saw of England until 11 April 1922.

The intervening year (as will be seen more fully in the next chapter) had not been easy. Not only did Robert loathe Japan, but Norah's parents were opposed to the marriage. In April he told Marsh that they were cutting her out of their wills if she married him,[20] and in May he wrote to Head: 'That grotesque old bandit of a villainous mother of hers [Norah's] is driving her frantic.'[21] By September a rival had appeared on the scene, Douglas Jones, who had more money than Robert and was favoured by the Dennys.[22] Nevertheless the engagement was intact and Robert apparently full of love for Norah when he arrived in April 1922.

There were various obvious objections to Robert as son-in-law: he had no money of his own, his bad health, mental and physical, made it difficult for him to earn anything, and it appears that he was still suffering from the effects of syphilis. What most antagonised the Dennys, however, was his politics. Mr Frederick A. Denny, a successful business man, was a Conservative of the most conventional kind; Robert was a member of the Labour Party,[23] and Mr Denny could not stand his mixture of socialism and anarchism, though it was completely harmless and in its own way almost as conventional. He probably disliked the whole literary, artistic and intellectual world in which Robert moved easily and where his ideas were thought, if sometimes misguided, still nothing unusual. Ten years later Robert said to the Heads that the Labour cause seemed to him 'more just and less unintelligent than that of the Liberals or Conservatives. ... I am a born Menchevick and find the psychology of the working man difficult and am not upborne as the rank and file are either by (a) faith that the Millennium is round the corner (b) hate (c) constant contact with comrades.'[24]

Siegfried Sassoon's diary gives a glimpse of the difficult situation that existed between the Nichols and Denny families. He and Robert were dining at the Café Royal when

> Suddenly Bob became transfixed by consternation. A very large, powder-white, empearled, goggle-eyed, frigidly frowning dowager passed our table; she was followed by a leather-skinned, white moustached, angry-eyed husband; he had two deep furrows on each side of his nose. He also bowed to Bob, with volcanic embarrassment.
>
> 'Good god! It's the Dennys!' muttered the poet from Tokyo.
>
> So I got my first sight of his future deputy-parents. They sat at the next table. Bob was very much upset, but I enveloped him in a barricade of defiant and hearty unconcern, and soon we were able to appreciate the spectacle of the Dennys failing to do full justice to an expensive dinner.
>
> They appeared to be an odious pair. (I know for a fact that they are outrageous snobs.) As we were going out, Bob went across and apologized for the spontaneous episode, but the old woman merely glared and said '*We don't want to see you.*' So we departed to the Coliseum and thoroughly enjoyed the show. The incident made me feel affectionate and protective.'[25]

Sassoon had a very just understanding of Robert. The previous evening, complaining about the horrors of life in Japan, he had said 'I'm always wondering if I'll go off my rocker.' Sassoon replied: 'It'll be your own fault if you do.'

Robert seems to have spent the next couple of months mostly in

London or at The Hut. He had a mortifying glimpse of Daisy Kennedy looking happy with John Drinkwater, a poet not worthy, in his opinion, of her beauty.[26] On 24 June he wrote from London to his brother, then Second Secretary at the Embassy in Vienna:

Things have come to a head at last and after a very trying struggle with her people, who wouldn't give their consent, I am to marry Norah Denny at St Martin's in the Fields on Tuesday 11th July at 11 o'clock. Her father refuses to attend and 'any of his family who go will go without his consent'. Father is going to let us have Lawford to stay in afterwards. O dear what a frightful rumpus and how foul they have made it for her – all on account of mother – so they say – but largely because her father, though he pretends not to have any personal feeling, loathes me. He has cut her out of his will – entirely disinherited her and is even taking away her dress allowance of £200 a year. (N.B. He is a very rich man!) Such, he says, are his principles. He spends a large portion of his time and energy abusing me – calling me names, among them 'socialist' and 'atheist' – he's like a person in a bad play. At one time he threatened personal assault. Father has been absolutely splendid. He doesn't theoretically approve of the marriage but he says 'I'll never desert my son.' I think he's touched at the way we've stuck to one another, and as for the girl – why she's absolutely enchanted him. O Phil, I wish you'd come back to be my best man! Couldn't you? I haven't seen you for such ages and as we are off to Japan again (alas!) on August 21st I don't suppose I shall see you again for at least two years. And she does so want to see you. Also (beneath the surface) Mr and Mrs Denny regard it as a bad match socially (if you please! What next?) and a Second Secretary is something. But I dare say you are very busy. Isn't being best man to a brother a good enough excuse to raise a week's leave?

I do wish we hadn't to go to Japan, but it seems inevitable.

I should so like you to see her – she is so good, so calm and so beautiful. No one ever brought me the peace she brings.

Philip Nichols seems not to have managed to obtain leave. Sassoon, however, was at the wedding to support the bridegroom and gives a full account in his *Diaries*:

An emotional medley today. In fairness to Bob Nichols I must try to record it, as I feel I have been rather unfair to him earlier. He was at his best today; and when he *is* at his best one forgives him everything.

I called for him at his father's house in Bryanston Street at 11.30. My costume was a compromise between respectability and unconventionality. I wore my black coat (minus the abhorred tails) and a *soft* collar; a tie that had enough in it to be a little Radical anyhow; and a brown felt hat. I feel bound to describe this rig-out, owing to my previous diatribes about the dress-problem.

Bob, of course, was quite the conventional bridegroom (in a borrowed tail-coat which fitted him perfectly). He looked extremely nice, and his demeanour was as irreproachable as his garments; and just sufficiently imbued with the irresponsibility of the man of genius.

The bride, of course, was calm and dignified. The charming eighteenth-century interior of St Martin's Church was enlivened by some sketchy organ-playing by Eugène Goossens – a Wagner pot-pourri. Hanging about in the aisle with Bob, while he greeted his friends, I felt grotesquely self-conscious. My emotions were vaguely associated with the last time I wore my black coat – at Rivers's funeral. My emotions, probably, had a certain affinity to the sniffings of the old lady who 'always weeps at a wedding'. Eddie Marsh was there, in a top-hat and tears. He never misses an opportunity of exercising his lachrymatory glands.

There were no bridesmaids. Roger Quilter (uncle) immaculately gave away his niece. In the vestry the bride's mother sniffed thunderously; and a young man, whose name I couldn't remember,* pressed me to go to a party at the Piccadilly Hotel on Thursday. Afterwards I lurked morosely at the back of the church, and cut the Sitwells, and evaded the *Daily Mirror* photographer. Masefield was there, and Aldous Huxley. The Heads were beaming.

Robert led his bride down the aisle, throwing a chest which becomingly signified his victory over the Dennys, without being absurd. Schuster was playing the frivolous septuagenarian as usual. The firm of Chatto and Windus[27] were there *en masse*. And I shook hands with the one-armed fanatic J. J. Chapman, who denounced me at one of my New York lectures. Arnold Bennett

*Sassoon's editor, Rupert Hart-Davis, says this was Evan Morgan.

was unavoidably detained in Poole Harbour on his yacht, the *Marie Marguerite*. In fact the wedding was quite a bright affair, although the weather became so dark after it was over that I had to turn the electric light on when I got back here at 1 p.m. to inscribe a large-paper copy of Jane Austen's *Love & Freindship* 'for Norah Nichols' (having avoided the reception at Quilter's). However, I went to Liverpool Street to see them off, was kissed by Norah, and felt adequately moved by the thought of the difficulties which confront those two human beings.

The presence of Mrs Denny was a good omen, and at the last moment she gave Norah some pearls. One literary figure not among the guests, though Robert continued a warm admirer of his poetry,[28] was Robert Graves. He wrote to Edmund Blunden: 'Nichols never sent me so much as a piece of his cake or a slice of his father-in-law's prime bacon.* We were all against him marrying and producing offspring after his kind and I give him credit for sensing this.'[29]

In August, as had been planned, Robert returned with his new wife to Japan. Even his closest relatives agreed that he was luckier in her than he had any right to be. She suited him perfectly. He had warned her in 1921 that 'my work *must* come first'[30] and she accepted this.

People often say to me [she wrote in 1928] 'You have no particular work or job, how do you occupy yourself?' I answer them, 'I am the wife of a poet; that is my job and chief occupation.' For I am inclined to think that, unless you are contented with wifehood as a full-time occupation, and regard it as such, you had better refrain from marrying a poet, however much you love him.

The great exception to this rule is, of course, Mrs Robert Browning, who, a genius herself, yet found time to keep house, have ill-health, write poems, see after Browning, be poor and extremely happy, all at the same time. An amazing feat, yet possibly easier 80 years ago than in the modern hurly-burly. Today marriage with a creative artist becomes for the wife a highly specialised job, for particular temperaments only.

To begin with, she must be of the kind who really enjoys playing second fiddle, the kind who knows it is just as difficult, just as praiseworthy, to play second fiddle as to play first, and that one is

---

*Mr Denny's money was made from bacon. This was found surprisingly comical not only by Graves but by most of Robert's literary friends.

complementary to the other. Then she will play her wifely second fiddle proudly, knowing the first fiddle could not make just such music alone...

Of course, there are days when I think it would be more fun to make poetry than puddings, yet when the poet, after a day's work, produces 15 closely-scribbled foolscap sheets, result of a superhuman struggle to create perhaps five good lines of poetry, then I am not so sure he has the best of it.

Where the poet's wife scores is in the company she keeps. The poet, when not working, knows how to enjoy himself and his friends do likewise. He is intensely sensitive, intensely alive. His fun does not depend on money and motor-cars. With him can be shared a life of high adventure on very little a year, and by his side a wife will have the sensation of marching through the heart of life instead of sitting about somewhere on the edge of it.[31]

II

Japan

The SS *Kitanu Maru* which carried Robert to Japan in January 1921 went through the Mediterranean. The sea always inspired him and he composed several poems on the way. A lady who was particularly struck by four lines in one of them[1] wrote to him in 1925, and his reply[2] provides some details of the first part of the voyage.

> The day I set sail in bitterly cold weather from Gravesend was the most miserable of my life: my heart literally shook in my body and that evening I verily believed I was going off my head: I never knew such anguish could exist. I walked the deck till late at night in a state of incoherency feeling as if I had been engulphed by a whirlpool.
>
> In the Mediterranean I experienced another anguish – we passed through the gates of Messina and I had to see the Sicily I longed for and the ruins of Taormina go by. This was my first view of Italy and the ancient world of heroic mythology, and I had to see that world only to see it go by...
>
> The next day, thinking of D'Annunzio, reputed at that time – after the Fiume smash*– to be wandering on the shore of the Adriatic a broken man, I wrote a poem to him called *Lines from the Adriatic*... A big sea was running – a very big sea, accompanied by a violent wind and the wildest sunlight. The Adriatic, curiously fawn-coloured, as if the waters were full of sand, boiled like a cauldron and the spray rose into the air like flights of white gryphons. Salt was on my face, my clothes were sticky with it and my hair stiff with it.

The opening stanzas of this poem, which appeared in the *London Mercury* soon after and later in *Such Was My Singing*, try to capture this scene:

---

*At the end of the First World War D'Annunzio captured Fiume (Rijeka) with a private army and set up a short-lived ideal state, based on music.

Loudens the sea-wind, downward plunge the bows,
Glass-green she takes it, staggers, rolls and checks,
Then sheers, and as she buffets back the blows,
There comes a thundering along the decks.

The surf-smoke flies, the tattered cloud-wings haste
And the white sun, sheeted or glaring cold,
Whirrs a harsh sword upon the spumy waste –
Now ancient grey, now weltering dizzy gold.

From the Adriatic he passed to the Aegean, and here he expressed
what he had felt when he was unable to stop and see classical Sicily:

Now after six most cruel years
Spent as I never thought to spend –
In task where the battle sows its flame,
In toil where the victim hides his tears,
Or sent where my country might me send
To shield her faith or serve her fame –
I view, hung in the ocean's glass,
Those Grecian isles, my constant end.
I view them – but to view them pass![3]

Robert was later to see something of Italy, but this was the nearest he
ever came to Greece.

Robert's misgivings about America in 1918 had proved prophetic,
and those about Japan were fulfilled even more quickly and abundantly. 'In the first place,' he wrote to Head,[4] 'I loathe the East – ever
since Suez there has been nothing but dirt, hypocrisy and metaphysics
and I hate all three.' Then when he arrived he was presented with a
contract quite different from what he had been offered in London. This
he managed, with the help of a sympathetic lawyer, to get changed, and
in particular got written in enough leave to return to England the
following year. In the University he found that his pupils could not
speak English. And his privileged background and his ignorance of
civilisations other than his own made it impossible for him to see any
merit in Japanese customs or culture. 'The people in the street', he said,
'are so ugly that I have to turn my eyes to the ground: they revolt me so.
Their mode of thought is as unintelligible and as unpleasant to me as
their language – as persons they are about equal parts of childishness
and iron pedantry.'

He was himself lodged in what he describes as a 'clergy house'.

In the clergy house bedroom, with its ugly scriptural prints, I had such a bout, my mouth opened and closed so convulsively and I could hear myself making such queer noises – quite unlike any sounds I ever remember making before – like a series of little tears in silk I now see they sounded – that I wondered dimly whether if I had a fit I should be found – the house was empty save for a cowering Japanese.

The letter concludes with a diagram showing 'self' standing alone and watching while Norah, the Heads and 'all yours' like a 'very white glistening city island' are receding into the distance behind a silvery blue-white wave, and an encircling mass of darkness ('The End: death? oblivion of some sort, perhaps mental nothingness') is coming up behind him.

The subjects of Robert's lectures included Shakespeare, Walt Whitman and Meredith. He had done some preparation of them on his journey out,[5] and they were well received. His audience rose from 30 to 70, not a common experience even for the most seasoned university lecturers. But he

was never suffered to lecture without the presence of a Japanese professor. Why? To make sure that in taking my students through (say) *Romeo and Juliet*, I did not undermine the purity of Japanese morals. For though the Ministry of Education was prepared to wink at what we'd call matter-of-fact and indeed all-too-sordid sexual immorality among students, it was not prepared to countenance any teaching which might sublimate instincts in terms of western romance.[6]

At the end of his first term he wrote to Head:[7]

I cannot possibly stay here. I am wasting my life ... The Japs provide me *with no art material that I can use*: if I knew them very well, if I lived here ten years and knew their language and wasn't a professor whose life is a rut the material might just be usable ...

Imagine living in a country where nobody is a *person* to start with. Everybody is a cipher here – a communal cipher. No one exists except as a unit in something else – a family, a business, a university or a clan. There is no privacy. (When I read letters or a book people come and read over my shoulder!) No one has any responsibility. If you want to change anything or do anything – if you want to consult a professor (the head professor, your colleague!) on some simple point – he smiles, dithers and doesn't know till he has called in three or four other persons (persons? – they are all like eunuchs!) and confabulated with them. Then you are living with a people who have no art – only styles of art. Everything is done according to precedent. A painter is a master in this style and that style and another style – never in his own style. Imagine everything I dislike in my father multiplied by 100 and pressed on one at all hours of the day and you have some sort of idea of what life is like here. Again the professors, lecturers and readers in the university cannot speak English properly and very few of the students can do more than stumble out conventional phrases. In addition to which the students can't think. It is against the tradition of the country to do so. They at once loathe and admire me. Admire me because I am probably more interesting (because person- and not text-book-learned) than any teacher they have ever met ... and loathe me because I tell them straight out that they are ignorant snobs (or words to that effect).

Having Norah join him would be no improvement:

When I think of her among the Japs it gives me the horrors. They have no opinion of women ... For them a woman is simply good to bear children, arrange the house for her lord and master (master in the sense that she is a slave – they bring their concubines into the house) and to copulate with (they do a great deal of copulation – indeed there is something rabbity about their whole life – they don't *have children*, they *breed*.)

The criticism was not entirely one way. The gossip column of a Japanese paper said:

Mr Nichols is a good-looking youth and we are not surprised that he is pursued by the brazen western women. Our reporter tells us that the young professor was driven from the Imperial Hotel by the addresses of two young ladies who had fallen in love with him. Later he retired to the clergy house where our reporter perceived two more young ladies lying in wait for him. So great is his attraction for the fair sex that two white women – one of remarkably good looks – have come to attend his lectures. We hope his head which is certainly effervescent will not be turned.[8]

'Fabrication from beginning to end' said Robert. He left the hotel because it was too expensive, and the Protestant mission took him in until he arranged to share lodgings with an English lawyer called John Gadsby; though it was true that 'two missionary girls have appeared in the class'.

As to material for his art, in the event, Japan *did* supply some. His play *Komuso*, on which he was working at intervals for twenty years, is set in Japan. It draws both on Japanese culture and on the Japanese climate, and shows that Robert acquired at least a smattering of the language. Its very full stage directions reveal also that he learnt to appreciate Japanese painting and interior décor. Nevertheless his first year there remained in his memory as a time of particular unhappiness. When he got back to England he told Siegfried Sassoon: 'It was worse than the war.' Sassoon says in his diary 'But he was only *at* the war for about three weeks, so I wasn't greatly disturbed.'[9] Robert did, however, have some sort of breakdown in the summer and, after being dosed with tuberculosis-infected milk, on which he blamed all his subsequent ill health,[10] he had to be rushed to Yokohama General Hospital by a female American missionary who took a romantic interest in him.[11] In September he was writing from there and his doctor was recommending that he go home and rest for a year.

Instead of that he revived sufficiently to publish a slim volume of aphorisms, *A Year's Grain, 1920–1921*,[12] and to start writing articles for the *Japan Advertiser*. He began with a long piece on Paul Claudel, recently arrived in Tokyo as Ambassador of the French Republic.[13] In spite of, or perhaps because of, Claudel's profound Catholicism he admired his work, and the friendship which grew up between them may have done something to lighten his spirits. This article was followed by a series entitled 'Certain English Novelists Who Are Artists'. The articles are short and informal, but have not dated in the eighty years since they were written.

He will not, he says, 'dilate on Thomas Hardy, George Moore, Joseph Conrad, Arnold Bennett, H. G. Wells, Hilaire Belloc or Max Beerbohm'; their works 'are already classics'. He starts off[14] with E. M. Forster: 'Of all living English and American novelists he is … the gentlest and the wisest.' His work 'is rather feminine in approach' and his mind 'is one that is eminently reverent and understanding towards women'. Of his novels, *Howards End* 'completely overtops the remainder'.

The following week[15] he discusses Compton Mackenzie and Gilbert Cannan. Though conceding to each a book (*Guy and Pauline* and *Old*

Mole) that is 'worth reading' and not merely 'worth perusal' he explains how both writers, in his opinion, have lost their way, the former through 'living on the immoral earnings of his Muse', the latter through taking Samuel Butler for his guide without appreciating the need for his sincerity.

He has comparable criticisms of Hugh Walpole, but in D. H. Lawrence he again spots a winner – something harder to do in 1921 than ten years later when F. R. Leavis started to proclaim his merits. About Lawrence personally he continued to have mixed feelings, but 'I have yet to discover a novel of his which is not worth reading, – crude, violent, perverse, formless, irritating, nervous, hysterical sometimes, as they always are.' His work 'is said to be immoral... On the contrary, his books are monsters of morality, terrifying in the deserts and abysses they disclose.'[16] In the same article he warmly recommends Frank Swinnerton's *Nocturne* and also gives the sympathetic picture of Swinnerton himself quoted in chapter 8.

The remaining articles in the series deal with women writers. Robert likes Bridget Maclagan's *The Romantic Woman*, 'a most brilliant study in the influence of background upon temperament'. As one would expect of someone so much at home in Bloomsbury, he says the right things about Virginia Woolf: 'It is the sensitiveness of this author which makes her work at once so distinguished, so painful, so exquisite and so intriguing. You cannot help wondering how such an acute, tender and rare spirit survives at all in this world of hogs, dogs, apes and thrusters. For nothing escapes her – neither the flood of living passion nor the least twitch of any nerve of it deemed dead. Indeed, a sort of terrible lucidity seems to inform her exposition, at once powerful and delicate, of this emotion' etc., etc.[17] Robert might be one of her own characters, rising off the page to salute his creator. But the place of honour, last and most spacious, is kept for Dorothy Richardson. Two whole articles are not too much to devote to her 'revolutionary method, the method of a subjectivism carried further than any hitherto known'. 'There is', he says, 'no pose in it – even pose of sincerity. It's beyond that. The figure [of the central character, Miriam Henderson] has – if it is pure invention – an artistry of the rarest kind because the artist fits so entirely into figures that we never catch her arranging the folds of the dress with that slight pursing of the lips which tells us the artist is thinking "That, I think, just about does the trick."'[18]

Robert's writing was not limited to journalism. In April 1921 he told Marsh he had resumed work on his *conte Sir Perseus*[19] and in March

1922, in a letter jubilant with the prospect of impending departure, he announced it was finished.[20] To confound Sidney Colvin who had said a poet cannot write prose, he had put in 'the most highly coloured, elaborately harmonised, complicatedly rhythmical prose I possibly could'.

The main theme of *Sir Perseus* was supposed to be 'the contrast between Romantic Mediaevalism and Romantic Hellenism'.[21] Andromeda is the familiar heroine of Greek legend, treated in a light modern fashion that recalls Disraeli's *Ixion in Heaven*. Perseus is a medieval knight returning from the Crusades with powerful sexual inhibitions: at the sight of any attractive woman he 'crosses' himself. Rose Macaulay in a review in the *Guardian* complained that Robert 'vulgarises good themes', but Marsh wrote 'Perseus is to me almost a sheer delight, it is exquisitely written and full of masterly pictures.'

In his darkest hours in 1921 Robert dreamed of going to America, staying with the Lamonts, and finding a job at a famous girls' school in Connecticut.[22] This vision did not materialise. But he found a ship back to England via New York and visited the Lamonts before landing in England in April 1922. For the rest of his time in Japan, America, despite his experiences in 1918–19, figured in his thoughts as a blessed land beyond the horizon to which he hoped to make his way eventually.

But life with Norah when he got back to Japan in autumn 1922 seems to have been an improvement on his time there alone. There are no more depressed letters home. They rented a house in the grounds of an ancient temple which Norah described as follows:

The house was old, very heavily roofed and eaved, the woodwork darkened by weather to a soft grey-brown. Facing south, it looked into the tiny rock-garden, and was completely hidden from the road. It contained the right number of rooms, but no drains, no heat, and no furniture, except an American ice-box. The rent asked was higher than that of a furnished house of similar size containing all modern conveniences, either in England or Western America. Still, I thought, I would gladly pay extra for the sheer beauty of the place. The strange workings of the wooden bath-tub, in a lean-to shed at the back of the house, were then revealed to me. One end of the tub contained a little furnace with an iron chimney that disappeared up through the roof; you lit within a fire of charcoal, filled the tub with cold water, waited four hours or so, and then the hot bath was ready. Time is no object in this land, I remembered ... I felt so happy that tears came into my eyes. I would have a dwarf tree of plum-blossom in my sitting room; I would slide back the walls, let in the sun, seat myself on a purple cushion on that floor of golden straw... [23]

Financially their position was improving. It appears that Robert was receiving an allowance from his father, and that in 1923 Mr Denny came to accept the *fait accompli* of the wedding and made Norah an allowance of £500 a year.[24] They were also making some Japanese friends. Robert was on a committee for establishing a permanent orchestra in Tokyo, and also had 'a finger in various "Education Reform" pies'.[25]

In autumn 1922 Robert renewed his work for the *Japan Advertiser*. There had been an anticipation in America of McCarthyism, and at the same time a Chicago court had issued an injunction preventing strikers from picketing and even assembling near railroad property. On 29 October he wrote a satirical article criticising this injunction and also making fun of the League of American Pen Women who were afraid that the purity of the American ethos was being corrupted by foreign influence in philosophy, music and literature. This broadside evoked some protests to which he replied in further articles.

He gave offence to a larger group of readers in November with 'Some Reflections on the Treatment of Horses in Japan'[26]:

I am informed that the Japanese treat animals with great consideration. I have not noticed it... Fully three long walks out of five are completely spoiled for me by miserable memories of unneeded torments inflicted on animals who seem to have no one to protect them.

Horses were overloaded and then beaten because they could not do what was demanded of them.

You hit your horse, it flinches, you harden your heart and strike it again – and each time your heart becomes more like the stony heart of a fiend. And when this happens nearly every day you become callous and presently you will treat your wife or poor child as your treat your horse.

He recalls his two years' experience with horses in the war:

On the great retreat and on the extension to the sea the Royal Horse Artillery and Royal Field Artillery repeatedly saved the day.

How? By their mobility. The success of cavalry rear-guard actions was due in an immense measure to the past care given to the horses and their fine condition and to the care given to them even on that terrible retreat. Neither the German cavalry or artillery possessed the same stamina (with consequent mobility) on that retreat. Why? Because they treated their horses after the manner of many Japanese today – that is, as machines, instead of treating them as the English treated them, as noble animals and humble friends.

In the next fifteen months Robert wrote on a wide variety of subjects. He reported on concerts, plays and art exhibitions, contributed light reading in the form of essays on letter-writing, Elizabethan food, and cocktail mixing. He had considerable talent for journalism and it is a pity that only in Japan did circumstances force him to work at it. But there are some series of articles that go beyond the ephemeral.

While full of admiration for Darwin, Robert hated what he called 'the Huxleyan school of Darwinists' who held that progress comes solely through cut-throat competition of individual with individual and community with community. He blamed them for 'Prussianism in Germany and the doctrine of the survival of the fittest in unlimited commercial competition in England and the United States, the one leading to the European War and the other to the theory that goods are manufactured not with regard to service but only with regard to sale.' In December 1922 he attacked this social Darwinism in an article entitled 'Gensan and Mutual Aid'.[27] A large number of Russians had fled from the Bolsheviks and become stranded in conditions of miserable destitution at Gensan (now called Wonsan) in North Korea. Certain communities in Japan heard of their predicament and provided relief. Robert defied the Darwinists to explain this. It was no use saying that the charitable communities were acting stupidly or wickedly and that they ought to have left the Russans to perish instead of encouraging 'the weak and the broken and the diseased elements in society'. The notions of free choice and obligation were not available to the Huxleyans. 'Evolution cannot contradict itself. Either all evolves or nothing, and consequently the hospital no less than the machine-gun.' What must be recognised is that mutual aid is just as important a factor in nature as competition. Robert appeals to Kropotkin and other writers for evidence that this actually exists in many species, and quotes passages that prove Darwin himself left room for it.

Robert replied to criticism in a further article a fortnight later.[28] He justifies what he had said about Prussianism by quotations from Tre-itschke and Bernhardi. 'We have now agreed' said Treitschke in his essay *On International Law* 'that war is just and moral and that the ideal of eternal peace is both unjust and immoral and impossible', while Bernhardi in *Germany and the Next War* declared 'The Christian duty of sacrifice for something higher does not exist for the state, for there is nothing higher than it.' And he writes perceptively of T. H. Huxley himself:

> He was a great liberator. But the war of liberation, especially with such pig-headed nobodies as Bishop Wilberforce, tended to make a temperament already combative see life always in terms of battle... I would never accuse so scrupulous a man as Huxley of perverting the truth, but temperament does decree the approach even in a scientist and influences his interpretation of facts. In that he resembles the artist. The dogmatism and lack of subtlety which characterises so many figures of the Victorian age is also to be found in the glorious and most formidable opponent of its wretched smugness. The great man seems to have been unable to see society as part of nature.

Huxley, he says, 'did not know that society is anterior to man'. He borrowed Rousseau's account of the origin of society; and later social Darwinists were prisoners of 'the acute individualism of Darwin and the preceding age'. Social Darwinism with its individualist assumptions is still with us, and Robert's attacks on Sir William Bateson and other prophets of the 1920s read curiously like Mary Midgley's attacks seventy-five years later on E. O. Wilson and Richard Dawkins.

Early in 1923 Robert drew upon his university lectures for a series of articles on Shakespeare. The most interesting of them is the third, 'The Conditions of the Elizabethan Theatre and Their Effects on the Drama of Shakespeare'.[29] He saw clearly the relevance of the structure of the Elizabethan stage, jutting out among the standing spectators, the fact that plays took place between two and five in the afternoon, the lack of means to produce special effects. More is now known of these conditions than was known in 1923 and he would have been keenly enthusiastic about the rebuilding of Shakespeare's Globe and the methods of Mark Rylance, the Artistic Director. In April 1999 'the pursuit of eloquence' was made 'the primary aim of the oncoming season' and this aim was explored by the actors in the Globe's Research Bulletin 14a. Nothing could better illustrate Robert's words:

Why was the Elizabethan stage an eloquent stage? Because the age was an eloquent age... But if the Elizabethan age had not been eloquent, yet eloquence would in all probability have appeared on the Elizabethan stage. Why? Because that stage, given to stirring speech and action, necessitated it by the very nature of its structure.

Robert's article is only a summary of a longer study, 'The Elizabethan Theatre in Being', that he prepared for his students. This presents historical detail in the form of an account of a visit to a performance of *Romeo and Juliet* by himself (interestingly described as 'Master Robert Nichols, an Essex squire's son'), Evan Morgan, Tommy Earp and Mary Hutchinson,* all four projected back to the year 1599 and Elizabethan dress. They take a boat down from Westminster Bridge to the Globe, which is thus placed in relation to the whole London scene, and Robert describes the appearance of the playgoers, the stage, the tiring room etc. He then goes on to draw some conclusions for modern productions and recommends much that has now become standard: reducing scenery to a minimum and obliterating 'to some extent these divisions into acts and scenes which are not by any means to be found in the earliest editions'.

A third series of articles is concerned with education. In April Robert reflected on the difference between the English and the German systems, and criticised the latter for trying to develop only the intellect and not the whole person.[30] There followed in May four articles in which he set out his own ideas. He might have had a more substantial set of proposals if he himself had been more educable. 'Teachers would do well to aim at producing in the pupil rather, perhaps, the attitude of the open mind and caution in accepting any finality in argument... than any very strict adherence to the logic of the day.'[31] However that may be, the series is an application of his ideas about competition and mutual aid. Governments, he recognises, wish to make education a matter of implanting nationalistic ideas. He himself views nationalism 'as one of the most dangerous creeds extant' and pleads for presenting international cooperation and world service as an attractive alternative to war.[32] 'We want to get into the child's head and heart the idea that man can radically change his position', but not, in Dean Inge's words, that 'All progress hitherto has been the result of bitter competition and struggle.'[33]

*Mrs St John Hutchinson, mistress of Aldous Huxley and Clive Bell, cousin of Lytton Strachey and author of *Fugitive Pieces* (1927).

In June Robert and Norah went to North America, partly in the hope of finding work either in Canada – their ship put in at Vancouver – or in the United States. Robert's friend Maurice Browne was running a summer school in acting at Santa Barbara and invited Robert to attend free of charge and give a lecture or two.[34] He and Norah seem to have liked California enough to decide to try their luck in Hollywood when the appointment in Tokyo should come to an end. Robert told Marsh[35] that in many ways the Americans 'are nearer to Athens than we'. This may have been because of what he saw on the beach at Santa Barbara. 'There the young men and women are divine to look at – more like gods than any race I ever saw: lithe and golden brown. No bunched muscles, no short legs. (The women's legs made my wife and me quite rapturous – they were as long and as lithe and as beautiful (though different) as the men's.)'

On the way back to Japan, besides rhapsodising to Marsh, he wrote a letter of forty-five closely written pages to Sassoon, 'probably,' Sassoon remarked in his diary,[36] 'the longest letter I shall ever receive. It is all about himself, and written on a boat, going from California to Japan. The word-cascades of his convey very little to my brain. The sentences go by like low-flying rain-clouds, amorphous and colourless, with suggestions of brandishing forms but no definite design.'

While the Nicholses were away, Japan suffered a catastrophic earthquake. When they arrived at Kobe, near Kyoto, Robert reported:[37] 'In Yokohoma the ground rose in places *four feet*, fissures opened exuding sulphur fumes which choked those who inhaled them. The oil tanks burst and the oil flowing over the water caught alight... Tokyo is under martial law and it's going to be difficult to get up to it. I shall probably make a solitary expedition – taking knapsack, food, disinfectants and maybe a gun in my pocket. The great danger now is revolution.' The authorities were frightened of communism and of Koreans ('there are about 3,000 in and around Tokyo – the Koreans correspond in politics to the Sinn Feiners.') Robert made Norah stay at Kobe while he investigated, and fearing that he might not come back he deposited with her a formal valediction to his friends which began 'I write these brief lines to assure my friends that mine has been a very happy life.' Had the occasion arisen for delivering it, his friends would have found this opening absolutely astonishing.

In Tokyo he made some notes for Head of the 'psychological vagaries' he observed, the heavy drinking and vanishing of inhibitions. 'One man rescued a very pretty girl from a bath high up in a hotel. He pick-a-backed her down and swam about with her in Yokohama harbour for four hours. She was stark naked.' But he did not confine himself to observation. The University Library of 700,000 books had been totally destroyed. Robert wrote a long memorandum to the British Ambassador urging that His Majesty's Government should send an immediate generous grant of cash. He pointed out the good effect this would have on Anglo-Japanese relations, and mentioned the influence Germany at present enjoyed with Japan. He also wrote to the Oxford University Press and to affluent friends including the Lamonts, who sent a private donation of $5,000 in addition to $25,000 from Mr Lamont's firm.

In January 1924 Robert wrote to Marsh from hospital where he was recovering from appendicectomy.[38] The operation disrupted his last term's teaching, but on 12 March he delivered a farewell address to his pupils. It is more personal and political than literary. He apologises not only for any deficiencies in his own lectures, but for the behaviour of Western Europe in the nineteenth century. 'Your fathers were forced to open this country against their will and to appropriate to themselves many ugly usages and all the cruelties of the West for this country's preservation... You have been wronged – that is a fact, however it may have come about, however unconsciously or through mere lack of fore-sight the wrong may have been inflicted.' At the same time he ventures to assert that if the East had been subjected to 'the violent changes of the years 1750–1850' and had had placed in its hands 'the power, the resources, the inducement to use and abuse both and the extraordinary organising ability which the West during these years displayed', it would have forced the opening up of the West no less than the West forced the opening up of Japan. He goes on to hold up the ideal enshrined in the motto of the Princes of Wales, 'I serve': 'Serve and seek not happiness, and happiness will come unsought.' He warns his pupils, too, against the 'dream of drunken greed that at present oppresses the world' and 'the many miseries and corruptions that char-acterize what Nationalism and Capitalism and (let me add) Commu-nistic Materialism (so singularly like capitalism) mistake for greatness today'.

These words would not have been well received in English universi-ties, then as always sympathetic both to capitalism and to communism, but perhaps one or two students who heard them remembered them twenty years later. The *Japan Advertiser*, at least, had said a few days earlier[39] at the end of the handsome article it published to mark

Robert's departure: 'A few more years will reveal an unmistakable change in the opinions and actions of the Japanese people. When that time comes, and it will come, Professor Nichols will find that the three years of his valiant fight in the conservative atmosphere of the Imperial University have not been spent in vain.'

12

Guilty Souls *and* Golgotha

While Robert was in Japan, Chatto and Windus published two books by him. The first was *Guilty Souls*. This is the play he wrote in 1920, preceded by a 76-page Preface composed in Japan in which he takes it upon himself to lecture the older generation on behalf of the youth of the entire world. George Bernard Shaw called the Preface 'pretentious'[1] and Arnold Bennett wrote: 'I have deeply reflected on your preface, and will definitely state my opinion that if you had let the MS lie for six months you wouldn't have sent it to the printers. It is not cooked enough. It is full of stuff, but not cooked enough.'[2] Since we are told it should be read *after* the play, not only is its name a misnomer but it could perfectly well have been omitted; though if it had, his biographers would have been deprived of twenty useful pages about his religious experiences between the age of twelve and the time of writing.

Of the play itself Robert had high hopes. 'If I get it as I should like to get it, it will be one of the greatest plays Europe has seen for a century,' he told Marsh at the outset.[3] 'But I don't expect many of the intelligentsia to like it or even understand it.' In the event the reviews neither came up to his hopes nor fulfilled his fears. *The Times Literary Supplement* gave it a balanced column and summed up: 'Far from being a perfect play or even a good play, but its weaknesses are not in essentials, and its virtues are.'[4] 'I commence', Robert says in the Preface, 'with two lawyers and a deed box, and I end with two guilty souls and God' (p. lxxiii). 'No easy transition' commented J. B. Priestley. 'It is very much to his credit that ... he has been able to make such a transition, and, further, to make it with what seems to be such astonishing skill... He has written a play; not a great play, perhaps at times even a crude play, but still a play. His great burning theme is reached inevitably by drama that flows naturally out of character and action.'[5]

The play starts, in fact, with two solicitors and two deed boxes. Their firm is not flourishing. The senior partner has a young wife who finds her life limited and dull, the junior partner is in debt and desperately needs £140 – more than half of Robert's annual allowance at the time. One of the deed boxes is the firm's, the other a client's. The senior partner surreptitiously transfers £4,000 of bearer bonds from the client's box to the firm's and brings it about that when the client comes to look into his affairs, the junior partner is arrested for stealing the bonds and condemned on perjured evidence. This is the first of the four acts. Writing to Marsh Robert speaks of 'four interminable acts'[6] but originally it had five and the first two were boiled down into one at the instance of his friends Harley Granville Barker and Maurice Browne. Robert found the process acutely painful, but anyone reading *Guilty Souls* is likely to think that the first act moves fast and readably, and that the whole play would have been better if the rest had been subjected to the same rigour.

But although the theft and the treachery are exciting, the play is fundamentally religious. The mood of the last three acts is not unlike that of T. S. Eliot's *The Family Reunion*. Eliot found his way to religious plays some fifteen years later, and in *The Family Reunion* does what *The Times Literary Supplement* said Robert ought to have done, makes his crime occur before the play starts. Robert's subtitle 'Dramas for the Theatre of Tomorrow, Number One', though absurdly boastful, turned out to be prophetic.

After his spell of ascetic mysticism in 1917–18 Robert found himself torn between emotional feelings inspired by the betrayal, passion and death of Christ, and an intellectual conviction that miracles are impossible and that Christ was nothing more than a human being. He was drawn to the Christianity of Julian of Norwich, Thomas à Kempis and Pascal, to Jansenism and the religious life, rather than, say, to the Anglican *via media* or the lay devotion recommended by Francis de Sales (whom he had read).[7] But he could not part company with the sceptical tradition of his father and friends like the Heads, Eddie Marsh, and Aldous Huxley. *Guilty Souls* is written to resolve this tension and make a definitive statement.

The three last acts are set seven years after the first. Vyson, the junior partner, has completed a long prison sentence but been drowned, we hear, when the ship on which he was emigrating in search of a new life hit a derelict in the ocean. The senior partner, Bentley, after gambling successfully on the Stock Exchange with the proceeds of his crime, has left the law and is now a rich tycoon. But he is devoured by guilt and remorse. He stands in the middle of the drama, representing Robert's own religious dilemma. He is flanked by two women, on one side his wife Clara, still beautiful, totally devoted to him, and personifying the scepticism of Cambridge and Garsington. On the other side is Lois, the stepdaughter of his dead sister, now aged twenty-three and a believing Christian. Bentley upsets his wife by saying that society ought to forgo profit and establish a commonwealth 'after the teaching of Jesus of Nazareth', and that he means to give an example of renunciation. Before she has recovered, the manservant they have just engaged reveals himself as Vyson, not drowned but returned to force Bentley to confess. We are to understand that confession will not result only in Bentley's being disgraced and going to prison. He is now in partnership with the son of the client from whom he originally stole; this man and Lois are in love; and the scandal when Bentley confesses will drive them apart. Vyson demands the ruin of their lives as part of the price Bentley must pay for redemption.

The later action of the play consists of responses by the characters to this situation. Lois accepts that both she and Bentley must make the sacrifice; human beings have no right to happiness and the two days for which she has been happy since her lover asked her to marry him are 'too long for a God who suffers' (p. 111). Only by misery and shame is it possible to imitate Christ. Clara wants to fight for her husband no matter what he has done. Wealth, reputation and human love seem to her obvious goods, and religion not only false but cruel. As Bentley moves towards paying the price demanded, Vyson shows he has been motivated only by spite and revenge, and unable to bear Bentley's repentance, he tries first, Judas-like, to hang himself and then shoots himself. This suicide gives Bentley a chance for reconsideration, but when the police arrive to investigate it, he hands them a written confession of his embezzlement and perjury.

J. B. Priestley found the complication about Lois's engagement less than convincing, and it unnecessarily overloads the choice facing Bentley. Bowyer Nichols, usually too discreet to criticise his son's work, said 'I think possibly the last two acts should be merged into one and a good deal of Bentley shortened. He tends to repeat himself and to be static.'[8] These faults, however, as *The Times Literary Supplement* observed, concern inessentials. The play has genuine power. This derives from the fact that while 'violent, crude and uncompromising' (to use Robert's own words, p. xxxiv) religious ideas prevail, the sceptical but loyal wife comes out as a convincing and attractive character. Again and again her voice rings clear, because although she is defending a superficial kind of happiness, she has disinterested loving concern and practical wisdom. The outlook she expresses is what Robert understood best. Unfortunately this merit in the play defeats the purpose of making a final statement. The Preface, as Shaw says, proclaims a new religion; 'but you do not make any attempt to define the new religion; you produce the effect of a man in the wilderness, shrieking for he knows not what.'[9]

The play was performed on 16 November 1924 by the Three Hundred Club, a body directed by Phyllis Whitworth which was formed to put on plays aimed at the intelligentsia in a theatre that would hold just 300 people. Robert was then in California but arranged for his sister Irene to keep an eye on rehearsals, and she sent him an account of it. She said it was too long. 'Though cut extensively it took three and a half hours.' The wife, she went on, comes out best and was certainly the most alive person on the stage. Bentley, though acted quite admirably, 'was never a real creature and his struggles left one curious but unmoved'. Robert's father was put off by 'the business with the crucifix' which has a prominent position on Bentley's writing-table in the last three acts: 'It didn't go down.'[10] These two close relatives were perhaps the last people that could be expected to enthuse over a religious play, but there was a good turnout of Robert's friends, Frank Schuster coming all the way from Paris.

The main parts were cast as follows:

Bentley:	Claude Rains
Vyson:	Ernest Milton
Clara:	Muriel Pratt
Lois:	Dorothy Holmes-Gore

The general opinion was that the actors did well,* but that the character of Lois failed to come to life. Perhaps that was not the fault of Dorothy Holmes-Gore. She wrote to Robert thanking him for a kind letter he had sent but saying:

> I personally had a peculiarly unsatisfactory feeling in trying to 'be' Lois which I should rather like to explain at the risk of being unbearably egotistical. You see, I like when I have a part that has some real brain and feeling in it, to 'be' that character instead of acting it so far as it is possible for anyone to sink their own personality in another's. I hate 'acting' from the outside which is only just a game of charades. 'Lois' after the second act baffled me entirely for I have never experienced any sort of religious fervour or spiritual exaltation such as she lived through – I have never even seen it in others. So instead of losing myself in the emotions I

---

*So J. C. Squire in the *London Mercury*.

portrayed as I have always done when they were within my own imaginative grasp I was feeling utterly detached – doing my damnedest to give the true expression to your ideas and saying to myself 'Oh I hope to God this is not too awfully unconvincing – *what* ought I to be feeling now, I wonder?' Fortunately I do believe the sincerity of my wishes overcame the lack of spontaneous emotion in me, for I have been told by everyone that they were moved as I think you meant them to be.

But, oh Mr Nichols – it was a cold and ghastly feeling of nullity I carried in my heart when I most wanted to be exalted with poor Lois herself!

I believe I should have been much more at home with Clara though my personality may not suggest it to anyone else. But if you ever write a play where you want passion and humour and faulty humanity and a loving temperament – you won't forget me, will you?[11]

In his letter to Marsh from Pittsburgh Robert expresses distaste for the 'bowler hatted' slaves of modern capitalism but a desire that they should find a better life. This theme is touched upon momentarily by Bentley when he speaks of giving away the riches he accumulated from speculating in oil. Bowler hats surface in the Preface of *Guilty Souls* (pp. lxi and lxxiv) and social relations are mentioned there (p. xxviii) as constituting with religion and sex 'the three sovereign problems of modern life'. But Robert comes to address social and economic issues directly only in *Golgotha and Co*. This novel-length story takes up most of the second of Robert's books published while he was in Japan, *Fantastica*.

In the Epilogue to *Golgotha* Robert says that anyone with the least knowledge of science who 'turns his eye on the powers that rule in that den of thieves, mountebanks and filthy urchins known as the Ruling Classes of Europe, cannot but feel his blood run cold with indignation and horror as he discerns the fact that those in power, so far from appreciating the position of man on this planet, seem to be bent solely on behaving like a pack of irresponsible, sometimes furious and nearly always greedy lunatics' (p.506). 'They insult the living,' he cries, 'they defile the memory of the heroic dead. ... Spawn of hell, how my heart would burn at you!' His objection is not simply to capitalism. 'Insofar as Capitalism is cynical, conservative, pessimistic and uncreative, I detest it. But in a large number of cases it is not so'

(p. 504). In 1921–3 the Bolshevik revolution was surging forward in Russia, but Socialism appeals him no more than Capitalism: 'I dislike Bolshevism intensely' (p. 503). Nor is he sympathetic to 'the Mystical Efficacy of the Peasant Mind' (p. 499). He repudiates both the Tolstoyan and the Chestertonian ideals of agrarian happiness. 'To claim that to live in a state of holy vegetation is the highest good possible to man, seems to me the worst legacy of thinking the Middle Ages has left us.' He wants industry and technological progress, though, following Kropotkin, he would like to abolish the antagonism between town and country. But how is this to be achieved without the miseries attendant on capitalism and socialism? By a moral revolution. Human nature can be changed. And this brings us back to the theme of *Guilty Souls*: the instrument of change must be religion. In *Fantastica* Robert indulged himself not only with an Epilogue but also with a Preface, and although he was taken to task for this by Osbert Sitwell[12] it does enable him to explain himself more fully than he did in *Guilty Souls*.

Just as the ideal economic system is not all that different from the system actually prevailing in England and America, so the ideal religion is not impossibly removed from enlightened forms of Protestantism. Robert wants to strip Christ of his supernatural attributes and identify him with Prometheus (p. 496). 'To me, what is sovereign and sacred in Christ is that he did believe and that he was not detached' (p. 32). That he did believe *what*? Robert does not say, but he would probably have applauded the position taken by the present Prince of Wales when he said that he would like to be not, like his predecessors, the Defender of the Christian Faith, but the defender of faith or faiths generally. Anyhow, Christ is to function as a 'symbol of the Integrating Factor in Human Evolution' (p. 497). The evils of capitalism come from seeing (or pretending to see) competition as the sole principle of evolution. They will disappear if, as Robert urged in his newpaper articles, mutual aid is put in its place, and a Promethean Christ is what will provide the inspiration for this change of attitude.

Golgotha is intended to put all this across in the form of a philosophic *conte* or, indeed, a massive prose-poem. An impossible project, one might think. But Robert received an encouraging letter from Bertrand Russell, to whom he had sent a copy. Russell was not a close friend, but one of long standing who was to show himself reliable in a way no one else did when Robert died. In June 1923 he wrote: 'I read *Golgotha & Co* with the greatest appreciation. I liked the idea, I admired the development, and I thought some of the writing very fine. It seems to me altogether a distinguished piece of work.'[13] And after some discussion of the differing functions of the artist and the scientist he said in a postscript: 'I was interested to observe what I took to be the effect of the East on your outlook. It makes one see our civilization as a whole. I wonder whether you read my book on China, and if so what you thought of it.'

Unfortunately Robert was not content with these compliments from the greatest of living English philosophers. He had hoped to be rewarded with the Hawthornden Prize. When it went to David Garnett for his shorter and far slighter *Lady into Fox* he wrote to Marsh, who had been on the judging committee:

> It would be a lie were I to state that I was not extremely disappointed by the Hawthornden award. I was and I am. That's not to say I don't think *Lady into Fox* is good. I do think it good, but I also think it small, and I am surprised that the committee should have made the award to a *first work. Golgotha* is big.'[14]

Marsh managed the difficult task of replying with considerable tact:

> I'd have given a lot to be able conscientiously to vote for it, but the plain fact is (and now I wonder if Apollo will blast me before I finish the sentence? shall I whisper it or shout it?) it wasn't good enough IT WASN'T GOOD ENOUGH. The book [*Fantastica*] stands or falls by *Golgotha*, and of that the first 200(?) pages are an absolutely undigested, unmanaged, un-*done* outpouring – Talk of taking a pill. You could have, and ought to have, got the whole sense of them by distillation and clarification into about 20 pages.[15]

This should not have come as a complete surprise to Robert, because Marsh had sent him some serious criticisms in May, complaining of the long opening and also of a long speech by one of the characters later in the story, and saying:

> Once you get onto your 'ideas', you treat language *like dirt*! To begin with points of elementary grammar, you use indifferently the third person singular and the second person singular inflections with the second person pronoun – 'Thou plaineth' – (p. 319) 'soundeth thou' (p. 320) 'thou testifieth' (p. 439). These can't all be the printer! Then you have 'Let HE' for 'Let him'

(p.322). '*He* that comest to me I will no wise cast out' (p. 441). And what kind of flowers of speech are 'sepulchretide' and 'peri-papatious'?[16]

Robert eventually came to admit: 'You are, I suppose, quite right about *Golgotha* – confound it.'[17] The trouble was that whereas *Guilty Souls* had been written in Oxford and exposed all along to criticism from Robert's friends, *Golgotha* was written in Japan in the winters of 1921–2 and 1922–3 when he had no one to curb his tendency to run on and on.

The opening sentence of *Golgotha* is not unpromising:

It was after the Second World War had been brought to its sublime conclusion; when the starving peoples of the earth began to emerge from warrens beneath the crust, wherein they had huddled from the triumphs of Applied Science scattered by the Onward March of Progress; when all but the houses of the Overlords, who now as ever proved fittest to survive, had been flattened in those merciful ruins which did much to clear Europe of the slum dwellings to which the Underling so foolishly clung; when the Peace of the City of Fiasco had been signed by the smiling dele-gates by the smiling waters of the Mediterranean, that there assembled in the palace of Cyrus Magniferox, above the shards that had once been Paris, a collocation of the Brains of Power.

Golgotha was written nine years before Aldous Huxley's *Brave New World* and might have been an equally successful novel of the future. Robert's prophecies about such developments as air travel, the cinema, loudspeakers broadcasting in public places, are close enough to the mark, his satire at its best is quite as sharp as Huxley's, and his convic-tions were less conventional. (Huxley would never have attacked every possible potential ally as Robert does in The Preface and Epilogue.) He also lacked Huxley's weakness for sex scenes. But the reader is immedi-ately battered by a succession of lectures that go on, if not for 200, at least for 137 pages. Mr Magniferox reports that though slavery has been rendered comfortable and deprived of its offensive name, the proletariat want freedom, and he has invited Professor Ulysses Mammon, occupant of a Chair in Herd Psychology, to make some proposals. Professor Mammon argues that the people need a religion that will make them submissive to social Darwinism and its Natural Law that the rich rule and the rest obey. The best religion for the purpose will be Christianity, and he proposes it should be imparted to the people by means of a film of the Life of Christ. Although he is heckled by the Wandering Jew, present among the Brains of Power under the name of Dr Ahasuerus, his proposal is accepted and a company is set up to make the film and orchestrate the advance publicity, a task the nature and importance of which Robert sees pretty clearly. This company is called Golgotha and Co.

Once this monstrous convention is over the story starts to move and it becomes clear that Dr Ahasuerus, who had hitherto seemed less important than Magniferox or Mammon, is in fact the central character. We find him, two years after the opening scene, cruising the Pacific in his luxurious yacht, and hearing from his spies the progress of Mammon's plan. Although a vulgar revivalism is spreading, the sample documents he sees reassure him that it is harmless folly. There is a charming advertisement for the Church of England:

> *For the* CHOSEN FEW
> *who cannot be satisfied with*
> *anything less than* THE BEST
> *it goes without saying and*
> NEEDS NO EMPHASIS *that*
> *there can be but one altogether*
> *satisfactory Religion:* THE
> CHURCH OF ENGLAND.
> ESTABLISHED *in* 1534 BY
> *the Act of Supremacy of the*
> *illustrious* HENRY VIII, *it has*
> *continued* UNDER *persistent*
> ROYAL PATRONAGE
> *to this day.*

Robert also uses his poetical skill to effect in an up-to-date hymn:

> *A fire-mist and a planet,*
> *A crystal and a cell,*
> *A jelly-fish and a saurian*
> *And caves where cave men dwell;*
> *Then a sense of Love and Duty*
> *And a face turned from the clod,*
> *Some call it Evolution*
> *And others – call it God.*

But among the material he has been sent, Ahasuerus finds a photograph of the unknown actor who is to play the part of Christ, the Protagonist, in the religious film, and recognising it is Christ himself, makes all speed to Jerusalem, where the last scenes of the Life of Christ are being shot on location on Maundy Thursday and Good Friday. At this juncture Magniferox announces that the Protagonist will really be crucified.

Ahasuerus finds the Protagonist on the Thursday night praying in the Garden of Gethsemane, and addresses him for eighteen pages that bring the story to a complete halt. This is the long monologue to which Marsh objected. Besides being incredibly ill-mannered (imagine banging on at a silent praying man for half an hour), it is totally out of character, being simply an outpouring of Robert's own dissatisfactions with Christianity. We then jump forward to Easter Sunday, which Robert dates to 1 May in order to have it coincide with workers' demonstrations, apparently ignorant that Easter can never be that late. Mammon, following Bentley and Vyson in taking on the role of Judas, has committed suicide. The story ends with the radio reporting that Christ is risen, and Ahasuerus raising a shaking fist.

Fantastica had a good many serious reviews both in England and in America. Nearly all paid tribute to the author's sincerity and depth of feeling. Edward Shanks said: 'One cannot help crying the word genius' and William Kean Seymour used the same pulse-quickening word: 'What is triumphant is the quality of imaginative genius which so often lifts Mr Nichols head and shoulders above his contemporaries.'[18] Several readers, however, did have difficulty in seeing where the story was going. 'A perplexing performance' was the verdict of *The Daily Telegraph*.[19] 'It would take a clever man', thought J. C Squire, ' to construct either a religious or a political system from Mr. Nichols' effusions.'[20]

A few reviewers thought that *Golgotha* has a happy ending. 'That which was intended as mere make-believe, a device for keeping the people quiet, turns out true. The kingdom of Christ comes again.'[21] In fact, however, it is not absolutely clear that Promethean Christianity *does* triumph at the end. Then while Robert satirises the idea of using religion to support plutocracy, he betrays a fancy for invoking the same techniques of hype to enable it to help the proletariat. *Golgotha* is dedicated to Claudel, and in graceful letter of thanks Claudel delicately points this out. But above all, the figure of Ahasuerus is fatally ambiguous. We are told in the Epilogue that he is the 'Incarnate Enemy' of

Robert's religion (or at least of H. G. Wells's religion, which is surprisingly presented on p. 494, like a rabbit out of a hat, as an anticipation of it). 'He appears', says Robert, 'under all forms common to that enmity.' Since these are widely different, Ahasuerus's character is inconsistent. But he is still the nearest thing Robert has to a hero, and it is hard to reconcile the sympathy with which he is treated with this declaration of him as the enemy. Gerald Gould quoted Byron on Coleridge: 'I wish he would explain his explanation.'[22]

13
Hollywood

In March 1924 Robert sailed for California in high hopes. When he was there the previous summer, he had seen – besides Maurice Browne and his wife – the director Rowland V. Lee, and made plans with him to work on an ambitious silent film involving battleships.[1] He also wrote a short satirical scenario on the film industry which he sent to William C. de Mille. Not surprisingly, de Mille turned it down. 'It is a matter', he said, 'of "trick photography", difficult and wearisome, and the story has no human interest.' Robert, however, was not discouraged. 'I am going', he announced to Marsh on his way back to Japan, 'to write for the movies ... I go to Hollywood to live among civilized people who know what one is talking about ... The medium is new, so are the people, thank God.'[2]

To someone who knew this correspondent as well as Sassoon, it can have been no surprise to receive in July 'an immense epistle from Bob Nichols (in California) lamenting his enslavement to the brainless barbaric cinema people'.[3] The immense epistle has disappeared, but in July Norah told Bowyer Nichols that Robert was 'homesick not only for England but for Japan; anywhere where there is some sort of culture and background'[4] and at the beginning of September Robert wrote to Ruth Head: 'The film-game here is slow, tedious and exasperating... Unless things mend we shall return.' As for the civilised company, he later told his brother Phil: 'In Hollywood there was for the most part nobody – though I had a few good Sunday nights – some four perhaps in two years – with Maurice Browne ([Rupert] Brooke's friend) and my friend Abraham Plotkin the Labour leader and his wife. But Browne was the only one with sufficient knowledge to stand up to me.'[5]

Robert's friends came to understand that these swings in his letters from manic hope to misery were just a kind of steam arising from his personality, and gave little insight into his actual circumstances.

As usual [wrote Marsh in October 1924] you give no news of yourself at all, except what I can read behind the expression

'Damn the movies'.[6] I've often had to complain about the inhuman character of your correspondence, which consists solely of panegyrics or diatribes on third persons – and makes me feel immodest and irrelevant if I tell you my own news in my replies.[7]

With rather a bad grace Robert yielded up the following mundane details:

We are neither of us very well – a little overstrung perhaps. But we are moderately cheerful and love each other more than ever. I have not made *a cent*. The Movies are hopeless. We are at present trying to get enough money to get out and come home. After that – if we can persuade my in-laws – life in Italy on our allowances and work, work, work for the same old object. We live in a little bungalow. Norah does all the housework.[8]

Marsh's reply is rather touching:

My dear Bob,

I'm very much ashamed of myself. First I write you several complaints of your 'inhuman' letters. At last you are moved, and send me just such a letter as I always wanted – and I carry it about in my pocket for weeks without answering! I've wanted to write almost every day, but always some variety of tares has sprung up and choked me. Don't think I was ungrateful for your concession. You know, Bob, I don't and can't live on your high plane – and sometimes I wonder why you ever bother your head about me at all. I expect you don't realize how much I am one of those persons 'ignorant and unworthy of life' who 'think about pleasure and happiness'.[9] 'I admire you as a 'voice and a thinking machine' but that is not why I am fond of you – and I enjoy your writing to me about 'third parties', but a few little details like 'we live in a little bungalow and Norah does all the housework' are essential to make me feel that I am listening to the voice of a friend.[10]

The little bungalow had the address 6228 Glen Airy, Beechwood Drive, Hollywood. Norah gives this description of how they found it:[11]

We [she and the house agent] headed for the hills. A belt of eucalyptus trees stood on a low brow to the left. The houses here were plain boarded and old-fashioned-looking. I instantly liked the look of them 'A bum locality,' pronounced the house-agent.

We left the paved road and bounded for a little way over
a dirt track, then pulled up at a small house on the hill-side
right under a huge feathery eucalyptus. 'This is lovely,' I
murmured. ...

The living-room was long, running the length of the house. ...
A smartly dressed woman in a silk frock covered with an apron
appeared from the bedroom. Her blonde marcelle might have
aroused envy even in the waxen bosom of a perruquier's model.
She led me to the bedroom, bathroom and kitchen. 'I must show
you where we stand the ash-can,' she said matter-of-factly. 'The
garbage men come round every two days to empty it – you put
it out on the front porch.' Here was something I had not
reckoned on.

The daughter of a rich family in the 1920s would never have had an
ash-can on her front porch, much less put it there herself. They decided
to take the house, and the same evening they had moved in and 'I was
frying my chop on the gas stove.'

Robert's unpublished manuscripts contain this description:

The blue air quivers. It is as if flakes of that sparkling powder with
which window-dressers besprinkle Christmas trees at Yuletide
were slowly settling down through the sky into the heat-haze
above the further ridges, already cloven by roadmakers and
dotted with cube-like stucco bungalows. Here and there clusters
of eucalyptus trees quiver silverly and the idle rustle of the breeze
among the leaves, whose shadows move across the peeled trunks
beautiful as the bare limbs of athletic maidens, sounds like the
rustle of the sea over the roseate sands along the Pacific verge,
which can be vaguely descried half a dozen miles away. An oriole
has flown into the pepper-tree that droops feathery fronds over
the lawn of glistening emerald close at hand, and around a moun-
tainous heap of purple-flowered creeper a pair of humming birds
dance upon the air.

In November 1924 Robert and Norah produced a short book called
Winter Berries consisting of ten poems, five by each of them, arranged
alternately. Norah's contributions are all about nature, birds, trees, the
starry sky and so forth, and characteristically display little human
emotion. Robert's include a couple of love-poems. 'Rapture' gives an
idea of how things were going between them:

Thou art my boundless treasure,
  My garden and my house,
My miracle of pleasure,
  My love, my life, my spouse;
Thou art my hands, my tongue, my eyes,
  My breath, my hearte's blood,
Thou art all brightness in me lies,
That soul of light in me defies
  Time's change and Chance's mood.

Robert began by trying to sell scenarios – he offered quite a juicy melodrama entitled 'S.O.S, or The Honour of the Sea' to Jesse Lasky, to whom he had an introduction from J. M. Barrie,[12] at Paramount[13] – and this accounts for his not having made a cent by October. But he made contact with the English director Charles Brabin and later obtained a salaried[14] job with Douglas Fairbanks Sr. The hours were not what he was used to:

I am absolutely worn out. Week after week I begin work at 8 a.m. (rising 6.30) and continue till 6.30 at night: most of the day I am dodging round the cameras on my feet. It's killing work – but chiefly killing because though Doug is a prince among men (not, of course, an artist of *genius* but of tremendous talent and a wonderful flair) all his assistants are not (though they are better than in other studios) or rather Hollywood scarcely allows them to be. What wears me out is the continual 'politics' and intrigue ... and worst of all the jumping about trying to get in a word edgeways (the director when he sees me hovering dashes in on any excuse to prevent me getting at Doug or if he lets me in only lets me in when it's too late.)[15]

Robert found Fairbanks both impressive and likeable.

Even when Fairbanks' body is not so much still as maintaining that momentary pose which precedes the sudden suave accomplishment of such a feat of agility as places him among the foremost scientific athletes of the world, his eyes, black as a hawk's, dance glances everywhere. As on the screen, so in life he enjoys a boyish frankness, blitheness, intelligence and vitality which persuade the onlooker that life is a jolly adventure. Further acquaintance discloses beneath the surface a 'straightness', a vein of discursive meditation and sympathy (especially with animals) that recalls something of Meredith's Crossjay and Jefferies' Bevis.[16]

Fairbanks was making *The Black Pirate* when Robert was working for him, and Robert wrote the following poem about him:

> Attend all you who would forget
> The humdrum round and daily fret,
> The black ship rocks upon the bay,
> The bo'sun pipes – we must away
> To where upon the sunset Main
> The golden galleons of Spain
> Like whales besieged by ravenous sharks
> Battle with privateering barques,
> Where on a lone reef in the West
> The bleached skull guards the treasure chest,
> Where fierce grog prompts a fiercer greed
> And who shoots last shoots late indeed,
> Where plank or noose or knife await
> The man who masters not his fate,
> Where yellow gold shines bright above
> All splendours but the eyes of love,
> Where red blood flows and black flags fly
> And bold men *live* before they die!
> Away! Away! We need but these –
> High courage and a spanking breeze.
> The buccaneers crowd at the rail,
> See there the black flag upward sail!
> The bo'sun's whistle shrills again,
> Cheer boys, we're off to the Spanish Main.[17]

Robert later claimed credit for the trial by night sequence in *The Black Pirate* and the walking of the plank.[18]

Robert went on trying to place scenarios for over a year. He particularly admired Chaplin and wrote a comedy with him in mind, *Destiny*, which Chaplin seems at least to have considered.

I had hoped [Robert told Marsh in May 1925] to be able to get enough here to sit back for one, two, three, four or even five years and write what I was born to write. But it requires too many lies, too much intrigue, too much truckling to scoundrels. It is undoubtedly difficult to 'make out' in the Movies with clean hands unless one has the good fortune to work with such men as Doug Fairbanks. The day before yesterday I heard three decent men – one English and two American – declare the whole show was a 'crooks' paradise' and they are about right. I shall make frantic efforts to sell one story and then home. I only grieve for my wife – I had hoped we should have been able to afford a child and live not too shabbily and in not too great dependence on my wife's relatives.

But though his stories found no takers, he acquired a fair knowledge of how the industry worked. He made a special study of crowds – how to film them, how to alter their shape and movement, the potentialities of crowds of different sizes and so forth. He also prepared a memorandum on improvements for picture theatres covering such matters as logos, lighting, curtains, tickets, public telephones. After he had been in Hollywood a year his experience led to his writing a series of nine articles for *The Times* which appeared in August and September 1925 under the general title 'The Future of the Cinema'. They were introduced by a leading article which described cinematography as 'this young and little known art'. Although cinematography in England goes back to the nineteenth century, there was still no British film industry and in his articles Robert urged that it was time to start one. The articles contained interviews with five leading Hollywood figures – Jimmy Cruze, Adolph Zukor, Douglas Fairbanks, Mack Sennett and Charlie Chaplin (something of a coup, this last). But their main thrust, 'since over 80% of the world's "movies" are produced and consumed in the United States', was 'to enquire whether there exists in the United States any movement towards better pictures'.

The main source of mediocrity, he said, was that by far the greatest proportion of profits came from 'hick' audiences, especially in the Middle West, and the 'opinions, prejudices and peculiarities of the "hicks"' therefore had a decisive influence on film-making'. Two other economic factors to which he pointed were the production of pictures for sale by 'block', and the ownership of chains of theatres by producers. For these obstacles he could suggest no remedy. But he also spoke of the 'want of appreciation in the industry of what the medium really is, confusion with the curtain stage and unwillingness to follow the medium'. As an illustration of what he meant he said that *Alice in Wonderland*, as 'one of the most widely sold books ever written', must have entertainment value, yet 'though the screen is the only medium in the world wherein Alice's becoming thin can actually be visualized, nobody yet has had the courage to do it. And again, how often while sitting on a bus do we see people about us who resemble particular animals – donkey, pig or giraffe? Yet no one has yet got the entertainment value out of this fact.'[19] This was two years before Walt Disney produced his first Mickey Mouse cartoon.

The *Times* articles were well received, both in England[20] and in America,[21] but they needed to be followed by a development of these positive suggestions. Robert drafted three longer articles entitled 'The Movies as Medium' but they were perhaps too daring for anyone to publish. In the first he develops some general principles: that 'visual flow', unlimited by the physically possible, is 'what differentiates the medium', that 'in what we present to the camera and how we make the camera receive it lies the art of the motion picture', and hence that the camera is 'the soul' of the medium. He goes on to argue that naturalistic realism such as producers chiefly strive for is a blind alley: the true way forward is in the direction of the cartoon. 'The nearer the artist [i.e. the director] comes to using the medium as the Movie Cartoon artist uses it today, the correcter will his use of the medium be.' He has suggestions about how naturalistic themes might be imaginatively handled which seem more obvious now than they would have done in the 1920s, when films tended to be filmed stage-plays. But his preference is for myth, for characters like Prometheus, Achilles, Gargantua and Don Quixote, and for adult fairy stories; and here modern producers are still only making a beginning. His articles close with

A vision of what the Art Motion Picture and its art circus will be like in a hundred years' time, when we have colour, synchronisation of sound and motion, and creation of image-in-the-round … In order to combine the advantages of the Greek and Curtain stages our circus will be a crescent moon with the horns somewhat bent towards each other. The audience will occupy the crescent, the spectacle taking place within the arena and in the gap between the horns, this gap corresponding to the proscenium on the Curtain stage. The audience will be vast – ten thousand at least. There will be tiers of seats for those who wish to view the spectacle from a distance and from one point, as opposed to walking round three sides of it. The synchronised projectors will be about the outer edge of the crescent and will cast invisible beams through the darkness onto an invisible and uniform point

of focus above the arena. The house being full, music will gradually well into being. As it waxes, there will rise in the arena a
pale mist which will slowly climb, as vapour climbs in a gigantic
test-tube, until it reaches the roof. In that mist, to the sound of
music, forms will take shape, body, colour, and these forms will
be either gigantic, august, Michelangelesque, or myriad. ... I
think I see a Don Quixote, huge as a Titan, lying in his death-
trance, with the figures of those mere men, who are are you and
I, bent over him.

Vera Mendel of the Nonesuch Press asked Robert to write a full-
length book on the cinema based on the *Times* articles,[22] but nothing
came of the proposal, partly, perhaps, because he was under contract
to Chatto and Windus. Regrettable, since a Nonesuch volume on the
cinema in 1925–6 would have been a bibliophile's treasure.

In September 1925 Robert was approached by T. A. Welsh who
with George Pearson was starting to produce films in England. They
asked him for a scenario as soon as he returned from America, but this
did not happen for another year and the proposal was not pursued.
He remained, however, an acknowledged authority and did on his
return write a further series of articles for the *Observer* in which he
urged the Government to fund a British Film Corporation along the
lines of the British Broadcasting Corporation. 'A wild scheme? Perhaps,
but the writer feels a scheme worth airing (so desperate is our plight) if
only as a provocation to other schemes on the only scale that will aid
us. Guild Socialism of a sort? Why not? – if it will produce the desired
results.' He was still so respected in 1929 that *The Times* asked him for
an obituary of Chaplin to keep on file, though Chaplin was to turn out
to live many years longer than he.

Although Robert hoped to support himself by scenarios for the
movies, he went to California with plans for no less than eight plays.[23]
He was, in fact, in process of mutation from being primarily a lyric poet
to being primarily a dramatist. Before long the list of dramatic projects
had lengthened from eight to twenty-seven. Being pregnant with so
much art was a heavy responsibility. While he was in California he
accepted an invitation to take a flight and, becoming nervous about his
aircraft, wrote another final message to Norah:

In case something should happen to me I am writing this after
refreshing myself with a bath and while you are asleep.
   I don't much like the notion of this flight, but I have enquired of

my inner spirit – Destiny or whatever one calls it – and it says that this flight is a matter which I must be left to decide. ...

No one [he goes on handsomely] could have been a better wife to me than you have been ... If I am not disfigured and my face is not set in some terror, have a death mask made ... This is not vanity but because I am thinking of the morrow and of other young men who might possibly get something from seeing it. ...

Bury my heart in England under a stone with the first bars of Schubert's *an de Musik* on it and the last stanza of Shelley's *Prometheus Unbound* final chorus. Let my friends have such of my books as they wish. I leave you my love and the memory of what I tried to be.

The envelope was sealed 'Only open in case something happens.' Fortunately this condition was not fulfilled. Nor were any of the listed plays completed, at least at that time. But a play not on the list was.

While in Los Angeles Robert met Jim Tully, one of the most remarkable literary personalities in America at that time. He was the child of poor Irish parents and when he lost his mother at the age of five his father put him in an orphanage. On growing up he spent ten years as a tramp. Becoming interested in literature and wanting to earn enough money to write, he became a professional boxer and eventually published two extremely impressive autobiographical books, *Emmett Lawler* and *Beggars of Life*. He moved to Hollywood with the aim of writing for the movies and joined Chaplin's staff. In 1924 he gave Robert a copy of *Beggars of Life* inscribed: 'To Robert Nichols, a delightful faun among the wolves of Hollywood.'

They collaborated to produce a play, *Twenty Below*, based on Tully's tramping experience. It is set in a town gaol 'somewhere in the Middle West of the U.S.A.', where six tramps have taken refuge for the night from the cold outside, where it is 'twenty below zero'. One of them turns out to be a young woman in man's clothing. At first it looks as if she will be raped. Then the men draw lots for her, but she is allowed to draw too, and having won, to choose the man who has already shown himself the dominant personality, a 'yegg' or cracksman of powerful physique. When the two are left by themselves, instead of sex they have conversation, and love springs up between them. But the next morning when they are about to leave together the yegg is shot in the back by another of the tramps and dies cursing the injustice of life.

Robert says of the collaboration:

One day Jim, brought me some characters and a situation for a play. 'Where do we go from here?' he asked. I spent two days on it. 'Right!' I said. 'I see it. We go on this way... ' I sketched the myth to him – for to me the art of the theatre is the incarnation of myth – and in his Yegg (cracksman) I had glimpsed an underworld Prometheus, in Blazes [the girl] a nymph of the roads, in the situation the promise of an ironical comedy. 'Good,' he said. 'Shoot!' In two weeks, thanks largely to the advice of my friend Maurice Browne, I rang Jim up. His chortles buoyed me up still further for I felt we 'had something'. That's how *Twenty Below* was made.[24]

The play is forceful and, unlike *Guilty Souls*, very tightly written; 'I think', said Masefield, 'it is the most complete thing you have done.'[25] It was published as a book in 1927, Robert managing to hold himself to only two pages of preface. He hoped it might go on the London stage, but a very similar play, *The Wolves*, reached production ahead of it.[26] Robert and Maurice Browne suspected plagiarism but took no action and Robert had to be content with a limited run the following year. This was at the Gate Theatre in London in May with a strong cast including Robert Speaight, Dennis Wyndham and Beatrix Lehmann. The critics praised the acting – Robert himself considered Lehmann 'superb'[27] – but found it strong meat. The language, characters and situation are all violent and unheroic. A modern audience would be less shaken, and it deserves revival.

But although *Twenty Below* is gripping to read and suited to the modern stage, Robert's heart was with two other works. One was to be a Greek tragedy set in the present with the title *Orpheus*. He mentions this in letters to Marsh dated 7 April 1925 and 2 February 1926; in the second of these he describes it as 'a *modern* play with a *modern* hero which I am going to try to make have a classic quality: to be a running wave, smooth, clear, limpid and powerful - not like *Guilty Souls* a vehement flame surrounded by distracted gusts and much black smoke.' For this there survive only fragmentary notes. The other, *Don Juan*, also mentioned in the letter of 7 April 1925, was quite different in character. It was all in verse and destined to overshadow Robert's creative writing for the rest of his life. A version of part of it was completed by May 1926, when Robert received some slightly discouraging feedback from Ruth Head.[28] Two poems which appeared in 1928, one showing Don Juan in conversation with a priest in Toledo, and the other a drinking song 'Let the World Wag', may be by-products of early work on it.[29]

Most of Robert's creativity while he was in America went into plays, but not all. He admired Landor, and probably under his influence wrote some dialogues with the dead, at least two of which appeared in print. One, which took advantage of a new edition of Erasmus's essay *In Praise of Folly*,[30] was called 'Erasmus Revisits His Old Haunts'. This updates the original treatment of the theme with references to Leopardi and Aldous Huxley, but starts with a dutiful family tribute. 'I thought', says Erasmus, 'I was forgotten save by such elderly country gentlemen and scholars as your grandfather, who graciously translated my Letters in three volumes, taking eighteen years to do it, and finding, perchance, about as many readers.' The second, 'Petrarch in California', was prompted by a new translation of *The Life of Solitude*[31] and discusses Robert's hero D'Annunzio and a more general subject always prominent in his thoughts, the vocation and function of the poet.

Robert also wrote a small number of poems in addition to those included in *Winter Berries*. In June 1924 he sent Marsh a couple of promising lyrics about the sea, presumably the Pacific as viewed from Glen Airy. In the *London Mercury* of January 1925 he had a meditative poem about night, 'City of Angels', which he later included in *Such Was My Singing*. This deals more with the city of heaven than with that of film stars; his feelings about Los Angeles are better summarised in a satirical poem about the energetic lady evangelist Mrs Aimée McPherson not published until 1928.[32] It is entitled 'Hymns, Incantations and Songs from the Boosters' Breviary, Compiled by an Authority for the use of faithful Angelenes, Number One', and begins:

> I like Los Angeles
> It contains Aimée Semple McPherson,
> Who washes the human sheep
> In a so convenient dip.

14
Yew Tree House, Early Years

The Nicholses' departure from America was repeatedly delayed. In July 1926 they were still in California.[1] But Robert was then assuring the Heads that they would be back by the end of August and in September they joined Norah's parents for a holiday in Scotland.[2] In October Robert was writing from Spange Hawe, Ewhurst, Surrey, and this was their regular address until the following summer, when (thanks to the Dennys who put up the purchase price[3]) they moved into Yew Tree House, Winchelsea.

Robert could always dramatise his doings, and the following sonnet was probably written to mark his return:

> Twice round this perilous globe's gigantic girth
> On sea-peaks shouldered, in earth-billows shaken,
> Have I through ultimate seas and ultimate earth
> With hungry heart my bitter voyage taken,
> And now once more I view the quiet hills
> Of England, shining golden, firm, serene,
> My England, so long craved through so many ills, ...

The sonnet's sextet taxes England with having in his absence gone astray:

> Your greed's ill fame
> Has dogged me wheresoe'er my footsteps led;
> When men have named your name - your glorious name! –
> 'Twas in such fashion I needs bow my head;

Another unpublished poem says explicitly that 'a city desolate and wandering swine' are what it provides to greet:

> one whom the harsh sea
> Flings bruised upon that dazzling stretch of shore.

But in fact he entered now upon some peaceful and not unhappy years. He had a loving wife who in some measure shared his literary activities – in 1928–9 she contributed several articles to *The Sketch*; for the first time the Nicholses had an abode they could regard as a real home; and he accomplished as much and received as much recognition as any writer could reasonably wish. In February 1928 his doctors told him he had tuberculosis, but although he received the news as a death-sentence,[4] he was never incapacitated and the disease was eliminated by a successful operation in 1933.

Winchelsea is an old Sussex town a mile from the South Coast. Robert may have been attracted to it by its literary associations. In the nine-teenth century Dante Gabriel Rossetti had been accustomed to stay there as a visitor. Conrad Aiken lived there briefly in the early 1920s. It is close to Rye, hallowed by the former residence of Henry James. David Gar-nett when invited to stay in 1930 said: 'I think I could make a plasticene model of Winchelsea. I stayed there for a few days with the Hueffers (now Ford) during the South African War... I had a Brownie Kodak and we went over to Rye and I took a snapshot of Henry James. I remember I told him to take his cap off because it made him look vulgar.'[5]

Yew Tree House is a rambling abode with plenty of rooms and a pleasant garden. It was staffed first by a couple and then by a cook and two maids. Robert's letters show him working fruitfully, entertaining his friends – the Arnold Bennetts and Aldous Huxleys were frequent visitors – and taking a part, if more as observer than as actor, in the life of his family.

This family, it will be remembered, included two sisters, Irene, born in February 1896, and Anne, the youngest of the family, born in May 1902. Irene studied Architecture at the London School of Economics and afterwards worked among the poor in East London – like Robert, in politics she inclined strongly to the left. In October 1926 she married George Gater, a man who had served as a soldier with distinction during the war – he became the youngest brigadier-general in the Army – and who then entered upon an equally illustrious career in the Civil Service. He ended covered with honours, including the KCMG and the KCB. Robert wrote an enormous letter to the Heads describing the nuptials. 'You are a real Archangel to give such pleasure,' Ruth told him;[6] 'H. H. listened to it with the fascinated attention of the Wedding Guest in the Ancient Mariner, although luckier than he was, there was never any occasion for us to beat our breasts.' The letter is too long to quote entire, but some excerpts, besides showing Robert as a raconteur, will provide a backward glimpse of his earlier years.

The celebrations were orchestrated by Phil whose sociable tempera-ment and experiences as a diplomat made him the family expert in stylish entertaining. They started, a couple of days before the wedding, with a dinner at Claridge's. Robert and Norah arrived only for the end of this.

We were conducted into a choice saloon - more white and gold, relieved by scarlet curtains, where a friend of Phil was giving a dinner in Irene's honour amid an atmosphere redolent of champagne and coronas. In the midst sat my little father, smaller than ever and even more distinguished and, poor man, more than ever subject to delicate vagueness as to who was who and what was what, but enjoying himself all the same and obviously, if a little uncomfortably, pleased to be being made much of by what was really a rather fine little set of handsome young English men and maidens – for if Phil's friends seem a little ineffective, no one can deny the distinction of their faces, the grace of their manners, the dexterity of their wits and the omnipresence of something one calls charm. And here I had my first shock and felt the first whisper of that old magician Time cause an indefinite stirring and strange music to respond in my breast. For there was Judith Waggett – the doctor's daughter – smiling at me with the merry eyes I last remembered in a little girl wearing a short frock as she led her children's cotillon heaven knows how many Christmases ago. And opposite her a worn but distinguished looking woman of about thirty – looking however about thirty-five – with grey hair falling around her ears, Christina Rossetti fashion, whose name appeared to be Clare Mackail.* Clare! – why, when last seen, she was a nymph just about to graduate into the aspect of one of Burne-Jones' younger oreads who, leaning over a silver pool, marks with wistful awe the sky and the secret mystery of her own beauty which has come to be – for what? For what indeed? There she sat and I could hardly look at her though I made an effort and went over and touched her on the shoulder and said, 'Well, dear Clare, how are you?' 'Robert!' she said, and it was obvious that I too had undergone a transmogrification. 'I haven't seen you for – ' 'Not since we bent over a little toy box with a glass lid. When one rubbed the lid with a silk handkerchief the tiny pellets of pith within jumped up like little angels pressing their faces against the panes of heaven.' 'They were scarlet and green,'

*Daughter of Bowyer Nichols's old friend J. W. Mackail and granddaughter of Burne-Jones.

she said. 'There were two boxes and you sent me one,' I answered. 'But the others are going to dance; will you dance with me?' 'I don't dance; I'll sit by your father.' So I danced amid occasional subdued and friendly guffaws from Phil, who apparently is under the impression that I am too moody-minded for that sort of thing.

From Claridge's the party moved to Hanover Terrace where there was supper and more dancing under the auspices of Phil's friend Mr Cottrell-Dormer of Rousham.

The next evening we dined at home, finding my father a little fatigued but obviously having much enjoyed himself. He said to Norah, 'That was a most enjoyable dinner at Claridge's, but I think I drank quite as much wine as was good for me. I was quite right not to have had any more in Hanover Terrace.' Norah went into peals of laughter. 'Why, you and I had some more together directly we arrived.' 'Did we indeed – I don't remember that.' Norah gave him a kiss. 'Of course we did and great fun it was.' 'Yes, it was great fun.' And he meant it. He hasn't had much fun, poor man. We were all very glad he liked it in his quiet, vague, delicate way.

The wedding itself was the following day at Holy Trinity, Sloane Square, with a reception at Kent House. Robert and his sister Anne took the going away clothes to Kent House before going to the church. 'Anne was very quiet. We smoked a cigarette together – poor Anne pale as a leaf you find pressed between the leaves of an old book. Her great eyes glowed. I said, "You can lean on us, Anne. We won't desert you." For Anne must not be left with Father. It isn't really necessary: Miss Dickinson agrees in this.'

At the ceremony 'Nobody could tell what Anne was thinking', but Bowyer Nichols's emotion prompted Robert for once to refer to him as 'Dad':

And there was Dad taking the bouquet from Irene as she put her hand into George's and marvellously, incredibly characteristic, Dad, realizing his Irene was leaving him, was softly putting his nose into the lilies of the valley as one who, in receipt of a blow from Fortune, with a mixture of Stoicism and Epicureanism is careful to recall to himself that beauty is always with us – though it be small and fragile as a lily of the valley – and not only is to be, but can be, however distractedly, enjoyed.

After the reception Norah and Robert visited Violet Dickinson who had been too frail to attend:

She was lying in a little room full of flowers. Her front hair had gone quite white. We came in softly and laid Irene's bouquet, as Irene had bid, upon her bed. 'Did it go well?' she said. 'Did Irene look happy?' 'Yes'. 'So that's all right. Then tell me about Henry and Ruth.' We spent about an hour with her and she asked a great deal after you two. 'I did my best to pass away,' she said, 'but it's evident, my dears, I wasn't born to pass away.' She took the bouquet in her hands. 'So the chicks are all happy,' she said, 'and old Bow, the Squire? I hope you didn't all get horribly drunk. What a beano it sounds. I wish I'd been there.' The same old Violet, you see; an angel disguised as a lamp-post.

The Nichols family dined out that night at the Carlton Grill. 'Anne was due. I met Father on the stairs. He said briefly "Anne can't come. She says she's off her feed."' She joined the party after dinner 'and when I kissed her I saw that she had rouged her cheeks: a thing that, as far as I know, she had never done before.' A final detail Robert records is that late that night his mother's sister Ethel Braye rang up asking after the bouquet that had been taken to Miss Dickinson: 'Might she have a rose for Mother?' This is the solitary mention of the unhappy mother of the bride.

Robert's account of the wedding reveals more than once his concern for his sister Anne. There was clearly a danger that she would feel bound by duty or pity to devote her youth to nursing her father – though he did in fact have a nurse, a Mr Flatman, who also functioned as a butler. She escaped this fate by brisk action. Irene's wedding was on 27 October. Just three months later, on 29 January, she eloped with Henry Strauss, later Lord Conesford, a barrister who had met Irene during the war when she was working in a Government office, and who had wooed her afterwards for seven years.

Whereas Irene's marriage to George Gater had the warm approval of all the Nichols family, this runaway match aroused grief and indignation. Robert, now comfortably in his saddle as a family chronicler, gave the Heads daily bulletins of the uproar. Unfortunately only one has been preserved. On 7 February he wrote:

What is painful in the Anne affair is not for me so much the fact that she's married Harry Strauss – though I rather fear that four or five years may possibly see it out – or even the way it was done, as the ungodly awfulness of the way it has affected my brother and sister. As to how it has affected Father we don't yet know. But Irene is difficult and I think her George is going to be difficult too as he detests the very sight of Harry. According to Phil, Irene will have it that Harry kept on coming to Lawford to see Anne, and in order to keep seeing Anne had to keep making love to her. The other side is, of course, that Irene kept him hanging about for want of a more suitable cavalier, turning him down but never wholly turning him down and then, seeing no one turn up, later repented and intimated to him that she would accept him if he made another offer, whereat Harry turned *her* down and so no fury etc. What the truth is, I don't know, and Phil says neither Harry nor Irene can see straight on the subject of each other and that the truth will never be known. All that I know is that at lunch on Wednesday Irene – George, Uncle Watty, Phil and myself being present – slumped down into the chair at the head of the table with 'Well, I suppose I may take the head now Anne's (scornfully) Mrs Strauss; for I shall still at any rate be the senior married daughter.' And afterwards sitting with Uncle and myself she suddenly bursts out sardonically 'D'you realise that Anne's initials now spell ASS?' (i.e. Anne Sadelbia Strauss.) And again, on the talk veering to how the rest of the day was to be spent, 'George and I are going this evening to buy Anne a little present – not too big. We don't intend to find anything for the other person. And a girl who runs away to get married can't expect to get anything at all like a girl who stays and is married in the proper way.' I was thunderstruck at this – so thunderstruck that I couldn't even for the first moment feel angry. Tears came into my uncle's pale blue eyes. He brushed them away with his finger tips and, leaning back, said mildly, 'Poor little Anne, I think (apologetically) I shall give her a cheque.' 'Yes,' I said, 'that's what she'd like.' Then, glancing at my sister and not without a sort of indignation giving me a sort of heartiness I said 'Well, all I know is that she's going to get the best thing I've got in my house – my Jowett landscape, it cost me £30. I've already written to ask her if she'd like it.' At that Irene said 'Very good of you,' and made deprecatory noises and looked rather abashed…

My reactions? Well, I read her matter of fact little letter through and felt distinctly stunned but, resolved not to give up, I read through my other letters. Then I went and telephoned to Phil whose voice sounded very queer – I had to threaten never to speak to him again at one point when he began to get fierce (then we both laughed, it was so absurd) – and sent some wires for which I have been blamed. I sent one to my aunt Belle begging her not to reproach Anne and was in London ticked off by Phil for so doing when it was he himself who told me over the phone that Aunt was likely to break out in reproaches to Anne for damaging the being (my father) she (Aunt) is most attached to in the world. Phil informed me that 'it was felt' (i.e. they'd all been getting into a stew over it) that I had 'no business to tell people what to do – especially obvious things – as if I was, as usual, the only person who knew anything 'at all'. Mais que voulez -vous? They were all in a stew, going round and round like mice in a trap, making little noises, giving each other little bites, making it up and fussing and fussing and going over every detail of the past like a lot of bookies over a crooked deal on a race course.

Bowyer Nichols was at this time in Italy. Robert wired to him 'that I thought Anne had done it that way in the hopes (erroneous perhaps) of that way sparing him an accumulation of slow pain.' He then wrote a letter 'urging on him a complete and utter forgiveness of *BOTH*'.[7] Reconciliation did follow, and the Strauss marriage did not break up after five years but lasted, like that of the Gaters, until the husband was removed by death.

It was probably between these two weddings that Robert started a short novel on the theme of gambling. Entitled *Under the Yew*, it is set in 1786 and told in the first person. The Narrator – his name does not appear – is an addict of twenty-three who has already gambled away two-thirds of his patrimony. On a Saturday afternoon in December he is invited by a neighbour to come over and spend the night gambling in a party that will include a rich young man called Sir Anthony Noble. (Robert was on friendly terms with Cynthia Noble, sister of the Northumbrian baronet of that surname, but the nomenclature seems accidental.) Sir Anthony turns out to be a sinister kind of fallen angel who challenges the Narrator to play until one or the other is cleaned out. The play starts slowly, but at midnight after supper the other gamblers are seized by a bizarre desire to laugh and make alterations to their attire, and this is the signal for Sir Anthony to transfer a notable ring from the little finger of his left hand to that of his right, and to start playing high. During the rest of the night he gradually becomes a steady winner from the rest of the company, while the Narrator waits for a turn at single combat. Sunday morning arrives, and its beauty urges him to 'leave these abominations while it is yet possible', but Sir Anthony detains him as if by hypnotism. Throughout the day he wins against Sir Anthony while the other gamblers look on in mounting envy. The Narrator's success, however, takes him out of elation into a mood of helplessness, guilt and 'intolerable distress'. When night falls Sir Anthony has nothing left but his ring. The Narrator insists on playing for that too. He loses, and thereafter loses consistently and fast until he is totally ruined. At two o'clock he sets off in the moonlight to return home. On the way he comes to a huge yew (mentioned on his outward journey). From its shadow an old woman and a youth of about seventeen in the last extremity of poverty and emaciation emerge and ask for alms. He is utterly overcome with shame at being unable to give them anything, and runs away. Then, with a supreme effort summoning up the courage to face them, he goes back, but they have disappeared. This experience cures him of gambling once and for all.

The story might not ineffectively have ended here, but in fact it goes on for another twenty pages to tell us that the Narrator becomes a prosperous merchant, and twenty years later revisits the house where the gambling took place. This house, which had not been described earlier, is now revealed (whether or not Robert realises the fact) as Lawford, complete with lime avenue and magnolia grandiflora trained up the middle of its perfectly proportioned Georgian front. Infested, however, with Sir Anthony Noble. He has bought it and now lives a Faustian life in one room, his angelic looks having undergone a horrible transformation like the portrait of Dorian Gray. In the gambling scene Sir Anthony had been calm and the Narrator feverish; now the Narrator has achieved inner peace while Sir Anthony curses God with a vehemence that recalls *Golgotha and Co.*

'As for your gambler story,' said Lady Head when Robert wrote to her about it,[8] 'the trouble seems to be that it must be all spun out of your imagination.' Ten years later Robert admitted this. 'The story is a piece of imaginative virtuosity – for, save an occasional small bet on a horse, I have never gambled and when I went to Monte Carlo – entering the salle privée on three separate occasions – I found I had no desire to gamble.'[9] He was not, however, trying to handle the theme in the same realistic fashion as Dostoevsky. His story is, as he said to Marsh, a fairy tale,[10] – a gothic fairy tale, we might be inclined to call it – no more about gambling than about rock-climbing, martial adventure or anything else than can destroy its votaries, lyric poetry included.

Under the Yew had a mixed reception from Robert's friends. Sassoon wished the style had been simpler and more left to the imagination.[11] David Garnett, reading it in 1930, pronounced it 'damned good' and said 'It has the go and brio of the best Conrad story.'[12] Reviewers found it puzzling. 'The first essential of a reviewer', said the *Observer*,[13] 'is the comprehension of what the author is trying to do; and that essential, in reviewing Mr. Nichols' book, I cannot provide. I have read every word of it with care, and several passages several times; I remain impressed, but bewildered.' Of these remarks, much more generous than silence, Aldous Huxley, who was staying with Robert that weekend, said: 'Purely silly, not to say imbecile',[14] and Robert himself exclaimed: 'If ever there was a perfectly simple straightforward narrative!' Perhaps; but one might wonder why Robert wanted to write it.

In January 1926 he had completed a work he entitled *The Rake's Progress*.[15] This was a 'scenario for ballet and cinema [silent, of course] founded on the works of William Hogarth' – chiefly on *The Rake's Progress* and *The Harlot's Progress* 'but subsidiary figures from other of Hogarth's pictures appear'.[16] It was originally written for music by Léon Goossens in the hope that it would be staged by Diaghilev.[17] After Goossens and Diaghilev had fallen out, Jack Lindsay printed it at the Fanfrolico Press – Robert collected well-printed books and was a friend of Lindsay – in *The London Aphrodite* of December 1928. Read in conjunction with it, *Under the Yew* lights up in intelligibility.

The Rake's Progress starts with an orchestral prelude: 'Darkness. Sudden shattering eruption of furious laughter, full of ferocious and brutal *bonhomie*.' The uproar passes. 'Bow Bells subduedly chime and are answered more subduedly by yet other bells and by uneasy murmurs.' There is silence. Then, 'from all over the countryside which hems in this eighteenth century London, floats the crying of cocks.' The curtain rises on 'a cobbled space in the midst of Hogarth's London', suggested by pictures like *Beer Street*, *Gin Lane* and the first plate in *The Harlot's Progress*. This is filled up gradually by vagrants, musicians, limbless beggars, Mohocks, the watch, headed by a beadle, etc., and there is a succession of scenes of quick-moving buffoonery: 'The Mohocks knock the Beadle's hat over his eyes, spin him round while he strikes out at them with his pole, then scatter and disappear. The Beadle reels into the door under the pawnbroker's. The casement above flies open: a chamberpot is emptied on the Beadle's head. His lanthorn is extinguished. He splutters, then blunders across toward the peg-legged sailor', and so forth. The interwoven stories of the Rake and the Harlot unfold on Hogarthian lines. But crowded and grotesque as Hogarth's pictures are, Robert's scenario goes further by adding movement and developing audible themes like cock-crowing.

> There appear from different directions a dancing master, a teacher of the flute, a French fencing master, an English master of the quarter staff, a bravo. All compete for the Rake's interest. The Rake signs for one at a time. The dancing master points his toe and flourishes his handkerchief till cracked on the head by the flute of the flautist, who in turn makes haste to avoid the passados of the fencing master, who in turn is driven away by the flourishes of the master of the quarter staff. Then they all close in on him and he gives them each a guinea. But they demand more. At this moment the bravo arrives and, pushing them all aside, displays his letter of commendation as one disposed to undertake all kinds of service. The Rake points to his persecutors. The bravo drives them out. No sooner is the bravo driving these creatures before him than a herd of others come running – a jockey, a gamecock fancier, a peruke maker. The jockey prances in front of him, riding a bridle he has in his hands over imaginary jumps and belabouring an imaginary horse with his switch. But suddenly over the jockey's head the gamecock fancier arrives carrying two baskets of cocks. He flings the baskets on one side and, pulling the jockey's cap over the jockey's nose, squats down on his heels and springs at the jockey like a gamecock. Twice or three times the couple spring at each others as if they were cocks in a main, then the fancier bowls over the jockey, stands up and crows.

The Rake is fitted out by the perukier 'while his assistant, a monkey in full costume, dances round in front holding up a mirror'. The cock-fancier 'pulls a cock from his basket. It crows. The Rake, highly pleased with himself in his new garments, seizes the cock, pulls a feather from its tail, shoves the cockade into the three-cornered hat which the perukier offers him, thrusts the fancier away, and flapping his sleeves like a cock, crows louder than the cocks in the basket.'

The Rake runs his sword through the Earl as in *Marriage à la Mode*, plate 5, and is duly hanged in the best Hogarthian style, off stage, but with the characters on stage scrambling over each other to watch. But the following morning his ghost makes a triumphant come-back to

greet the New Rake of the next day. The New Rake gapes. The final
episode in the scenario may be quoted in full:

> The Beauty sees the New Rake and is amused at the way he is
> taken with her. Lightly she plucks a rose from the wall and tosses
> it toward him. The Corpse of the Rake crows suddenly, piercingly,
> ironically, callously and with challenge. The New Rake stoops,
> picks up the rose, sweeps off his hat, would greet the Beauty,
> throws her an impassioned glance. Louder and ever more frightful
> laughter from the Mohocks. Then, as the New Rake gazes
> passionately at the Beauty, all the cocks in the world crow glori-
> ously, stridently, in a paean of almost unimaginable vehemence,
> the crow of acceptance to life. They are prolonging their crow of
> an unexampled sonority when there is a double crash as of an
> earthquake that sets free all the dead to cry their salute to life and
> THE CURTAIN SWIFTLY DESCENDS.

Robert's knowledge of Hogarth was inherited. 'My great great
grandfather wrote the first *Life of Hogarth* ever written in English.'[18]
He refers to the massive three-volume edition, written and printed by
the eighteenth-century John Nichols, which contains all 'The Genuine
Works of William Hogarth' and is 'illustrated with biographical anecdotes, a chronological catalogue and commentary'. He became interested in the masked comedy and *Commedia dell' Arte* that developed in
Italy in the sixteenth and seventeenth centuries, and this probably
suggested to him ways of turning Hogarth's pictures, frozen instants,
into drama. But what provides the motivation, the fire to carry out this
tour de force, must have been that manic elation which was so marked
and to his friends such a redeeming feature of his personality.

The Rake's Progress seems never to have been produced, though in
the last month of his life it looked as if someone might take the financial
risk.[19] But its mixture of hectic exuberance and self-destructive vice
seeks expression in other works: in *Don Juan*, the Sisyphus task of his
later years, and earlier in *Under the Yew*. It was the fate of Robert's
characters to be symbols rather than real people, and the turbulent
force which the Rake symbolises in the scenario is embodied by the
Don in the poetic drama and by the Narrator in the novella. Of the
three vehicles the narrative form is perhaps the least natural, but it runs
quite smoothly and effectively, at least until the last section.

H. G. Harwood in *The Outlook*[20] said: 'The end is a mess.' It might
be more accurate to say that it reveals a certain disorganisation in the

author. 'I had only the vaguest notion of my intended close', he recalled, 'when I started the tale. But one day I suddenly saw the Epilogue – it, as it were, burst upward from depths within me.'[21] He told Marsh he wrote the whole book in four months,[22] and a work on which a creative writer is prepared to risk his reputation ought to stay in the drawer longer than that. Robert was conscious of imperfections and made some alterations while the book was in proof which his publisher, Martin Secker, refused to incorporate, and a different set of alterations which did get incorporated when the story was reprinted in *Argosy* in 1938, but the oddity of the epilogue remains.

In January 1927 Robert was working on *Under the Yew*. In February he wrote to Marsh about a different project:

> The following is *strictly* between ourselves. So many paragraphs have appeared in the papers that I am setting out to write my play about the release of energy in the atom *at once*, and hope to write it, if my poor head holds out, as fast as I can for fear that someone else may step in and snatch the subject. Do not even mention the subject to others.[23]

Marsh wrote back:

> Bob, I am rather unhappy at the idea of your rushing the play through as you propose. You won't mind my saying that I think the fault of nearly all your work except a few of your best poems is that it is too *primesautier*, and would have gained by lying by and being gone through critically. I dread the lava-torrent of your inspiration.

The play to which they were referring was *Wings Over Europe*, and Robert was so far guided by Marsh's wise advice as to work on it for some nine months[24] in collaboration with Maurice Browne before sending it to look for a stage.

The conception is original and powerful. A young physicist has discovered how to split the atom and harness the forces that hold it together. In 1927 this was an ambition of scientists, but no one knew when, if ever, it would be fulfilled or what would be the result. Robert's physicist is able to draw on sufficient atomic energy to meet all the material needs and desires of mankind with minimal effort and at negligible cost – thereby threatening to make nonsense of the existing economic system. He also, since he can resolve matter into its subatomic elements, has the capacity for large-scale destruction. He wants his new knowledge to benefit mankind and, mistrusting the League of Nations, communicates it to the British Government. Though Robert had been out of temper with his native land when he returned to it, he now concedes that the 'political entity representing the maximum variety of races is the British Empire' and judges its having held together so long 'an extraordinary tribute to its government', showing that it 'relied on the good will of Mankind rather than on fear'. But his scientist is disappointed. When he explains his discovery to the Cabinet, everyone wants him to suppress it except the Secretary of State for War who wants to use it for military purposes. After some angry exchanges he gives them a week in which their chosen experts are invited to verify his claims and they themselves to think up a program for putting atomic energy to beneficent use. That is the situation at the end of the first act.

The whole play takes place in the Cabinet Room, and contains no woman's part. Robert obtained information about Cabinet meetings from Marsh and was shown the Cabinet Room in 10 Downing Street by him. In the second act the Cabinet resolve, if they cannot persuade the physicist to suppress his discovery, to keep him a prisoner incommunicado for the rest of his life. But he has anticipated this. He has, he tells them, the means to blow up England at any moment, and he will do so unless they are 'prepared to formulate, under my supervision, a constructive program satisfactory to *me*' by noon the following day. Any attempt to interfere with him in the meantime will simply trigger the catastrophe. In the final act, the following day the physicist announces that he has changed his mind. The human race is clearly unable to make use of his knowledge, but since, even if he himself conceals it, other people will arrive at it soon, he has decided to obliterate the planet and let nature try again elsewhere. He gives the Cabinet a quarter of an hour to compose their thoughts, while he himself takes a last look at the narcissi in St James's Park. In this interval they go collectively and individually to pieces in a most disedifying way. Their religious beliefs are exposed as hollow, the Lord Chancellor turns out to be having an affair with the wife of the Chancellor of the Exchequer and weak characters give way to puerile abuse. But when the physicist comes back the War Secretary pulls himself together enough to draw a pistol and shoot him through the heart. His death brings a moment of relief and the other Cabinet members begin to recover their dignity. But then a message is delivered that the scientists of the world are in possession of the secret of atomic power already; they too say the force must be used constructively, and their aeroplanes, equipped with atomic bombs, are stationed over every capital in the civilised world. The sound of these aeroplanes is heard as the curtain falls: they are the wings over Europe of the title.

Thanks to the efforts of Maurice Browne, who was credited as a co-author, this play attracted more attention than any other work of Robert's. It was first performed in New York in the winter of 1928–9 and received enthusiastic notices. It was published in book form in America in 1929 by Covici Friede and in England in 1932 by Chatto and Windus. Waltzer Preusler produced a German translation in the winter of 1928–9 (he had already translated *Twenty Below* the year before[25]) and it was put on in Germany in 1930. Finally it was produced at the Globe Theatre in London at the end of April 1932. That production happened to be excellently timed; for on 1 May Lord Rutherford (who is mentioned in the first act of the play) announced that he had, in truth, split the atom. Aldous Huxley pointed out the coincidence in an article on the 14th in *Time and Tide*.

Wings was a more popular success in America than in England. It ran in New York for several weeks and then toured the outlying States for several months, bringing the author a substantial income. Robert's name rode so high that (always eager to help aspiring writers*) he was able to persuade Covici Friede Inc to publish a volume by the Los Angeles poet Leroy MacLeod.[26] 'I see your hand', said MacLeod, 'pulling the strings of destiny in my behalf. Thanks! Thanks.'

The London production might have run for longer if Robert had not fallen out with Maurice Browne over the making of cuts. The play as it was performed has a serious weakness. The character of the young physicist is too much Robert's own. His very name, Francis Lightfoot, is one Robert liked to give himself. The description of him in the stage directions of the printed version is an embarrassing self-portrait. He cut out of the proofs, thank goodness, 'His face is very beautiful and rather unearthly', but left in 'His voice, a high tenor, becomes eloquent with an eloquence which is, however, slightly marred by shrillness of timbre; and his gestures and bearing display a certain nobility as fiery as it is un-English.' But far more serious, whenever Lightfoot has a chance, he speaks exactly like Robert himself in his prefaces and newspaper articles:

---

*In the last years of his life he was trying to find publishers for a novel by Anna Whyte and poems by Edward Lowbury.

Must I tell you what every Board-school urchin knows? – that among the myriad orbs of the Milky Way there gyrates, in a minor solar system, a negligible planet, and that on this pea of a planet creeps a race of parasites? ... [But now] at last Man is free to enlarge the Kingdom of the Spirit; and so, whether the Sum of Things is justified or not, to justify himself. And do you think, because the Spirit of Yesterday in *you* is afraid, the Spirit of Tomorrow in *me* will run away?*

It is to be hoped that the critics were not conscious of this identification when they spoke of 'the pigheadedness of your utterly uninformed zealot' (James Agate in *The Sunday Times*) and 'the prose epitome of the Socialist Song-Book' (Ivor Brown in the *Observer*) or said, like Peter Burnup in the *Sunday Referee*, 'The young man's reading appears to have been confined to the odd cocktail of Maxwell Clark [*sic*] and Shelley. So that, having lived his short life in a vague Shelleyan trance and in juvenile innocence of the pavements and the excitements of lesser men, he can think only that mankind will henceforth be "free".' Francis James had the task of playing this unsympathetic character. Everyone said he did so admirably, and he himself wrote a graceful letter to Robert thanking him and Maurice Browne 'for giving me Francis Lightfoot. He will always be an important and thrilling landmark in my life.'[27] But the play would probably have had a wider general appeal if Francis Lightfoot's speeches had been considerably shorter.

The play had another weakness which though odd was less damaging. It had two different endings. As Robert originally wrote it the Secretary for War intends to shoot the physicist, but in fact Lightfoot is run over when returning from St James's Park. When the play was performed in New York the Theatre Guild, which was producing it, substituted the ending in which the physicist is actually shot in front of the Cabinet. The American printed edition has both endings, one after another. The 1932 London performance was the same as the New York performance except that the Censor, Lord Cromer, required the excision of those remarks by the panic-stricken ministers which were blasphemous towards God or the Royal Family, and also the Lord Chancellor's love affair. As Maurice Browne said to Robert, 'Members of the British Cabinet may commit murder but not adultery.'[28]

---

*In justice to Robert it should be acknowledged that *Country Life* (14.5.32) quoted this characteristic speech with the comment: 'I do not believe that even the most casual theatregoer can listen unmoved to rhetoric of this order.'

Though the London run was short, it had *succès d'estime*. The press coverage was not only copious but largely favourable and supporters turned out in force: not only the Huxleys, but H. G. Wells. H. W. Nevinson, Lady Colefax, and Lady Astor, who had recently become connected with the Nichols family by marriage and now brought along Bernard Shaw. The Denny parents were there, 'obviously delighted,' according to *The Sketch*, 'with their son-in-law's brilliant play'.[29]

Robert had seen the play already at the Beck Theatre in New York. In October 1928 he told Marsh: 'Mrs Lamont is transporting Norah and myself thither (and back) and putting us up while there.'[30] They set off on 4 November and Robert wrote a graphic account of the rehearsals, the dress rehearsal, and the First Night.[31]

The Theatre Guild's new ending was sprung on him only when he arrived. He seems to have agreed to it quite readily, though in a letter to the Guild on his departure he says he is 'still in a condition of doubt. There seems to be an irreconcilable breach between what is effective in the theatre and what is proper to the thesis. Undoubtedly the new form is more dramatic and there can be no question but that it produces a moment of extreme interest in the theatre.' In the end his doubts must have been resolved in favour of the Theatre Guild, since the motor-accident ending is not included in the Chatto edition of 1932.

Apart from this shock he and Norah greatly enjoyed their stay in New York, though on the evening before the First Night performance it looked as if the excitement was going to be too much for him. 'I went to pieces and felt I would never "make it". I was so weak I could hardly stand.' Fortunately Mrs Lamont and Metcalfe, her butler, were equal to the emergency.

> Florence took me upstairs and laid me down and talked angeli-cally to me. But I was so done I said 'I'll have to tell Nornie I can't go to the theatre.'
>
> Metcalfe arrived. He got me into a dressing gown, poured menthol on my forehead and cognac down my throat. He rubbed my legs and arms.
>
> 'You stay quite still. I'll put out your clothes. Don't come down to dinner if you don't feel like it. And finally this – and it's most important – when it is time to get up, take a hot bath followed by one absolutely cold. Stay under water in the cold seven seconds. Rub yourself down as quick as you can. Then get into your clothes and directly you're dressed, don't wait a moment or think about

anything, but come straight upstairs. And you'll be all right. I give you my word for it.'

The treatment worked, and Robert 'jumped out of the bath a different man'. He not only 'made it' to the theatre but when the time came for him to take his curtain call and he advanced to the centre of the stage he experienced 'a feeling I can only describe by saying it was like a still, unconquerable flame standing straight up in my bosom… My heart was full but I felt perfectly controlled. I bowed low to the audience, then, turning on my heels I lifted my right arm high above my head like a toreador who has killed his bull, and lowering it blew a kiss to Norah and Florence and Tom in their box. Then – the hubbub continuing – I bowed again and made my speech' – a speech consisting simply of thanks to the audience, the actors and the producers.

That, at least, was Robert's impression; St John Ervine had a different one. He sent a long report to the *Observer*[32] on 30 December which described *Wings* as '*the* play of the season' but said at the end: 'I venture, very reluctantly, to offer some counsel to Mr Robert Nichols. When next a play in which he has a hand is performed in New York, will he please abstain from coming on the stage and making a speech?' Robert wrote to expostulate, but Ervine stuck to his guns:

It was a bloody performance, and when I say that it was an anticlimax and that it caused cold waves to flow over the audience, I am speaking not only of what I myself felt, but of what I heard other people say. A girl whom I had taken to see it – she was deeply moved by the play – moaned with rage after you had been talking for about a minute, and was ready, if dared, to go on to the stage and pull you off it. My dear fellow, why will you indulge in all this high-falute? Your very manner as you came on to the stage, blowing kisses and holding up your hand to stop the applause, annoyed people. Then the speech itself, in its delivery more than in its matter, was appalling… You simply must not do this sort of thing. Either keep off the stage altogether, which is the proper thing to do – authors rarely take calls here: I've only seen three calls taken during my visit, two of them by English authors, Lonsdale and you – or make your bow and clear off.[33]

Robert later looked back on that appearance of his on the stage as one of the supreme moments of his life;[34] for once he experienced what he understood by 'glory'[35] and Ervine's remarks 'hurt and angered me a good deal'. Their correspondence continued and Robert left Ervine's letters, rebukes and all, to Trinity College, Oxford, but their friendship was damaged.[36] The reception of the play in America was in general gratifying. It brought Robert in all £2,000;[37] ran for eight weeks in New York, longer than the Guild had expected, and had an extensive tour in the provinces. Robert and Norah, however, returned to London on 14 December in the *Berengaria*, the Lamonts sending them first class (where they had the company of the future King George VI) with a large pot of caviare.

15
Deaths and Quarrels

In January 1929 the Nicholses went off to Majorca for the rest of the winter. There they met D. H. Lawrence, who was not in good health, helped him and Frieda to find a house, and renewed friendship with them.[1] However, though Robert lent him *Thus Spoke Zarathrustra*, they did not get onto very easy terms. Lawrence, he recalled in a letter to the Heads[2]

> had no scruples about wading into one's inner sanctum and denouncing the furniture and throwing it about... (a) I didn't think it right. (b) I like being on terms with people and am prepared – usually – to stand a certain bill for breakages in my own sanctum as the price of keeping on terms. (c) If I do get in their sanctum and begin throwing things about I frequently, nay usually, lose my head, and throw them about with a will, a will quite often actuated by hate... More than once I felt tempted to wade into D. H. L. Perhaps I ought to have done so – perhaps that is why to this day, though I feel I loved and love some of his characteristics, my main feeling for him as a man – as a person called David Lawrence – is one of contempt (I worked this out this week) tempered by physical dislike... There was a certain element of impatience and condescension in D. H. L.'s attitude toward me in Majorca which was irritating. I bore it and stuck to patience and gentleness though we nearly had one big row and I cannot to this day make out whether his dropping of this condescension was due to the persistence in gentleness or the signs of violence when we nearly came to a row. ... Such affection as I had in connection with Lawrence was affection for what he stood for – a sick and independent writer of some genius – and not for the man himself (in so far as I had affection for Lawrence personally it was for a sick little man who was in a bad way and had a certain attractiveness as long as he remained a rather weak, extremely sensitive, somewhat evasive man and had the dignity of such. When he started kicking about I disliked him and rather despised him. For

though he set up – on the plane of world literature and world thought – i.e. where one meets Nietzsche and Dostoievsky – as an aristocrat, he hadn't, so far as I could see (I may have been wrong), any stoicism whatever, and at long last your aristocrat who is the genuine thing always has a streak of the stoic in him.)

Apart from this sticky social interaction, the Nicholses seem to have enjoyed their time in Majorca. Robert was at first shocked by the raw Catholicism of the Holy Week ceremonies, but later came round to them, and it was probably because of having attended them that two years later he was able to carry out a commission for the Bishop of Chichester and produce his poem 'For the Eve of Palm Sunday', which was set to music by Eric Fenby and published in the *London Mercury*.

On returning to Yew Tree House Robert applied himself to two plays, the poetical magnum opus, *Don Juan*, and *Karin* or, as it later came to be called, *Komuso*, in prose. These were to occupy him for many years to come. Against the background of work on them, entertaining in Winchelsea, visits to London and Lawford and so forth, the events which stand out in the nearer future are mostly sombre.

There was a bizarre incident in September 1929. Five of Robert's poems, including 'Night Rhapsody' and 'Last Words', were read by Ronald Watkins in a BBC broadcast. A woman in Bromley, Kent, committed suicide by gassing herself after the broadcast and her husband, Mr Frank Davis, blamed the tragedy on their depressing character. The inquest heard that the woman had other sources of unhappiness – in particular she wanted children – but it was naturally a shock to Robert.

A larger and darker shadow was cast over 1929 by the failing health of Romer Wilson. Like several other of Robert's women friends, she was just a little his senior and had had early literary success. She was born in 1891, her first novel was published in 1918, and she was awarded the Hawthornden Prize for *Death in Society* in 1921. Edward Shanks who wrote an appreciation of her for the *London Mercury* describes her as 'one of the most exciting' writers of her generation, and says 'She gave me the feeling that, so long as she was at work, literature was live and that, between one moment and the next she might do anything.' Robert admired her enormously. Both had a propensity to manic elation. 'Nobody except me', she said, 'ever walked so permanently on such a wild windy hilltop with such a marvellous view as you.'[3] They also valued the same things and were close even in literary style: some of her writing is much in the manner of *Fantastica* and *Under the Yew*. He liked to compare her with D. H. Lawrence.

He was a queer sort of hero with a great deal of sensitivity and not much imagination as I understand that word. She was a spirit. I place spirits above heroes. And she was all imagination. In a word, however brave he was – and he was very brave – he belonged, so to speak, to the Underworld. Of spiritual entities he seemed to have little perception. (Look at his gallery of portraits – is there a spiritual personage among them?) She belonged to the Overworld, yet she was not at all out of touch with the world of sense. On the contrary, she liked luxury and power and honour, was indeed rather avid of luxury (of which she had precious little, poor soul) and she confessed to being – and probably was – sensual in the strictly physiological sense of the term (so am I!). It is typical of them that D. H. L. should describe rapture in terms of darkness, redness and obscurity and she in terms of light, of greenness, of blueness and of clarity. She was companion to me – through any bother – as he could never be. I would get exhausted and exasperated after seeing D. H. L. – my fault partly! – while I was refreshed and strengthened by seeing her. His eyes never seemed to meet mine directly – it may be that he was shy and uneasy. Hers looked at you and while they looked you forgot everything else in the world: they were as blue black as the darkest stillest midnight sea and there dwelt in their depths an extraordinary fire.[4]

These words may suggest a more amorous feeling than admiration. The year after Robert married Norah, Romer married the American writer Edward O'Brien, but they first met before this time and Robert told the Heads, what he felt he could not say publicly, 'that she was a very beautiful woman and that I knew it in my power very possibly to possess her on that first meeting and that all the circumstances were more than propitious for such a possession and that she was fully aware of that propitiousness.'[5]

Their acquaintance was renewed when Robert came back to England in 1926 and in January 1927 she sent a sprightly letter inviting him for the night. 'If you want Mr Houghton very much I will ask him, but would rather concentrate my charm on you. Remember, unless you want to forget, I have "spent but one hour with thee" in all my life.'[6] It looks as if the charm was too effective or Robert misinterpreted her signals. At any rate, after the meeting he wrote a letter to her which has not survived but to which she replied:

Dear Bob

Your letter is such that willy nilly I must answer it, and you force me out into the market place, so in the market place I will stand and say out loud exactly what I think and feel.

In the first place, *I am not Saturday Symphony* [her latest novel]. That book is my statement of a deplorable situation, my sudden view of certain circumstances, when as a spectator I suddenly came back to England after years.

That is not my idea of love, nor have I lived that way, nor in those circumstances. They are alien to me and disgust me.

While you were here the other day I wanted to say a number of things but could not because you were not well and were tired and I felt could not possibly hear properly, but I will say them now.

I saw you years and years ago in circumstances that were superficially frivolous. But I saw you, do you understand, and have never forgotten you. I have never since then wished for any trivial passionate episode with you, nor wished to marry you, nor wished to be adored by you from afar. How I saw you, who shall say? I have very few people I love, but you are one of them. I love John Goss,* another man and two women. Edward and I are so entirely at one that I need not say anything about our love to anybody. My love for you and Goss has no need of that enjoyment which you call a bye-product, nay, I would not between now and heaven go that way with either of you. And I don't care what you say or do, whether you stand on the other side of the fence or run against me.

I have a feeling of recognition when I see you, a sense of love. When you are not there I remember you and feel the world is not so lonely because you are in it. ...

You hate *Saturday Symphony* because you feel it is a charge against yourself. You are not in that picture gallery, nor am I, nor, essentially, is anyone I love. You have justified yourself to me long ago. Come and go as you please. You have the freedom of my love though not of that (in this case) inessential sphere of passion I may rule. ...

Now you may rave against me if you like. I dare say I shall cry if

*A friend of many of Robert's friends, such as Heseltine, Moeran and Augustus John.

you do. There is a street musician at this moment struck up 'How can I live without you?'

Well, I shan't ever have to live without you, one never does live without people one has once really loved.

I shall see you in Paradise if not before, and then you will laugh!

ROMER[7]

This letter seems to have cleared the air, and a friendly correspondence continued in which they discussed each other's work in progress. In July 1928 Romer and her husband removed from London to Switzerland and she wrote congratulating Robert on *Under the Yew* but reporting bad health, in particular an 'inside complaint which keeps me in the depth of depression and fatigue'.[8] Her doctors told her it was not cancer, but of course it was. Robert wrote her a series of long letters which seem to have helped her through the series of operations and false hopes which followed. In October 1929 she said 'I can't tell you how you put the courage back into me when I was nearly flattened out and frightened. You have done a fair job for me. I thank you.'[9] And this was confirmed some years later by her husband: 'I don't forget', he said, 'what courage you gave to Romer... Her courage was greater than even you know, I think. She had to fight against madness in her blood most of the years of her marriage, and she won that battle too. I think she'd like you to know this.'

The courage she shows in her letters to Robert in 1928 and 1929 (Robert bequeathed them to Trinity College, Oxford) does in fact make them very impressive reading. She pressed on with her literary work, an edition of fairy tales for children, a biography of Emily Brontë, and a novel entitled *Once in May*. Leonard Woolf's review of the biography made her feel 'all the blasted things I felt before about West Kensington and Bloomsbury in one fell swoop. Blasted desiccated refined specimen of mummified good taste.'[10] *Once in May* was to be dedicated to Robert and the hero was to be (though she did not put it like that) Robert as he might like to be: 'Has the gift of love and speech. Lives in Byron's time and is a great free dog and carries off his girl in high spirits... God, I love you, Bob! and I'll make ye a fine roaring book. Very happy and glad to have survived.'[11]

This was the end of April 1929. But in July she was back in Zurich 'to be deprived of some more of my malfaisant innards by X-ray'. The X-ray treatment went on for weeks, but was unsuccessful. At last, on 6 November, she wrote 'Am about to be cut again. Do not think I have the dumps and dismals. I am in the hands of Prof Roux who got the Sorbonne D Litt with Einstein a few days ago. He is said to be 84 years old but even so has still got some golden hair... Not quite finished *Once in May*, but *shall finish it. This* is the last time.'

She died in January 1930. 'Your telegram', O'Brien told Robert, 'she read over and over day after day. It was light and air to her and the best kind of courage.' He said also: '*Once in May* is nearly finished and she would like you to finish it. She felt that it was written in your spirit, and she has left a synopsis of how it would have ended.'[12] In fact there was still a quarter of it to be written. Robert accepted the commission to finish it and did a draft in 1933, inspired by happy days he had had at Salzburg recently; but he did not finish it and the draft was lost. He probably thought there was no urgency. When Edward O'Brien died in 1941 he said that he was 'one of those people, those not very conspicuous people, whom one takes for granted in the landscape'; someone who 'would be there tomorrow, or so one took it'.[13] His own fairly untimely death was also something he did not foresee.

Just before Romer died, Robert's relationship with Robert Graves, always precarious, reached a crisis. Graves had parted company with Nancy Nicholson in May 1929 and was now living *à deux* (they had formerly lived *à trois*) with Laura Riding. Robert invited Graves to stay with him – this would be at about the time when he was writing his laudatory review of *Goodbye to All That* – and bring 'his lady'. This way of referring to Miss Riding gave offence to the couple. The offence was aggravated when [said Robert] an autograph hunter 'started pumping me on books, particularly about poetry. I recommended [I. A.] Richards and so on and said that I'd dipped in *A Survey [of Modernist Literature]* which seemed to me stimulating as indeed it was bound to be as a friend of mine, Robert Graves, who had a hard head, had had a hand in it, but that I didn't know Miss Riding or her work.'[14] This gave rise to an indignant letter from Miss Riding in Mallorca: he had caused the autograph hunter to write to Graves 'as the prevailing spirit of the book instead of the specifically second-named author of a work which specifically defined itself as a word-by-word collaboration... The manner of your recommendation of that book accords very well with your reference to me in a recent letter to R.G. as his "lady". And I wonder that you dare extend me any courtesy however remote in such obviously offensive terms.'[15]

Robert 'sent a new invitation and an apology to the lady – damn! I mean Miss Riding – of the gentlest sort together with the mildest reminder that life is not very long and that the sun prefers to shine on and not at us.' He was anxious to 'keep on terms' with Graves who needed friends but (Graves might have said this of Nichols) 'is always by way of defying the world, but as that world is largely a chimaera of his own imagining he's always landing in difficulties.'[16] Perhaps Robert's reply was not as gentle as he thought. It evoked, at least, an excoriating rejoinder:

Dear Robert Nichols

I am going to make a few statements to you about myself because you have made a few observations about me on my behalf. And there's no use your saying what a pity she can't let anything pass, and so on. It is one of the laws of the universe that you will have to accept: that when you make an observation about me you get a statement back. It just happens. For convenience please just think of me, as I am sometimes described, as an automaton. You make the observation on my behalf that if I realized what a very common form of expression 'your lady' was in your world, I would not mind its application to me. The statement you get back is that I resist its application to me the more common a form it is in your world. In my world in rendering an invitation to a woman it is not customary to add 'and bring your gentleman' any more than it is to say 'and bring your nightgown'. In my world it is a matter of indifference whether one wears a night-gown or not. You see in my world there are only people and people, not people and nightgowns.[17]

These sledgehammer blows continue for eight pages. Laura Riding had attempted suicide not long before[18] and if she was still in a disturbed state of mind she may have been trying to be funny. At one point she says: 'You make the observation that I am fallible. That is untrue, and I'm so sorry you are, for you. Please understand that I am absolutely infallible but that this doesn't prevent my being irritated by the fallible.'

Robert, however, did not find it funny: 'To me it looks like preten-tious bloody nonsense,' he said to Sir Henry Head. 'Do you think there's any way of keeping friends with Bobby?'[19] It appears that in the event there was not, and that the two did not meet again.

In January 1930 the Nicholses went for two months to a villa at Villefranche-sur-Mer on the Côte d'Azur just to the east of Nice. There Robert worked at his plays, grieved for Romer Wilson and also entertained his sister Anne for a couple of weeks. At the end of February, however, Aldous and Maria Huxley arrived bringing with them Clive Bell and his new mistress (replacing Robert's old friend Mary Hutchinson). Robert was moved to send the Heads a pen-sketch of Bell.

> Clive has toned down a lot. He's suffered – the break with Mary Hutchinson I suppose did it. I like him better. Indeed, I feel some sort of current running between us which might later become friendship. But one needs, I imagine, to be terribly tactful with Clive – there are so many people in him: he is extremely intelligent and of great sensibility. He keeps a buffoon-ego which he brings into play for self-protection: but it is really only a minor character though troublesome because importunate. There is also an XVIII century self which is more autochthonous but that too is not a final thing. The final thing tends probably to be candid and tremulous. I think life frightens him as it must frighten, at times, all who *really* know anything about it. He is probably, as I am, an apprehensive being. Clive keeps up an elaborate appearance of playing with life: one way of non-plussing the adversary – appear not to take him too seriously. But *au fond* Clive has his eye open and is watching every move.[20]

This was not, however, an ordinary social visit. D. H. Lawrence was dying at Vence, some twenty miles away. The Huxleys had come to see him and said that he wanted to see Robert too, something about which Robert had been unsure 'as we'd had one or two rather lively exchanges in Majorca'.[21] Robert prepared to go but Lawrence's end came quickly and Robert was in time only to glimpse his corpse. He described the day of the burial in detail to the Heads:[22]

> I drove through St Pol, a beautiful little town on a hill, and so to Vence. I found the Villa Chaubert without much difficulty. I knocked and was greeted by a tall young woman – Barbara – Frieda's daughter by her first husband. Aldous was seated in a smallish tiled room with Thys, the Paris publisher of *Lady Chatterley's Lover*. Almost immediately Frieda came in and grasped me by both hands...
>
> We sat down and chatted, smoking innumerable cigarettes. For some time I did not gather that Lawrence was in the next room. Mrs Lawrence opened letters and telegrams. A huge wreath of

dark crimson carnations arrived from three American families who did not know Lawrence personally but much admired his work. Frieda was much touched. (She was by turns voluble and silent and when she was silent she stared in an odd manner, the pupils of her all-but-hazel eyes like pin-points.) Barbara opened the door to take the flowers in and I saw Lawrence's nose 'sharp as a pea' and his little Greek satyr's beard sticking up (his feet covered by a sheet were toward me) ... This was all the view I had of Lawrence. I was not allowed to see him though I (later) asked if I might. I gather they thought it would upset me. But I am not so easily upset. I should have asked to have kissed him – not so much for what he was as what he stood for.

Little Maria appeared. She looked ghastly – her face was grey-ish and one could see the blue veins at her temples. From time to time she shivered and enormous tears gathered in her blue eyes. They are a peculiar colour – clear as sapphires – and their blue is not the blue of the sky but the blue of water in a white-tiled swim-ming bath – absolutely translucent and to me very beautiful. They seemed the bluer because the lids were rather red. I must admit that almost my first thought was 'This woman is a lot worthier of Lawrence than Frieda,' but I doubt whether Lawrence ever really appreciated her. Indeed Barbara told me later that when Aldous and Maria left to come down to me Lawrence said 'I like them but I don't love them any more.' 'Because they are in Villefranche?' I asked. 'I suppose so. I suppose at the last, he felt they weren't his sort.' 'The fact that they were lacking in human warmth?' 'Yes.' I can understand that. I take it he went back to his warm miners' world. Probably his pronounced mother-complex waked. But of course A. and M. have plenty of human warmth, only it is very civilized warmth. It is not body warmth. I dare say poor little Lawrence wanted someone to take him in their arms – and proba-bly would have recoiled from it at the same time.

Robert arrived in the morning. Aldous Huxley, who apparently took charge of everything, carried the party off to lunch at a hotel, and there was then a long, awkward wait till the hearse arrived at four.

The crawl to the cemetery was rather a nightmare. But then I suppose it always is. There is something of going to executions in it. But it had redeeming features. Every man took off his hat on the way... [Frieda] said: 'See how they take off their hats to

Lawrence – isn't it nice.' Yes, they took off their hats. More people took off their hats to him on that ride than had ever done so in his life.

Lawrence was buried in a beautiful position under a solitary cypress overlooking a valley with the sea in the distance.

There were present Frieda and Barbara, Aldous and Maria, a Mrs Webster (an American Buddhist) and her sister, Mrs Eastman, Francis Harbott with a lady, two Italian girls and a man, another man, young, dark and handsome whom I didn't know and who appeared much moved, Thys and a well dressed Englishman and two ladies.

There was also a reporter with whom Robert had a few sharp words.

He represented *The Daily Express* in which that hound [Lord Alfred] Douglas attacked Lawrence and which got *Lady Chatterley's Lover* suppressed. Oh, I forgot to mention that he had the impertinence to ask why there were so few flowers (they completely covered the grave as a matter of fact). I replied that there were few of us and we hadn't had much time. I think he was rather ashamed of that question.

Robert begins this letter 'This has been a week of losses.' It saw the death, besides Lawrence, of Charles Whibley who 'earlier got me the job in Japan' and Charles Scott Moncrieff who had been such a strong supporter of *A Faun's Holiday* and other of Robert's pre-war poetry. 'The heaviest loss among these three', he said, 'is of course Lawrence. Romer Wilson was greater than any of them.'

The Nicholses returned to Winchelsea shortly after Lawrence's death. Robert there found himself engaged in an acrimonious local dispute about the low-lying land between the town and the sea. There were some weekend bungalows there which were threatened by the sea; it had come in the previous August and again in March, and the tenants being too poor to do anything about this, Robert had espoused their cause. The landlords and landowners, apparently, not only refused to spend any money on keeping the sea out but actually wanted the houses to be washed away.[23] In response to a good deal of agitation a temporary barrier was started, but the landlords resisted it. The climax came at the end of April when a big tide was expected. With help from Arnold Bennett and Enid Bagnold's husband Sir Roderick Jones,

Lawford Hall, the house in Essex where Robert Nichols grew up

LEFT Francis Morgan Nichols, grandfather, portrait by Sargent RIGHT Bowyer Nichols
with his daughters, Irene aged 18 and Anne (right) aged 12, April 1915

Catherine Louisa Pusey, mother, at the time of her marriage to Bowyer Nichols

Robert (right) and brother Philip playing chess, aged 18 and 17

April 1915: Philip (left) and Robert with (centre) their cousin Alselan

Middlecot, the house where Robert was sent to convalesce in 1916

LEFT Robert by Augustus John, 1921 RIGHT In 1935/6, by Catherine Dodgson

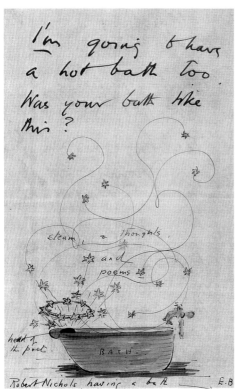

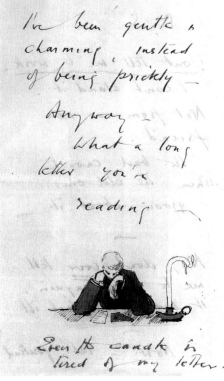

Extracts from Enid Bagnold's correspondence with Robert
during February and March 1918

Robert and his wife Norah in Japan, 1922

LEFT Norah in Hollywood, 1924 RIGHT Yew Tree House, Winchelsea: Robert and Norah
posing appropriately at the time of publication of *Under the Yew*

First night of *Wings Over Europe*: Juliette Huxley and H.G.Wells (from *The Tatler*)

LEFT Vivienne Wilkinson RIGHT As she appeared in the pages of *Vogue* (June 1937) when she was working for Robert Piguet's salon

How many half-smoked stubs I killed
I don't know. I could smoke no more.
But all at once I heard a clanking,
suddenly there came a roar
And the whole eastern arch was filled
With evening sunbeams, with sinking sunbeams,
With trumpets, with triumph, with rolling gold
With whirlpools of cloud among the girders,
With whirlwinds of cloud along the paving,
And through the clouds the engine came gliding,
Hurtling bright eddies along the floor,
Gliding and rolling and panting and grinding
With clatter and chatter and sudden shout
As brakes gripped red and the train ceased sliding;
And like a sun in cloudless weather
My love, a huge sun, came out in my heart
For there she stood at a sun-dappled door –
A robin hood hat with a pheasant feather,
Silvery tweeds, a crocus gloom,
A pair of huge eyes under the hat,
Eyes full of beseechment, fatigue and love.

Sample of Robert's handwriting from the unpublished poem 'Marseilles Elegy'
describing Vivienne's arrival in Marseilles

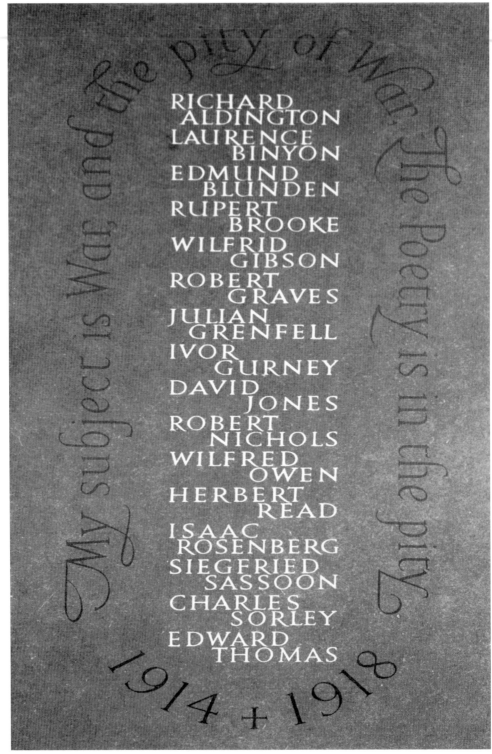

The memorial to First World War poets in Poets' Corner, Westminster Abbey

Robert alerted the London newspapers and they sent representatives in force including his friend Basil Murray, son of Professor Gilbert Murray.

The Engineer of the Ministry of Agriculture [Robert told the Heads[24]] had been that day on the barrier and had passed it as an excellent job but had stated that he was nervous about one corner and had put in one and a half hours himself with shovel etc. We were going to work anyway to make sure doubly sure: the big tide would culminate just after midnight ... I kept the reporters going in the inn with radio etc till 11.30. Then I went down to the barrier with Nornie. We had a big crowd there, close on 150 or so. There was some wind and the sea was choppy. We had just set to work when the local Napoleon – a burly ruffian named Merricks – turned up. Merricks has a dirty name round here. Though perfectly fit he stayed away from the war and made money. He has much land, two motors etc., and a big farm. He had planted his Sunbeam in the road to the barrier and I passed him – he was sitting in it – on my way down. ...

He began by ordering us off his land – abusing the reporters. I told him he had had plenty of opportunity to object before, and that if he wished to proceed now he had better go and get a policeman with his car. (The land is all mixed up down there and the sea's encroachment had further complicated matters.) The crowd began to boo him almost at once and the reporters became annoyed (they had police passes). They asked him who he was etc. I invited him to make a statement but he refused. A few minutes later he started to move a flaming barrel – lit to light the job – off what he called his land. I waited till he'd got it in the fringe of foam and then dashed after him to expostulate. He and I and the flaming barrel rolled about in the sea together. He got up first and I thought he'd go for me but I didn't feel the least afraid but floundered up and stood ready to do my best to give him the knock out on the chin. However he drew off and we went on with the work. A few minutes later there was a scuffle on the bank. He was trying to take away and smash a lantern. A clergyman, so I'm told, tackled him. I drew my electric torch and went up and stood by him. The crowd was now yelling 'Kill him! Throw him in the sea!' I kept the light on him. He stood with one or two bravos and said 'Put that bloody light away.' I said 'No, Mr Meyricks, I am going to keep it on you. Once you vanish in that crowd I won't be responsible for you.' 'He repeated 'Put that bloody light away,' and I could feel he was afraid. 'No,' I said, 'I quite understand your sort doesn't like the light. But I am here to prevent your being thrown in the sea.'...

By this time the photographers were after their shots and they wanted another tar barrel lit. The next I knew was that Meyricks was trying to rush the cameras. The crowd and the reporters became furious, a cordon was formed and the photographers tried to get on with it but it was a difficult job in the wind which had risen considerably ... Then Meyricks started laying hold of a tar barrel and Mac [a Mr Macdonald] and Swann (our engineer) laid hold of the other side. The crowd, which had been seething, became really dangerous, and Mac and I had to work hard for three minutes to prevent 'em doing him in (just before this a large woman had drawn me aside and bade me go home to bed: 'We'll settle him.') At length Meyricks withdrew (escorted, I believe, to his car). Waves were dashing twenty feet high above the barrier. Water (seepage) was coming through at the danger spot. We worked like niggers. At last it was over and the barrier held. I mounted a wheelbarrow and yelled 'Long live the liberties of the English people! God save the King!'

This drama apart, most of 1930 was quite peaceful. Edward O'Brien, Anthony Bernard, the Julian Huxleys, the Arthur Blisses, David Garnett, his old flame Elizabeth Birchenogh, now Dodds, and John Helston, a poet who lived by skilful backing of horses, were among the visitors to Yew Tree House, while Robert went up to London not only to consult his doctors, a regular engagement, but also to see various exhibitions and plays – including a remarkable production of Othello with Paul Robeson, Maurice Browne, Peggy Ashcroft and Sibyl Thorndike. It would have been even more remarkable if he had succeeded in getting Augustus John commissioned to do the sets.[25] The Nicholses also went to the Norwich Festival where there was the first performance of Bliss's Morning Heroes which included settings to some of Robert's poetry.

One London jaunt arose out of his being asked to write a poem in praise of Amy Johnson, the woman aeronaut.[26] There was a lunch in her honour, and his acceptance of an invitation to it resulted in a meeting with James Joyce. This was a major event, since he held Joyce to be 'the greatest virtuoso in English prose who has ever lived', as the creator of several characters (in *Ulysses*) 'each of whom could only be created by a genius', and finally as 'the greatest innovator and experimentalist with the medium of narrative we have ever had'.[27] He described this meeting to the Heads in loving detail. Indeed, he presented their conversation in the form of a dramatic dialogue. The letter is a composition worthy of the printed page. But admirable as it is, and unquestionable as is his admiration for Joyce, like the piece about Aurelia quoted earlier it seems to have been inspired as much by the comic as by the historical muse.

> After dinner [the account begins] Arthur [Bliss] and I set off to a house somewhere Chelsea-wards owned by Hughes the music critic. It was a large darkish room. James Joyce was seated at a long oak table. A couple of candles were burning at his elbow and he had a bottle of extremely good Chablis before him. Somehow there was something Shakespearean about all this.
>
> I was introduced and was at once struck by his voice which is very beautiful and very low, so low as to be like the voice of somebody who has come a very long journey, or of a spirit speaking from the shadows. There was a great gentleness about him. Directly I had taken his hand I turned away I was so scared and made off to the other end of the room and sat with Mrs Joyce and her daughter.

But this was not allowed. Mrs Joyce told him to go and speak to Joyce and Hughes 'hollooed to me to do the same'. Robert said timidly that he would like to take the opportunity to ask him a few questions.

> He poured out another glass of wine and seemed to look close at my face: at any rate the huge clear pebble of the left lens in his glasses suddenly turned on me and I saw an enormous velvety black pupil ringed by a golden green – more gold than green – iris. 'Very well,' he said with a little movement of the hand as if deprecating an honour.

Here the dialogue form takes over, and a reader of Stevenson might be reminded of the first chapter of *The Wrong Box* where Uncle Joseph Finsbury reads Miss Hazeltine 'the notes of a highly important conversation with a Dutch courier of the name of David Abbas, which is the Latin for abbot'. 'Mr Finsbury', Stevenson tells us, 'contributed about four hundred and ninety nine five-hundredths of the interview, and elicited from Abbas literally nothing.' So it was with Robert Nichols and James Joyce. Robert's questions are long and technical; Joyce's answers, if he did not merely 'relapse into reverie', were absolutely minimal. For example:

> R.N. Then there is the question of speech rhythm. That specially interests me as a potential dramatist for a fusion of rhythm can give the secret of character – as for instance in Congreve who though he works in a narrow compass does convey to us all sorts of characteristics merely by modulation of the rhythm. No one has ever carried this method so far as you have and I am curious to know and would ask if I might whether you have an enormous auditory memory or whether you made extensive use of your notebooks.
> *Joyce*: (slowly, smiling suddenly) No, I carried things in my head. The succinctness of this rather threw me off my track and I fumbled about for a bit.

Or again:

> I said to Joyce that some of his prose in its general effect, such as the decrescendo at the end of the seashore scene in *Ulysses* and the close of *Anna Livia* – approached so closely to music that I would like to know whether he actually made use of music to put him in the mood. For I said 'Some authors are wholly in possession of their talent, others are possessed by it, this possession is sometimes of a kind that can be induced.'
> *Joyce*: I begin work punctually at eight o'clock every day.

Robert asked only one question to which he got a really warm answer, and that answer was brief:

> R.N. I have enjoyed Bloom so much that I should like to know, did you know an actual Jew like Bloom?
> *Joyce*: (chuckling) Scores of 'em! (He seemed a good deal amused at this and poured himself another glass of wine, a proceeding which he somehow accomplished successfully though dreadfully blind. Then he sat back sipping his wine and there was something in him that sent a wave of affection through me: just Joyce sitting there, sipping his golden wine out of a thick brown glass with the spires of the candles on a level with his head; a very mysterious being in whose head, one imagined, many currents of thought flowed at once.)

Joyce for his part asked Robert only one question.

Joyce: (suddenly) What religion are you?

When Robert started to summarise the prefaces of *Guilty Souls* and *Fantastica* Joyce seemed to lose all interest, and Robert could see that he had had 'a notion I might be a Catholic. And from the expression on his face as he asked me for my religion I took it – indeed I am sure – that, were every other passion extinct in him, he would still preserve a most lively hatred of Catholicism.'

The year contained other good social occurrences. In April 1930 John Jay Chapman had been over from America, and Robert gave a grand lunch for him at the Café Royal, inviting a distinguished company that included Augustus John, Desmond MacCarthy and Henry Nevinson, and providing not only Château Beychevelle but Château Latour.[28] In the autumn another American friend, Conrad Aiken, took a house near Winchelsea at Rye.[29] Robert is Edward in his autobiographical novel *Ushant*. In December Paul Nash moved to Rye also. Robert, who had been complaining of lack of friends in the vicinity,[30] welcomed his advent, despite thinking him 'even more conceited that I am (if possible!)'.[31] Paul Nash was not too conceited to compliment Robert on his watercolours[32] and even put up with readings of his poetry.[33] But by this time a new quarrel of heroic dimensions was brewing up.

16

More Friends Lost

Though Robert, like Sassoon, felt that the Sitwells did not extend close friendship to anyone but each other, he was at one time on very cordial terms with Edith, and in spite of Osbert's occasionally saying unkind things about him in print, his relations with him remained amicable. 'On one occasion,' Robert said to illustrate this, 'to find out the source from which a friend now dead [possibly Heseltine] procured hashish, I took this drug and was rendered ill for the evening and was brought back to this man's [Osbert's] house and stayed the night, and I admit he treated me with consideration.'[1] Robert, for his part, gave Osbert introductions to America. But then in November 1930 Norah procured Osbert Sitwell's latest book, *Dumb Animals*, from the local library. 'I saw a story', Robert told the Heads,[2] 'called 'Alive – Alive O', and, attracted by the title, I plunged in.' He received a painful shock. The story seemed to him a treacherous attempt to parody his work, traduce his war service, and blackguard his character.

'Alive – Alive O' concerns a poet called Joseph Bundle who achieves success early in life but whose admirers expect him to die young like Shelley or Keats, preferably from tuberculosis. When he seems unwilling to do this, his sales fall. Then he goes to Italy, pleading ill health, and in due course his death is announced. Sales of his books now soar and his widow becomes rich. But he has only pretended to die. Many years later the narrator finds him living in a large villa in Calabria.

The idea is quite amusing, though the fifty-four pages Sitwell gives it are perhaps more than it needs for its development. But it is extraordinary that Robert should have thought he was Bundle. Bundle is primarily a Sussex poet who wins his laurels by writing about Sussex soil, village life and birds, subjects quite alien to Robert. When the war breaks out he produces some successful war poems, but it is his attachment to Sussex and birds that is chiefly ridiculed. Robert must have leaped to the conclusion that he was Bundle because in the war Bundle was a gunner, and fell down a chimney when using a roof as an observation post. Some such incident befell Robert,[3] and no doubt Sitwell heard of it, but to fill his fifty-four pages he had to gather material wherever he could find it. In all other respects Robert and Bundle were completely different. Nobody else made the identification; Marsh thought that Bundle was Edmund Blunden.[4]

At first it looked as if Robert's indignation would pass. Lady Head apparently told him not to upset himself, and next week he said 'I'm not bothering any more about Osbert. If I meet him I shall be unaware of the story.'[5] But in fact resentment sank deep into him and grew like an incubating disease or a monstrous embryo to burst out eventually in a terrific explosion of poetic spleen, a satire on a scale that had not been seen before in English or any other language for more than a century.

This, however, was not to be until after four years' gestation. In the next few days he sustained a different kind of blow. On 17 December his old and dear friend Heseltine died, apparently having gassed himself. 'The morning after learning of Phil's death [he told the Heads[6]] I hastened up to London to Arthur Bliss's. In the afternoon I went to see Cecil Gray [Heseltine's friend and biographer] ... and found him sitting in a state of sodden grief. For some reason or other I felt irritated by him. I fancy, too, that he regarded me as a self-important busybody.'

The facts, as Robert was informed, were fairly straightforward. The previous afternoon Heseltine had had a drunken tiff concerning his favourite brand of snuff with his mistress Barbara Peach, and Miss Peach had left him to cool down. Later he saw Bernard van Dieren and his wife and they had a drink. Towards midnight he bade them farewell, declining their invitation, offered because he seemed depressed, to stay the night with them. He went to bed, but rose at four or five, fed the kitten, put it out, sealed up windows and doors and turned on the gas. Heseltine's mother, Mrs Buckley-Jones (who had a bad press from his friends), was trying to put the blame on Barbara 'whom she took for some sort of little whore'.

'Cecil Gray apparently proposed to sit still and let poor little Barbara (who was good to Phil) get it in the neck.' Robert met Barbara's mother and found her 'of good appearance and breeding: a lady'. He then went to see Mrs Buckley-Jones and succeeded in convincing her '(a) that Phil's fame would not be advanced by a row, (b) that Fleet Street knew just enough about him as an erratic fellow to be thoroughly dangerous, (c) that poor Barbara would get it in the eye, (d) that once snuff was mentioned Fleet Street and the law would begin about imaginary cocaine, (e) that all this would harm the future of Phil's boy Nigel.' He also managed to introduce her to van Dieren, whom she had never met, at the funeral. At this 'pretty awful' event the family – the Buckley-Joneses – had been in one group, the musicians and artists in another, and Robert 'was the solitary link'. It was important to bring Mrs Buckley-Jones together with van Dieren not only in order that they might present a united front at the inquest, but also because van Dieren was Heseltine's heir. Heseltine's father had left a reversion of about £16,000 in which his mother had a life interest. Heseltine had 'concocted some sort of arrangement' by which Puma and his son Nigel were each to get a quarter, but the remaining £8,000 was left to van Dieren.

Robert stayed in London for the inquest, which went well. The post-mortem had found no alcohol, snuff was not mentioned, and 'John Ireland gave just the right sort of evidence as to Phil's discouragement over his work'. But there remained an anxiety about the £8,000. Robert knew that Heseltine had wished van Dieren to have this money in order that he might work undisturbed by financial worries. But he thought Heseltine would prefer that at van Dieren's death it should go to his own son Nigel and not to van Dieren's family. Wishing to be an unofficial channel between the parties, he agreed to help van Dieren go through Heseltine's papers and get his flat boarded up. This was the afternoon after the inquest, and Robert described it to the Heads in one of his most vivid narratives.[7]

Van Dieren, having given evidence, was 'all in'. Robert volunteered to pay his taxi to the flat and give him dinner. A fog came down. Eventually van Dieren telephoned to say his taxi had stopped in the fog, and would Robert meet him at Sloane Square Tube Station.

I met him and we got a carpenter and set off for Tite Street, crawling through the raw fog with myself hanging on guiding the taxi. The basement flat was very tidy and very silent and we went through the papers keeping a special look out for an MS score that Delius wanted (his *Dance Rhapsody*). I felt quite all right till van Dieren said 'Excuse this act of indecency. It is necessary at this hour.' I thought, since he has trouble due to kidneys and past gonorrhoeal infection, that it was something of that sort and, seeing him take out a little flat box, turned away. When I looked round there he was standing in the middle of the living room of the basement flat sticking a syringe into his left forearm. The needle was dug in as it seemed to me very deep and the arm was swollen above the syringe which was *full* of a clear greyish liquid like dirty sea water. I thought it must be morphine and this 'gave me a turn' as they say. Van Dieren seemed to think very little of it and said his doctor required him to take this treatment. I did not like to ask him what the stuff was.

We finished up in the flat and I asked him to dinner. We bundled two suitcases of MSS – but the Delius was not among the stuff – into the cab, and van D disappeared for a little and went and telephoned somebody. When he came back he said he wouldn't dine but would like a drink. I suggested taking charge of the two suitcases (a suitcase and a big oblong case) for the night. He agreed since Bloomfield Terrace [where Robert was staying at his brother's house] was near. We went to Sloane Street Tube Station buffet. I had a small whisky and he had two large double whiskies which he drank practically neat. I meant to ask him to eat something but he seemed pressed for time. The taxi was ticking up so I left with the suitcases after he'd borrowed £1 (after all I had asked him to dinner). After depositing the suitcases at Bloomfield Terrace I hurried back. But he had gone.

Robert was worried about the combination of whisky and the drug on an empty stomach, but van Dieren had told him 'he had an iron constitution'.

The discovery of van Dieren's habit put a fresh complexion on things: it might finish him off, iron constitution or no, before Mrs Buckley-Jones died. After much heart-searching ('as I don't like telling tales out of school') Robert had a consultation with the Buckley-Jones lawyer, and he, much to Robert's relief, thought the family might reach a compromise by which van Dieren would have an annuity for the present, and the reversion would eventually go to Nigel Heseltine.

The composer Elizabeth Poston was a friend of Heseltine, and came up to London when she heard of his death. She wrote afterwards to Robert:

I shall never be able to tell you what a firm assurance of support your presence was all the time – the one strong, sane tower of help and wise judgement in that waking nightmare of chaos ... You were really the only person who knew in the same way *both* sides of it all – ... in fact *all* sides of a thing far too many-sided and complicated to explain to anyone who did not know. And that in itself was a greater help than I know how to say.[8]

Heseltine died in December 1930. Three months later Robert lost another much valued friend in Arnold Bennett. For many years he had been an unfailing source of encouragement and good advice. Robert consulted him about all his books and also delighted in his personality, his 'sagacious sanity and Shakespearean breadth. The best of all writers as a MAN is Bennett.'⁹ Many visits from him and meals with him are described with affectionate relish in letters to the Heads. One letter contains an elaborate verbal portrait:

Bennett's peculiarities of deportment and speech, though pronounced in their major characteristics – which almost anyone could put down – are in their finer shades very difficult to catch since they depend so much on the poise of his body in his chair, the turn of his head and above all the nature of his glance. He has wonderful eyes – most wonderful and I have seen more than one aspect of genius burning in them. They hardly ever flash – I don't think I ever saw in them that sudden leap of light which, if hot, is like the fluorescent jet of smoky flame from a retort in the Black Country and, if cold, like the momentary uptoss of one spouting wave out of the darkness seen from a marine parade at night: both being the sort of flash I have seen in inspired men. No, Bennett's eyes are seldom sudden except in their change to vivacity from contemplative all-but-gloominess. Light *swims* into them like the sun behind thin cloud traversing a pond. When that happens the iris seems to change from sultry brown to golden brown - the colour of a bog-stream in mild sunlight. The first impression is that they are somehow ugly eyes asleep or quiescently unconcerned under his eyebrows – one cocked down, the other up – then he smiles at you with secretly-amused slightly melancholy benevolence and one forthwith detects a wide and deep and not a little ironical intelligence as animating that curious mien, on 'off' days so leathery and bilious a colour, on others slightly sanguine and even positively rosy. And so evident is the irradiation of that intelligence that one quite overlooks the weak chin, the ugly lower lip, the jutting upper teeth, the somewhat 'Old Bill' moustache, the nose that has got slanted a little sideways, and only feels the beauty of the eyes, so black and so brown (like an owl's) and the uncommon interest of and the obscure expressiveness of the face's asymmetry, for seldom have two halves of a face been as unlike each other as the two halves of Bennett: one dreaming, contemplative, melancholy, the other quizzical, alert, ready-to-be-mischievous.[10]

Three months after his death Robert wrote to Marsh: 'I cannot get the loss of A.B. out of my mind. It is like a stifling thunderstorm coming round and round again.'[11] He contemplated writing a biography, and later did write a long tribute to him in the form of a dialogue defending his best work – which he took to be his realist novels – as 'the greatest in its kind England has produced since Defoe'.[12] A shortened version of this was broadcast by the BBC on 8 September 1942.

These losses do not seem, however, to have interrupted his work. As long-term projects he had his plays – *Don Juan* at present taking precedence over *Komuso* – and his revenge on Osbert Sitwell, to be entitled *Fisbo*. In the earlier part of 1931 he was also working on a 200-line poem dealing with an episode in the First World War. In July 1930 Shane Leslie had consulted him about an epic he was writing on the Battle of Jutland.[13] Robert thought that the sinking of the *Nestor* would make a good subject. In November, feeling Leslie had mishandled it, he decided to have a try himself.[14] Armed with an introduction from Masefield he visited the Admiralty to get his facts right.[15] The poem was entitled 'The Souls of the Righteous' and printed in *The Times* on the anniversary of the engagement with the following note:

> On May 31, 1916, the *Nestor*, destroyer, led her Division in a brilliant attack upon the German battle cruisers of Jutland. Her officers included Commander the Hon. Barry Bingham (awarded the V.C. for gallantry in this action), commanding, Lieutenant Maurice Bethell, First Lieutenant (killed in this action), Engineer Commander Norman Roberts (killed in this action), and Sub-Lieutenant Dudley Rowe (awarded the D.S.O. for gallantry in this action). The Poem opens at the moment when the *Nestor* found herself lying disabled while the opposed battle cruisers, "furiously engaged", disappeared north-west.

Robert's poem is in heroic couplets. It describes the period of respite when it seemed that the *Nestor* could limp home if not attacked, and the return of the German High Seas Fleet. Bingham destroyed the code books, swung out the boats, fired the last torpedo and gave the order to abandon ship only when after heavy shelling it was already sinking. He and Bethell were the last on board and found the dinghy on which they had relied was shattered.

'And where do we go now?' brave Bingham said,
And Bethell with his feet among the dead
Feeling the slant plate sink, the waters thrust,
Answered him cheerly, 'Why to heaven I trust.'

O horn of Roland and the Frankish host,
Horn faintly holloaing from a phantom post
Beneath a red pine on the Pyrenees,
How do you echo in these northern seas!

And Robert here inserted a translation of the death of Roland from the *Chanson de Roland*.

The poem was very well received. David Garnett said it might help Robert towards being made Poet Laureate. But what pleased him most was letters of appreciation from Barry Bingham himself and from Bethell's father, Admiral Sir Alexander Bethell.

Some shorter poems date from 1931. 'Larus Marinus', which looks back, in its description of nature, to his Georgian days, was composed in memory of his uncle Walter who died in April 1930. His uncle was a keen ornithologist, and *larus marinus* is the greater black-backed gull. 'For the Eve of Palm Sunday' recaptures the mood of his early religious poetry. Both were finished in November and published in the *London Mercury*. In December he told the Heads plans for a complete new volume of poetry.[16] It was to be called *The Wreath of Iron*. The title was perhaps taken from an unpublished 'Invocation on Departure' which ends:

If so be I return, grant not empty-handed
Be it I return
But in my hands put blessing:
Phial of fuller love, light of an earthly Zion
And on my head a wreath
Though but a wreath of iron.

The poem is undated but could have been written on his departure for Japan in 1920. But whatever the origin of the title, the poems were to be different in character from his poetry of 1910–20. They were to be what he called 'Tyrtaean songs'. This phrase (taken from Goethe's Conversations with Eckermann) he explains as follows: 'I will give the name Tyrtaean poetry to that which not merely sings war-songs but also arms men with courage to undergo the conflicts of life.'[17] The volume was to include a number of poems already published: 'Lines from the Sea' (1921), 'Exile' (1924), 'Ishmael' (1922), 'City of Angels' (1924), 'Epic Wind' (1928), and 'Souls of the Righteous'; also 'Twilight Thrush' and 'At Forth-Faring' which appear in *Such Was My Singing*, all the extant songs from *Don Juan* and more poems yet to be written – 'Arrogant Eros', composed in 1933, was destined for *The Wreath*.

The Nicholses did not go abroad in 1931,* and the highlights of the year for Robert were visits from Aldous Huxley in February and October and a week in London in July. There were also visits in August to Norah's parents in Horwood House, Buckinghamshire, and to Robert's father at Lawford, but Robert, though he had come to like Mr Denny, never warmed to Norah's mother, and as for Lawford:

> In this house there is only one living thing – my grandfather's spirit. But it is growing feebler and fainter. I see the books he wrote in the shelves. Many are in duplicate. But I dare not ask for one. I did once ask for a copy of the Erasmus *Letters*. Excuses were made. I was not suffered to possess a copy. He [the grandfather, presumably] can no longer sustain the weight of despondency that has fallen on the house, the blight of the burden of those who have *given up*. ...
>
> This place gives me the multiple pip. However I got rid of some of it yesterday by taking notes from it for a play. Every other damn thing was symbolic – from the huge hideous toadstools I found in the park to the window covered with filth from the swallow's nest under the eaves, a nest which my aunt wouldn't have cleared away. The sundial my grandfather built and placed high up on the wall, which had the date of the present house [the Elizabethan house which replaced the medieval royal manor house] upon it and the date of his acquisition of it is peeling. You cannot read the time, for the figures are indecipherable because the paint has fallen in flakes. Why? *Because there is no time here.*[18]

Trips to London, in contrast, were a tonic, and Robert was finding friends to replace those who had died. At the Café Royal he renewed acquaintance with Rosamond Lehmann, whose first novel *Dusty Answer* had drawn fan mail from him in 1927. 'I am not in love with this woman, but I love her.'[19] The Café Royal had been a favourite haunt for many years, but now a group of literati were in the habit of

---

*Unless Robert visited Delius in France; Eric Fenby (*Fenby on Delius*, p. 121) speaks of several visits to Grez between 1928 and 1934 which are not mentioned in Robert's correspondence.

meeting on Wednesday afternoons at Ridgeway's Tea Shop. W. J. Turner and Ralph Hodgson were often there and Robert joined them when possible. There he met one of the rare people 'who waken sweetness in my soul... Koteliansky. He's a *man* by God. But he's difficult to get on terms with. He's very poor and very, very proud and he won't come and stay with us and I don't know where he lives.' Samuel Koteliansky, known to his friends as 'Kot', was a Russian Jew who had come to England in 1911, his liberal ideas being suspect to the Russian authorities. In 1914 he had met D. H. Lawrence and in 1915 moved into 5 Acacia Road, NW8, the house just taken by J. Middleton Murry and Katherine Mansfield. That is where he was still living in 1931, though Middleton Murry had left long before and had quarrelled with Koteliansky in the 1920s over the *Adelphi* – just as well if he was to sweeten the soul of Robert, since Robert and Murry were not good friends. Though not an orthodox religious believer he was of rabbinic stock and impressed everyone who knew him, Robert included, as a man of outstanding integrity.

Another person who entered Robert's life at this time and was destined to play an important part in it was Phyllis Spender-Clay. The daughter of a prominent Conservative backbencher – her father started the 1922 Committee – and the granddaughter of the first Viscount Astor, she had a gentle, tolerant temperament and was more interested in animals and the arts than in social life. She was attracted by the intelligence and charm of Robert's younger brother Phil. They became engaged at the end of 1931 and were married early in February 1932, the date being determined by Colonel Spender-Clay's need to be on the Spey for the opening of the salmon season. Robert had never filled the role of elder son with much confidence; after Phil had acquired a rich and kind wife he slid into that of a dependent.

He had given the Heads full accounts of the weddings of his two sisters, and over the splendid celebrations that attended those of his brother he surpassed himself. Forty pages were not too many to cover the dinner to introduce the Nicholses to the Spender-Clays, the reception and dance given by Lady Astor, and, a few days later, the wedding itself.[20] Perhaps as a result of his time in Hollywood, Robert's description is like a cine-film or a video-recording. He had a cameraman's eye for significant detail. At the Spender-Clay dinner he notes how, at a certain point, 'a ripple passed round the table', and every lady started talking to the man on her other side. At Lady Astor's house he captured a curious mannerism of Eddie Marsh: 'he made funny noises and waved his right arm up and down, sort of singing "Ho - ha- hum!" I am sure he has copied this from someone in a book of memoirs.' At the wedding party his lens tracked Boley, the gardener from Lawford, and Handy, his brother's servant and former batman: both very elevated and emotional. One of his most successful cameos was of his father, who had arrived 'looking more like a tired little bird than ever'. In the vestry after the marriage ceremony 'he went up to the bride and took both her hands and looked long and earnestly in her face with a most beautiful expression on his own, and raised those hands to his lips. That man is quite extraordinary – I never saw any action more eloquent and more discreetly and beautifully performed. It was, I am sure, quite spontaneous, and demonstrated once more Father's wonderful sense of the appropriate.'

Ever since 1928 Robert had been hoping that Maurice Browne would produce *Wings Over Europe* in London. There had been repeated deferments and disappointments. But in the course of 1931 a firm decision was taken, and immediately after his brother's wedding Robert threw himself into preparations for a staging at the Globe Theatre in Shaftesbury Avenue. There was, of course, no need for him to do this at all. Nevertheless he took a flat in the Marylebone High Street and must have tried Maurice Browne's patience to the utmost by finding fault with the casting and intervening at the rehearsals.

There was nothing wrong with the casting. Robert would have liked John Gielgud to play the leading part of Lightfoot. He admired Gielgud and fancied him also for Don Juan if his play should ever reach the stage.[21] 'Material there', he said to the Heads, 'for the greatest Shakespearean actor (but I don't think he could ever do Lear) of our age.'[22] Maurice Browne, however, decided against him in May 1931,[23] and the critics all agreed that the actor chosen, Francis James, gave an excellent performance. The notices found no fault with the acting. But on 6 March Robert had written to the Heads that the play was

> too intelligent. The audience for an 'intelligent' play is reckoned to be 4,000. That, in a medium to largish theatre, is exhausted in a couple of weeks. Unless of course the Elmhirsts, whose money will be behind the production, like to nurse it on the unlikely off-chance of the public changing its mind. The critics will praise it – you'll see. And it will die in between a fortnight and a month.

This forecast was extremely shrewd and there was little anyone could do. After the play had run for a few nights Browne proposed some cuts. Instead of leaving the decision to him, Robert 'went quite mad with rage,' and rang up the backer, Mr Elmhirst of Dartington Hall, Devon, who referred him to his lawyer. Robert told the lawyer that he had been warned long ago by Arnold Bennett that Browne was 'a crook', and there were scenes at the theatre with the actors – all, one might think, as bad for the production as could be. When the play came off, having fulfilled Robert's March prediction to the letter, he quarrelled furiously with Browne, and though by January 1934 he was prepared to shake hands with him[24] their friendship, which went back many years and had been both warm and productive, was never renewed.

17

Austria, Italy, Bavaria 1932–4

The closure of *Wings Over Europe* in May 1932 was a turning point in Robert's life. He had anticipated it in March, he understood why it was to be expected, but he simply could not accept it. He was like a spoilt child denied an unreasonable request. And this failure, not the illusory failure of the play but the personal failure to come to terms with its closing after a fortnight, gradually destroyed both his work and his life. He was never again really happy either at Yew Tree House or with Norah.

Taking the flat and intervening in the production had cost him £200 he could ill afford: it was a fifth of a capital sum his father had give him to increase his income. He went back to Winchelsea in a deep sulk and was unable to enjoy a very minor dramatic success scored by his wife. She had written a play called *Rank and File* and in May it was performed in aid of charity by an amateur company, the Dartmouth Players. There were several performances, one attended by a Royal Duke, Field Marshal the Duke of Connaught.

After a few weeks it looked as if hatred of Osbert Sitwell would pull him out of his misery. He resumed work on *Fisbo* and wrote one of the best pieces in it, the Invocation to Widow Clicquot.[1] This is decidedly lighthearted and begins:

> O Widow Clicquot, Widow Clicquot, queen
> Of all nymphs potable save the Hippocrene,
> Delicious dame in purest sunshine gowned
> And with a coronal of foam-flowers crowned,
> Who twice as gay makes fluttering candlelight
> Where the jazz croons the livelong summer night,
> Who sets love-wings upon the dancers' heels
> And the shy lips of damosels unseals
> To babble of starshine and the scent of flowers
> And of the privet-hedge's secret bowers,
> You I invoke!

Lady Head appears to have been sceptical about putting much effort into a piece of personal retaliation. 'I'm sorry you don't approve of my proceeding with *Fisbo*' he writes.[2] But he was unable to make any progress with *Don Juan*, so he worked away at the satire until he stuck there too. By August he was again unable either to work or to enjoy himself and Norah sent him up to London. There his doctor gave him some dubious advice. He should sell out a bit more capital, go abroad and have a casual love affair.[3]

This was just what he wanted to hear. It is doubtful if Robert's marriage to Norah had ever been very fulfilling sexually for either of them. In June 1934 he told the Heads that they 'had the profoundest affection for each other, in each case, however, almost without physical attraction'.[4] Whether or not it was like that from the start, the letters describing his visits to London in recent years[5] show his eye roving lustfully. It is significant also how he picked up his friendship with Elizabeth Birchenogh and kept watch for his other early inamorata, Daisy Kennedy, still wasted on John Drinkwater.[6] He now set off at once for the Salzburg Festival – he was a passionate lover of Mozart – and 'a tremendous five weeks'.[7] On 24 August he sent Lady Head a card saying 'Every day is a miracle. I am at home at last.'

A long letter on his return[8] fills in the details. On the first evening in Salzburg:

> After my meal I drove through the evening air to the Residence Place. At the corner I dismounted. Strolling round that corner I came on my home. I saw that Place under the clear sky and I knew that at last I had found what I had been seeking all my life – grace, proportion, harmony, quiet majesty (but with a slight theatricalism) under a clear sky, with a people I could love – independent, healthy and direct of gaze – walking up and down in the late afternoon hush. Here East and West and North and South, peasant and classical culture met. I was in the heart of European culture at last.

What about the casual love affair? On the train from Cologne he met a pretty girl who asked him to break his journey at Munich, but there she produced a husband, and though they had a pleasant evening it consisted chiefly of talk about Aldous Huxley. In his Salzburg hotel he met a white-haired lady of thirty-eight with gypsy eyes, the wife of an American professor of music, and they walked the streets (without the professor) till 4 a.m. At one point 'she stopped and placed both hands on my breast and it wasn't till the next day that I realized that it was then I should have kissed her'; but in actual fact 'I poured forth a wild flood of words.' The night before he went to *The Magic Flute* he had a romantic conversation with a waitress in the Café Mozart, and although she confessed to being an 'old wife' of forty-one, 'I dashed out and found a flower shop not yet closed and there I bought three carnations – one red and two white.' These he presented with the gallant words 'Two white and one red – two for your eyes and one for your mouth', and 'she pressed them slantwise over her heart and rocked softly, looking at me out of fathomless eyes, smiling so softly that I felt all the gravity go out of my face.'

So far Robert's fling may seem rather tame. But on the last of the sixteen pages of this epistle, Robert says he thinks it was also on the *Magic Flute* night that

> I first saw the most beautiful girl, Lesley Black. I shan't tell you about her. That's my secret. Suffice it to say that her beauty was with me in spirit day and night, that we drove out to Mondsee a day or two later and sat on a hillside looking at the Schafberg, and that during the ensuing days I came to understand as never before Bridges' rendering of Michelangelo's madrigal 'Gli occhi miei vaghi delle cose belle' – 'My eyes for beauty pine.'

This was to be no casual affair but a wedge that would split the Nicholses' marriage.

Having got back to Winchelsea Robert immediately put in hand the letting of Yew Tree House for six months, and at the beginning of October he and Norah set off for Vienna, planning to spend the winter there before going on to Italy, where Phil was First Secretary in Rome, in the spring. Just before they left they were visited by Eric Fenby on a mission from Delius. In 1904 Delius had written the music for an opera *Margot la Rouge* and wished Robert to write new words. Robert had no time to compose a new libretto, but suggested taking words from Walt Whitman's *Leaves of Grass*. In two hours he and Fenby fitted words to the best of the music.[9] Delius was delighted. He had been blind for some years, but Jelka Delius wrote to Robert on his behalf: 'The words you have found are simply exquisite and it is miraculous how they fit the music.'[10] The resulting work, *Idyll* for soprano, baritone and orchestra, was performed in October 1933 in the Proms.

Meanwhile autumn 1932 was a pregnant time in Austria. The Nicholses came with introductions to Jewish friends of Roger Quilter, and after a month in a flat where they found the décor too ugly, moved to another with a Jewish landlord. Going to a night club one evening (reluctantly; he much preferred the opera), Robert was surprised to see a Jewish actor playing the part of a Jew in an antisemitic sketch before an audience with a large admixture of Jews. He commented:

I fancy all Jews who are conscious of themselves as Jews are deep down within so proud that they believe nothing can lower their dignity. And when they are thinking of their dignity they are not thinking of it as an Englishman might among French, Russians and Germans or among a collectivity known as 'Dagoes'. They don't consider the 'Goys' at all. Their dignity is only considered by them vis-à-vis their own race. What will Jewry think? And apparently Jewry permits them to be abject in a way that would be absolutely out of the question for an Englishman vis-à-vis French, Russians or Germans and still more vis-à-vis the collectivity 'Dagoes'. I feel they despise us as we English tend to despise 'Dagoes', yet that didn't prevent this comedian permitting all sorts of abuse to be heaped upon his people and emphasizing all those characteristics which bring his people into odium, and I tried to analyse this and came to the conclusion that the Yiddish table of virtues differs so radically from that of the Gentiles that the comedian felt his brethren would only feel admiration for him for getting coin out of the Gentiles for exploiting the – to them – foolish predilections of the Gentile in matters of honesty, cowardice and so forth.

Jewish psychology interests me more and more – the more so because there is a real Jewish problem here. During the last few days it has become prominent again because the University here has a (rather disgraceful) tradition that it cannot be entered by the police, and traditional advantage has been taken of this tradition for the rougher Gentile elements to 'beat up' some Jewish students. This time however they have, thank heaven, bitten off more than they can chew, for among the students roughly handled were two or three American Jews. Now the American Minister, Stockton, has taken a strong line and given the Education Minister such a wigging that the said Minister has threatened to sack the Head of the University and half his underlings (so we hear) if this occurs again. I am glad of this, the more so as the University seems to me precisely the place where of all places this sort of thing ought not to occur. It is particularly criminal and foolish in the case of the

Jews, for the most valuable contribution the Jews have made to civilization is, I think, without question in the domain of learning and the sciences, especially philosophy, law and medicine, on schools of which this University particularly prides itself.[11]

Robert was supposed to be working on *Don Juan* and *Fisbo*, and he did give a reading of modern English poetry to the Anglo-Austrian Society;[12] but he was also in correspondence with Fenby over Delius's *Idyll*[13] and he and Norah seem chiefly to have enjoyed themselves going to musical events. They met some prominent figures in the Viennese music world and took every opportunity to urge them to include modern English composers in their performances. Over Christmas they stayed with 'Red' Sinclair Lewis at Semmering. Robert and he had had a bibulous time together in Vienna in November[14] and Robert's guarded report of this visit suggests some intemperance. The hospitality, he said, had not given him much chance to write. 'Red's hospitality was lavish. I like him. But as it would be very difficult to be precisely just about the whole show I shall say nothing. I've thought it over and that's what Bennett would have done I feel sure.'[15]

In January 1933 Lesley Black arrived in Vienna, officially with the object of learning German. Robert wrote:

> Under the influence of a feeling such as I had for her [in Salzburg] one might become a great human being, or if not a great one, at least drop some ignobility. Nornie likes her. Nornie's very practical. She sees that such a feeling lifts me up like great music. (I hope that I shall be able to use some of this feeling in Act III of the *Don*.) I have been able to be useful to Lesley – gave her letters of introduction to my sisters and to Arthur Bliss: her home life with an intensely neurotic mother [in Hampstead] not being satisfactory... She's in love, I fancy, with a chap in the South Kensington Museum. I have had long talks with her.

Presumably Norah saw that he was in love and trying to conceal the fact from himself. In the Nicholses' world one-to-one marital fidelity was not an ideal, much less the norm, and she decided to give him his head and hope the affair would work itself out. It was unfortunate for this strategy that Lesley went down with influenza – 'Poor Lesley, brought up by Christian Scientists, hadn't the least idea what to do with 'flu' – giving him an excuse to haunt her bedside and administer *eau de cologne*.[16]

Meanwhile the political situation was deteriorating. Nazis and Social Democrats were parading against one another and Robert's friend Abe Plotkin, the Californian Labour leader, who was studying conditions in Berlin, prophesied 'some fundamental rumpus during the next two or three months'.[17] The Reichstag fire came within weeks. Just after it, late at night on 5 March, Robert encountered a party of Nazis in a back street pulling down posters pasted up by the Social Democrats which laid the responsibility on Hitler. 'I wasn't', he wrote to the Heads, 'going to stand for that, the Social Democrats being a sensible sort of crowd and these Nazis a lot of idiots anyway and their German affiliations unspeakable, the veriest *canaille.*'[18] Though alone he chased them away. The Heads, perhaps afraid of his being beaten up, told him not to interfere in a foreign country's internal politics. He replied:

The Nazis don't correspond to anything in England. They are an organization pledged to practising *force majeure*. There is very little to choose between them and communists as to method, their methods being entirely opportunist and violent. In fact they are the exponents of precisely the ethic – or want of it – to down which we fought the war. There is in their leaders a strong pathological strain of sheer sadism. ...

The most terrible fact so far as Austria is concerned is that the Nazis in Germany are working for a Nazi *putsch* here (they have just sent down Patot, one of their big men). The Government here ... are trying to finesse. They are likely to be swept away. Result: Nazis in power. Once the Nazis are in power, the French will be faced with a sort of psychological Anschluss. That suits neither the French nor the Little Entente. Result: war. You in England have no notion of the gunpowder now lying about in Europe. Nor is the fire brigade's power (if any) to deal with things aided by the fact that the word neither of Italy nor of Nazi Germany nor of Communist Russia can be trusted. There is a complete return to barbarism not only in internal but in external politics. ...

It is incredible what is going on in Germany. The Nazi *putsch* is not, you understand, against the Communists only. It is anti-Jewish and is rapidly becoming anti-Centre. They will first ruin their country and then Europe, just when there was a chance of getting straight at last. And for what? For a nationalism that had Europe by the ears in 1914 and which in the various countries since has all but finished Europe. Don't make any mistake, Hitler,

Hindenburg and Co represent nothing but barbarism of the worst type. And just because we – such people as you and I – are not barbarians we are heavily handicapped in dealing with them. Today in Germany intimidation is the only law. And I as an artist, a good European and an Englishman cannot think it not my business.[19]

Robert's next letter reported the suspension of Parliament and riots outside the Parliament House.[20] The Nicholses' stay in Vienna was coming to an end, but his final letter described further violence. He, Lesley Black and a young American couple

> went to a restaurant in the Jewish quarter over the river. While we were there, the Nazis broke through and ran into the Jewish quarter. The lights were put practically out in the restaurant as a precaution. We heard feet running and were bidden to gather on the other side of the restaurant for fear of (a) attracting attention (b) for fear of flying glass. The place was then barred up and the few Jewish patrons present made ready (I don't blame them) to scuttle out through the kitchen and go out by the back. Sure enough a brick came through the window and there was hammering on the door. Meanwhile the proprietor had telephoned the police. I took my walking stick and stood with the others. We decided to stand our ground. If we ran we were likely to be set on like the others should the Nazi roughs effect an entrance. As I was in my best suit I decided that the best chance for us was to yell 'Englischer Gesellschaft' for then I thought they wouldn't (a) touch us (b) would think twice about wrecking the place (I liked the old Jewess in charge, she had lots of pluck) in the presence of supposed officials from an important foreign legation. At worst I thought Bitter's girl and Lesley could scuttle out at the back while Bitter and I held them up with words and, if necessary, stood our ground in the doorway.'[21]

In fact, after some shouts and banging the Nazis went away, and though Robert went back the following evening, on that occasion the Nazis did not penetrate into the Jewish quarter.

Robert must have left Vienna immediately after this since on 7 April he was in Florence having passed through Venice. This was his long awaited first visit to Italy. He made nothing of Venice. Apparently as a result of having parted with Lesley Black he was in a 'hopeless stupor'.²² Florence too was something of a disappointment, but he revived in Rome where his brother and sister-in-law were living in considerable splendour. They had taken a large house outside Rome, the Villa Spada, because 'Phyllis was unfortunately brought up with pedigree dogs... She simply MUST have them about her. So they had to get a big house with a garden for the dogs.'²³ Robert enjoyed both the luxury and the sightseeing. It was a wrench to leave after a fortnight and go back to Yew Tree House. 'I feel I need nutriment, spiritual and sensuous,' he said, 'and I get precious little of either in Winchelsea.'²⁴

He certainly found it hard to settle back into Winchelsea life. 'I CAN'T live that life,' he wrote to Lady Head. 'I CAN'T listen to them [to the small change of local incident]. They drag me down.'²⁵ He went up to London and introduced Lesley to the literary circle of Ridgeway's, and at the beginning of June was already thinking it would be pleasant to spend the coming winter in St John's Wood, a part of London conveniently placed for visiting Koteliansky and, no doubt, Lesley.²⁶ He had her to Yew Tree House, along with the Julian Huxleys, for Whitsun and again in July. His letters over the summer and following winter show him pretty well besotted with her.

Throughout this time their relationship was platonic. Robert was seventeen years older than Lesley, and imagined her saying to herself in later life, not 'I knew Robert Nichols the poet', but 'I had a useful friend once who helped me to a notion of what life could be for a private person.'²⁷ But her company had a good effect on his spirits. It helped him through an operation in September when he had a tuberculosis-infected kidney removed – something of which he would otherwise have made exceedingly heavy weather. It rejuvenated him: 'Last night', he wrote on 5 August,²⁸ 'I went bathing at midnight by the full moon with two girls – Margaret Ritchie, daughter of my next door neighbour [Lord Ritchie], and a girl friend, very lovely to look at.' And he found it easier again to write poetry. Although he had been working on *Fisbo* since 1931, before Lesley entered his life he had probably written only a quarter of it. In October 1933 it was accepted by Heinemann,²⁹ and he then had to write thousands of lines in a few months. She sustained him through the hard work involved and inspired two important constituent pieces, that 'Address to Fame', and 'Courage'.³⁰ He also returned to lyric poetry. In the spring in Vienna, despite the political tensions, he could write:

When you're in love and walking early
Through city streets, how everything amazes.

In June he composed a 'Paean' beginning:

> Blessed be love that has my sense unsealed –
> For now the glittering ash drips fire again,
> Happiness sighs about the harvest field,
> Sweet smells the honey-hedgerow drenched with rain.[31]

And the more substantial 'Arrogant Eros' which appears in *Such Was My Singing* belongs to this period too. In August he saw his friends the Chapmans who were staying 'at the dungeon called the Artillery Mansions Hotel'. John Jay Chapman said: 'There's a new fibre in you – something I never saw before.'[32]

This was the last time Robert saw Chapman. He died in November: 'Cheiron, the great King of the Centaurs, is dead,' Robert said to the Heads.[33] Cheiron was tutor to the Greek heroes, and had played this role for Robert when they first met in America and Robert was afraid his experiences in the war had damaged his mind. 'I don't believe you will have *lost anything*,' said Chapman. 'This process of being gutted by Fate and having one's insides removed – like cleaning a fish – though it is the unpleasantest experience (I believe) in the universe, is very good for the intellect.' Wishing to mark his death by doing something of which he would have approved, Robert addressed an appeal on behalf of Dimitrov,* then undergoing a show trial in Germany, to the German Ambassador, and got Eddie Marsh to vouch for him as someone to be taken seriously. He also wrote to *The Times* and the American Academy of Arts and Sciences. 'It wasn't difficult', he told the Heads, 'to write something – however inadequate – about John Jay Chapman. You see I'd thought about him for years until he had become a feature – a mountain – in my mind's landscape. I had only to stay still – and the news of his death threw me into a great stillness as a starry night does or the presence of a flushed sea at evening – I had only to stay still and limn the outline of the mountain.'[34]

The Nicholses were unable to let Yew Tree House, and apart from visits to London and Christmas with Norah's parents, Robert spent the winter in Winchelsea. Working on *Fisbo* gave him insomnia.

> As slumber approaches the chambers of my brain grow black – in fact this happens quite suddenly. Then, if all is well, I soon lose consciousness (hence my habit of 'thinking black'). But on this

---

*Georgi Dimitrov, a Bulgarian Communist, was accused of complicity in the Reichstag fire. He was eventually acquitted and went on to a career in Soviet Russia.

occasion there were a succession of shapes, resembling grasshoppers, vaguely seen and not determinate as grasshoppers, and only so named later, which sprang up in the blackness. Each of these was the *sensation* accompanying a word which requires a rhyme. Had the words been ordinary words – particularly one-syllable words – they would not have been grasshoppers. Each grasshopper leaped up with a little click and fell, if not abolished by the instant finding of a rhyme, only to leap up a moment later, during which moment another might have leaped up. These words were words with a feminine rhyme.[35]

Besides insomnia he suffered from depression. 'Would that I were in Vienna,' he said. 'In Vienna I felt AT HOME.'[36] Norah sent him to London to see Lesley[37] and had Lesley to stay for the weekend.[38]

Robert finished *Fisbo* in March 1934, but before he did so his relations with Lesley reached a climax. In London on 8 March she told him she loved him,[39] and gave him a 'marvellous kiss'.[40] He went back to Winchelsea in a state of rapture. In Austria she had said she did not intend to marry but would have two or three major affairs. Envisaging a three-sided relationship of the standard Bloomsbury kind, he asked Norah's permission to sleep with her. Norah 'behaved miraculously'.[41] But he had not told Lesley that he was going to reveal all to Norah and on the night of 4–5 April, when he was back in London about to start with Norah for a holiday in Naples and Rome, Lesley upbraided him and walked out on him.

He took this disappointment even worse than the closure of *Wings Over Europe*. He seems to have wept incessantly. He and Norah proceeded with their Italian plans, but in Anacapri, where they had been lent a villa by Francis Brett Young, he was in a state of collapse. Moving to the luxury of the Villa Spada did no good. Lesley wrote to say that she no longer loved him. Robert chose as his confidante Koteliansky, begged him to mediate with Lesley, and bombarded him with letter after frantic letter. 'O Kot, Kot, dear, strong truthful Kot,' he cried, 'if only you were here.' To this Koteliansky replied: 'As regards your state of mind at present I think really you ought to take yourself in hand quite courageously.'[42] He urged patience, but his negotiations brought no comfort. Lesley told him: 'There is not to be love, or a love affair, or whatever it is called.' 'She tried to explain it by saying that, had there been a love affair, it was bound to end in a sort of mess.'[43]

Robert's papers contain no letters from Lesley Black and no account of her by a friend. For a picture of her we have to depend on him, and he gives us two pictures which do not cohere well together. In 1933 he described her to the Heads as follows:

> She is about five foot ten high but looks taller. Her hair is a dark-ish chestnut and falls in little curls about her nape ... She carries herself with her head up and steps like a stag... Her body – she went in bathing with us when she was down here and I bathed with her in Austria – is the most beautiful I have ever seen: broad shoulders, shallow and beautifully shaped bosom, a long back with the muscles moving but the shoulder blades hardly showing under a perfect skin, long sides, the strong thighs of a rider, small hands, a long foreleg, fine feet... She has lots of courage, physical as well as moral – she has piloted her aeroplane at night and liked it so much she didn't want to come down – but more moral than physical. She is intelligent, very unprejudiced, somewhat opposed to the Christian concept and canons – and can give her reasons – fond of music and more than a little knowledgeable on the history of art, particularly early Italian. When she is decided she really does know her mind. Koteliansky, a good judge of human nature, likes her and says 'She seems to me strong and unselfish and dependable.' I have found her so – remarkably so – and with plenty of good sense, for though only twenty three she is in her mind and spirit – as in her body – which still however has at one or two angles something girlish about it – older than her age. Were I to meet her for the first time I should say she was a woman of twenty seven. She is already a somebody, a definite if somewhat mysterious (because so reserved) personality and will be more or so I think... With her courage, her intelligence, her beauty and her noble heart – for it is noble ... she could do a great deal in the world.[44]

But a little over a year later he said: 'Lesley has faded into the insignificance proper to her and her kind – a vain, evasive being unconsciously and sometimes perhaps consciously insincere.'[45]

The Nicholses set sail back to England on 26 May. At Marseilles, while Norah proceeded with the ship, Robert left it with the declared purpose of visiting the Aldous Huxleys at Sanary just along the coast. He did not tell the Heads, and may not have revealed to Norah, that he had a further purpose.

His desolation when staying at the Villa Spada had not been totally unrelieved. Also in Rome at that time was Nancy Jones, the twenty-year-old daughter of Sir Roderick ('Jonah') and Lady Evelyn Jones and the granddaughter of Lord Grey. Her parents had arranged for her to do a grand tour accompanied by a friend a year her senior called Vivienne Wilkinson. One day they were invited to lunch by the Philip Nicholses. Vivienne Wilkinson recalls:

> Robert Nichols the poet and his wife were staying with them and as Robert came into the room I felt I had known him for centuries, most strange. We talked about the [Augustus] Johns who were friends of his and then had coffee by the fountain. I thought his wife seemed rather silent. ... Next day a whispering grey Rolls Royce drove us out to Ostia and lunch in a superb restaurant by the sea where we chose our fish from a great basket. We stopped and bathed at the sulphur baths on the way home and there was a lady holding a locust which she had found, wearing the most elegant purple pyjamas. A memorable day for a young girl and I did enjoy it and went to bed early.
>
> I was woken by a tapping on the window pane, and looking out I saw a shadowy figure beckoning me to go out. Dawn was rising over the Colosseum and there was Robert Nichols waiting to show me the wonder of it. I crept out and we sat on the hillside gazing at the flaming rays going up into the sky. The almond trees were in blossom and he had thrown almonds up to wake me. Next day we were to go to Tivoli and the Villa D'Este, and it was in those gardens by the fountains that Robert and I realized we loved each other... [46]

This went unnoticed not only by Norah but by Phyllis Nichols, who thought only that Robert had seen for a moment that Lesley 'wasn't worth it'.[47] Robert, however, contrived to ask Vivienne to come and stay with the Aldous Huxleys. Vivienne was supposed to be chaperoning Nancy Jones, but the temptation was too strong: she decided to go to Marseilles for a week and rejoin Nancy at Florence, the next place on their itinerary.

She took a train to Marseilles and 'there', she says, 'was Robert to meet me and we had rooms in a most unattractive, primitive hotel. Separate rooms!' In fact she made Robert move into her room;[48] – she had come with the intention of sleeping with him and he later spoke of her 'unexampled generosity';[49] but she really won his heart when 'she took me into a field and laid me down between an olive and a fig tree and sang her little German songs till all the tears went out of me.'[50]

To return to Vivienne's narrative:

The days went by and I had to leave to meet Nancy in Florence. Robert came to the station and caused consternation by weeping loud and strong with all the porters watching. I felt dreadful for leaving him, but I thought he would be returning to England and Norah and I had pledged my word to Jonah that I would stay with Nancy. I felt entirely free and uninvolved, not knowing what had been aroused... [The girls had a jolly time in Florence until] suddenly there was a debacle, Robert Nichols had arrived, followed me from the South of France, and was staying in a hotel near us where he spent the whole day weeping and ringing up. Poor Nancy, she had to go and console him and try to get some sense into his head, in other words to go home and return to Norah. He took us to dinner at the very best restaurant in Florence near the Duomo and the following day for a long drive in a carozza by the banks of the Arno... He stayed for about a week during which Nancy had to console him for his deep troubles and unhappiness. Something grievously disturbed him and when he left I thought he would return to Norah.

Robert did return to Yew Tree House, but it was now like Peacock's Nightmare Abbey, where Scythrop Glowry recreates the complexities of Shelley's private life. Robert was still lovesick for Lesley and she played Stella to his Scythrop while Viviennne played Marionetta. Unable to work, he made up rival fantasies concerning his two charmers. In one case, he is at the Opera in Covent Garden. He has just had a big play produced and is rather the literary man of the hour. Between the acts:

Lesley walks up and down with me – she is more beautiful than ever. People look at each other as we pass. 'There's Robert Nichols!' 'Who's the beautiful girl with him?' 'I don't know, but I hear they are often together. Isn't she beautiful?' 'The poet and his Muse?' 'Perhaps.' 'What are their relations, do you suppose?' 'I don't know. Nobody knows. But it is evident that they are both more alive than they will ever be again. There is resolution in his face and serenity in hers.' 'I envy them. They are at the top of life: he in his creation through her and she in him through his creation. And each feels this state of being is what they were born for.'

The picture with Vivienne is very different. The scene is a workroom in a large cottage near a fishing village. The moon shines on the windows for the winter night has come. Robert Nichols is sitting in a deep sofa by the fire and Vivienne is by him with her head on his shoulder. Their child is asleep in a cradle which Vivienne rocks with her foot. One candle is burning on the table.

Robert I have failed, I suppose, but, you know, I don't care. I don't indeed really much care whether I write or not, though it is nice to make beautiful things.

Vivienne With no more pride in them.

Robert Yes, humble things, human affectionate things... [and so on for a protracted dialogue in which Robert does nearly all the talking].[51]

The best thing for his difficulties, Robert thought, would be to go abroad for some uncomplicated sex with Vivienne.[52] Norah, he assured the Heads, 'approves of Vivienne and her consolations.'[53] But a string drawn tighter and tighter will eventually snap. Norah had had enough and herself announced her intention of going off to live with a married man called Clem Gresswell. Robert informed his father of this in August.[54] Since Yew Tree House was Norah's property, Robert cleared out, leaving, he told the Heads,[55] 'not only a great and beautiful human being [Norah] but everything I had so toilfully built up there: the respect and, I may say, the affection of all classes of the little community which I had tried to help [he had just been made a freeman of Winchelsea], the house I loved, in which I had hoped to live and work and die.'

Although for the last two years Robert had been complaining about the deficiencies of his marriage and the loneliness and stifling triviality of Winchelsea life, these losses laid him even lower than he had been in April. He went first to his sister Irene and then to the Arthur Blisses. They must have found his tears intolerable. Then Phil and Phyllis Nichols took charge and sent him to Haus Hirth in Bavaria, a guesthouse run by friends. After a couple of weeks Frau Hirth found him too much to handle, so Phil arranged for him to be treated at a sanatorium in Munich. There they sedated him and tried to make him give up being a poet. After a few days of Dr Lampe's pills he was writing:

I've had enough of this absurd business with the pen. I have sacrificed far too much to it... All my life I've been horribly seri-ous and my brain is not good enough for all that – it's only pretence. Let me live like the ordinary reader of the *Daily Tele-graph*. To be an artist is far too expensive in every sense. Besides there's a sort of swank about it. What business had I with all these books and sitting down solemnly to record my thoughts – when I know *nothing* and in my blindness cared to know nothing how ordinary people live who mow the lawn and play with their chil-dren and have little jokes with their wives?[56]

But he must have realised that this was a denial of all that he had lived for, and stopped taking the pills. 'I have had two *terrible* days – worse than anything since Nornie left me, worse than during the war.' He asked to leave, but Dr Lampe forbade this; 'so, late in the evening, I got out of bed, dressed and ran out of the sanatorium and walked miles, having no money.'[57] He finally compromised by lodging with a Baroness Larinaga and her sister and receiving outpatient treatment for his throat and toenails.[58] Meanwhile in England his belongings were transferred to Lawford and the Nichols family lawyer started moving with divorce proceedings, it being easier, as the law stood, for Robert to divorce Norah than vice versa.

It was on 8 October, in the midst of these emotional tempests, that *Fisbo* finally appeared. Charles Tennyson, writing some years later, described it as 'some of the most brilliant and entertaining work in this vein written during the present century',[59] and the reviews at the time were excellent.

We have had to wait a long time [wrote Charles Powell][60] for the poem that would restore satire to its ancestral place in English letters, but it would seem to have been written at last. And the authorship is something of a surprise. Mr Robert Nichols' rep-utation as a poet was made during the war. His last book of verse (his third) appeared in 1920, and since then it has been the fashion to count him among the far-receding Georgians. *Fisbo* is one of time's revenges. It has in shattering derision the image that the new bardolatry has set up. Fisbo is a bogus poet, the pet of fashion, and the product of publicity. He is a compound of the ignorant, the incompetent and the ignoble. Mr Nichols car-ries his fantastic career hilariously through nearly five thousand lines. ... There was a dragon to be slain and it is a Georgian who has slain it.

Similarly G. W. Stonier in the *New Statesman and Nation*,[61] C. J. M. Turner in the *Poetry Review*,[62] L. P. Hartley in the *Sketch*, and also the *Observer, The Times Literary Supplement, The Sunday Times* and so on. But perhaps the best tribute came in a private letter from Eddie Marsh. He was anticipating the publication, he had told Robert, with 'holy dread'.[63] When it actually came out he wrote at once to say 'It seems to me a magnificent work, a miracle of sustained energy, immensely amusing and with many paragraphs of breath-taking beauty. ... I can't tell you, Bob, what a delight it is to find you once more at the top of your form as a writer.[64]

Fisbo is more than twice the length of any satire by Dryden or Pope. (*The Rape of the Lock*, to give a standard of comparison, has a mere 800 lines.) Byron's *Don Juan* (which Robert greatly admired) is longer, but it is in a different metre and quite different in character. There is enough connected incident in Robert's biography of Fisbo to carry the reader the full length of the course and he could claim to have achieved a revival of satire even more vigorous than his revival of pastoral with *The Faun's Holiday*. He proves himself a natural master of the heroic couplet. In his hands it is, as Charles Powell put it, a 'lithe, leaping thing', and it can achieve a wide range of effects, from the evocative beauty of the lines quoted by Marsh in his letter:

> Light so profound and silence so complete
> That it seemed snow not moonlight at our feet

to the knock-out blow in this description of Fisbo sitting down to write a poem:

> Creamy the paper was and broad and bland,
> Nobly expectant of the buoyant hand;
> The ink lay harboured in a silver swan;
> The new nib was a golden paragon
> Very Polymnia might use with zest;
> The blotting paper, too, was of the best.
> All seemed propitious, inspiration near.
> All that was wanting now was an idea.

The Heads asked him if he had been influenced by Horace. 'I have always loathed him,' he replied surprisingly. 'I read a certain amount of Byron (not so very much); a lot of Dryden in small snippets; I glanced at Pope but found him largely unreadable.'[65] In fact, while he may have taken Dryden as his model, there are several passages in *Fisbo* strongly suggestive of Pope. The description of Fisbo's dressing table, for instance (p. 15), brings back *The Rape of the Lock*, and the palace of Stultitia (p. 69) *The Dunciad*. But his witty description of London literary life is based squarely on his own experience.

There are also passages which he might have cut out, had he had time for second thoughts. They give rather too much information about himself, but at the same time they have considerable power: for instance pages 137–40 where he speaks for those who have 'the sovereign folly to be sick' and pages 40–1 where he expresses his own desire for fame:

> Small is Fame's company, her table spare,
> But the roast's excellent, the wines are rare,
> The peaches delicious and the conversation
> Outplatos Plato's best imagination.
> The dinner ended, Fame most often chooses
> To ask some music of her friends the Muses.
> They sing of gods, or demigods and heroes
> And, loveliest of all, they sing of Eros ...
> Won't you perhaps send me an invitation?

Heinemann printed 1,000 copies for sale at the price, large for 1934, of 7/6d, and in just over a month 700 had been sold. Robert had every reason to be delighted. But he had had misgivings when writing it. It was 'on a scale perhaps larger than the subject warrants'[66]; he wished 'the rabbit' were worthier of his 'heavy charge of shot'.[67] The resentment and malice which inspired it must given a sour flavour to the many hours of composition, and when the acclaim arrived in the winter of 1934 he was too distraught to enjoy it.

18
Vivienne

Vivienne Wilkinson, of whom Robert said in 1937 'She is the great love of my life, and I know quite well that I have never loved like this before nor shall again',[1] was born in India on 23 August 1912. Her father, a Wilkinson of the engineering family, was a successful architect at that time working for the British Raj in India. He returned to England in 1914 to enlist for the war, and served as an officer in the Royal Flying Corps. His mother, Eveline Neave, belonged to a family that traces itself back in the male line to the reign of Henry IV and received a baronetcy in the eighteenth century. In spite of this solidly respectable background Vivienne was drawn to the stage, passed from the Bar Convent in York to RADA, and danced in *The Miracle* in London for six months. At this time[2] she had a love affair which ended badly and caused her parents to adopt the counterproductive strategy of trying to keep her on a tight rein. In her seventies when she wrote her recollections she entitled them *Myself When Young, or, From Gum Tree to Gum Tree, The Story of a Wasted Life.* From London her mother took her to Portmeirion in North Wales. There Clough Williams-Ellis and his Strachey wife Amabel gathered around them luminaries like Bertrand Russell, Harold Nicolson and Diccon Hughes who can have done little to steady her. When she met Robert at the Villa Spada, if he was pining for Lesley Black, she was still sore from the unkindness of her own lover.

On her return that summer from the tour with Nancy Jones, Vivienne was found to have hyperthyroidism and was sent out to Hindelang in the Bavarian Alps to be treated by a Dr Gerl who was considered the leading European authority on the condition. She chose an operation in preference to a long course of treatment in order to get back to her stage career. While she was recovering Robert arrived at Garmisch desolated by the loss of Lesley Black, Norah and Yew Tree House. He visited her at Hindelang, and when she was stronger and he had moved to Munich:

> I went down to Munich for a few days and Robert took me to the Rot Hun, the restaurant where Hitler lunched every day. We had a

banquette by the wall and opposite was Unity Mitford looking
pale and rather ethereal with her straight blonde hair. Suddenly
the door opened and in strode some heavy men with hands in their
pockets, no doubt on revolvers. They looked quickly round the
restaurant and everyone leaped to their feet to 'Heil, Hitler'. Not
Robert and I, we were English and not interested and reading the
menu, we sat as we'd never sat before. Behind the strong men
came Hitler, a very tired-looking figure in a shabby mackintosh,
his face was white and drawn and there had just been the purge of
Roehm and others, but he had the strange, luminous look of the
fanatic, or ascetic. I had seen that phosphorescent look in Mother
Margaret [her old head mistress] but for a different reason. He
just walked through to the back room and that was over, and
Unity left.[3]

Vivienne went home in October, but came back again for a check-up
at the end of December.

Robert met me in Munich and had arranged a beautiful little
Christmas tree in the suite of the hotel. He was still living with the
Larinagas. He had taken infinite pains to make it beautiful for me
with little angels and bells on the tags and a pile of lovely presents
underneath. He took infinite pains to please and loved making
things beautiful.[4]

This really touched her. She once told him 'I love you for the little
exquisite things you do and think of, like the Christmas tree in
Munich.'[5]

After Christmas he accompanied her to Hindelang. Dr Gerl was a
friend of Rudolf Hess and in charge of SS troops on the Austrian fron-
tier. He asked Robert to interest Lady Astor in lending money to Hitler
to equip his army. 'Robert, of course, refused absolutely to have any
political interests whatever, as he was a writer and not a politician, even
though we were offered the doubtful privilege of meeting the Fuhrer
personally. NO THANKS.'

On the contrary, he wrote to his brother via diplomatic bag describing the manoeuvres of Goering's air force and recalling the conditions
of the Versailles Treaty; just fodder, presumably, for the Foreign Office
waste paper baskets.

Robert and Vivienne returned to England separately in January
1935. His sister Irene arranged for Robert to live as a paying guest with

a Mrs Robertson in two rooms at 3 Upper Cheyne Row.[6] Vivienne went to work with an interior decorating firm in Bournemouth where her Neave grandmother was living. He came down to her from London for occasional passionate meetings. By this time Norah had reached the end of her lover and since she and Robert had always kept on friendly terms, Koteliansky and others thought they might make it up. Through the first half of 1935 Robert was miserable with indecision between Norah and Vivienne. The indecision was compounded by Vivienne's wanting a baby and his conviction that no matter what happened they would never have enough money for this. He seems to have been receiving at the moment about £500 a year from his father, his brother and his sister-in-law. He calculated that when his father died these allowances would be replaced by a share of the estate that would give him £800 a year. His mother had always had an income of her own and the Pusey estate, which included Pusey House in Oxfordshire and land that had been given to the Puseys by King Canute, was entailed on her children.[7] But Robert seems to have had no expectations from this quarter. Vivienne had an allowance of about £100 a year and thought she could earn a further £300 a year as an actress or at least as a model girl – she did in fact earn something like this as a model for Piguet. To her and to many people it seemed that she and Robert could well afford to marry and have children. But Robert said to the Heads 'I am not one of your cottage poets, you know.'[8] He wanted to live in central London, to entertain leading writers and artists, to go to the theatre, to winter in a warm climate and so forth, and £800 seemed to him insufficient to support even one person in this manner of existence. Yet any encroachment on it would have an adverse effect on that work as a poet which, as he often said, he was born to do. The court hearing for his divorce came up in June. Norah then went to Sweden by herself for three months and although she did not afterwards return to Mr Gresswell, and would undoubtedly have been glad to remarry Robert, that is something he seems not to have considered. Norah ceased to be a rival to Vivienne but his muse did not, and lack of money always remained a pretext for indecision.

In February he had a temporary distraction. He was 'selected by H.M. Government to represent English literature at the centenary celebration of the publication of the Kalevala'[9] in Finland. He was at Helingfors for a week and made a couple of speeches; he also (he recalled later when on a strict diet) enjoyed having reindeer tongue and vodka.[10]

He treated himself to another holiday a couple of months later. On
26 April he took a steamer from Liverpool, stopped at Lisbon,
Madeira, Las Palmas and Santa Cruz, and got back on 14 May. At first
he found his fellow-passengers dull and buried himself in the *Iliad*.[11]
But Homer and the charm of Estoril awakened him, he felt a happiness
he had not known since Salzburg, and wrote non stop for four days and
nights. At Santa Cruz he hired a car and a driver, and sped round the
island scribbling in a notebook.[12]

A new volume had already been taking shape in his mind which
would be presented as 'a collection of poems by an emblematic personality' called Prince Axel of Salzburg and Estoril (the scenes of his
inspired elation). The Prince would be 'an uprooted aristocrat of
Austro-Spanish descent, of romantic instincts and quixotic propensi-
ties'[13] – himself, in fact, as he would like to be. The Spanish cruise
yielded several contributions to this volume: a poem beginning 'Night
looks down into the ocean', which remains unpublished, and four
others which are printed in *Such Was My Singing*. Of these the three
composing what he called *A Spanish Triptych* are some of the most
substantial poetry of his later years.

The *Triptych* has a Madonna on either side: a 'Virgin of Sorrows'
who looks across from high on a cathedral to a brothel, and a 'Virgin of
Joy' who stands in a garden between two ancient fig trees. Between
them is 'Prison Calvary', which is just what the title signifies. It begins:

> Within this torrid acre of bleached walls,
> Beneath mounds shaven like a criminal's head
> The condemned of man are lying,
> And above the row of mounds and white-washed stones
> On an iron Calvary hangs a bronzen Christ,
> Forever dying yet not dead, not dead.

Robert was pleased with this poem which describes the neglect of the
figure, 'green from many rains', the suffering represented, the thirst, for
which 'no sponge is ever lifted to that mouth', the inability to die,

> Since just so long as any sword can slay
> Such crown and such a cross must yet be his.

But nature shows compassion:

> Sprung at the calvary's very root,
> Vine of the passionflower upstealing

Day by day, hour by hour,
Leaf by leaf, shoot by shoot.
Twining and ever intertwining
In and out of the skeleton iron,
In and out up the cross's foot,
The vine clambers...

and

by the seventh summer
Not only the spike, but the ladder, the spear,
The riven side, the blood-bedewed bosom
Will be wholly shrouded in leaves and blossom,
The awful diadem slumber above,
Among the clouds a cloud of flowers,
And the very eyes of anguish be hidden
Behind the veils of beauty and love.

When *Such Was My Singing* appeared the reviewers tended to concentrate on the early poems it contains and overlooked the *Triptych*. Readers who knew Robert, however, were appreciative. John Masefield liked it best 'of the new work',[14] Dorothy Carrington, known at that time as Mrs Boulton* or 'Cappy', and a confidante of Vivienne and Robert, said it had 'all the intensity and observation of the earlier poems combined with a much simpler and purer more genuinely personal style – self-assured and not too ornate as well as deeply felt.'[15] It is illuminating to compare it with the early religious triptych, written before the 1914 War and printed in *Ardours and Endurances*. He included none of the earlier panels in *Such Was My Singing*. If he had, the reader would see not only how the poet's command of English had matured, but also how his understanding and compassion had deepened. He can now say what he thinks about God without, as he did in his youth, putting Judas in the place of Christ; and his 'Virgin of Joy' works over the theme of his original first panel 'The Hill', the virgin playing with her child, more naturally and realistically.

After his Spanish cruise Robert remained in London (apart from an unhappy visit to Lawford in June) until his landlords left town in July. He then had to find shelter elsewhere for three months. He stayed with a friend near Eastbourne, Stella Churchill, attended the Margaret

*Though only two years older than Vivienne she had already got through two husbands, Franz von Waldschutz and Darcy Sproul-Boulton.

Morris Summer School to improve his health by dancing, and went on to the Joos School of Dancing at Dartington Hall, where Vivienne thought they might both find jobs. Nothing came of that idea. He then appears at Place Farm near Didcot, still undecided about the future and dispirited because inspiration had run dry. On 12 or 13 September Vivienne, who was with her parents in Lancashire but about to come to London to work for Sibyl Colefax, wrote to him:

> My Dear Robert –
>   I can't say your letter hasn't depressed me because it has. You've succeeded in making me as despondent as yourself. ... If you want this thing [a life with her] and feel it worthwhile attempting please try to summon some effort of fortitude at any rate. I *know* it is worrying and difficult and I quite understand your anxiety to get down to the basic things [sc. writing poetry]. All I can say is that I am willing to do my level best to make you happy and to help you on in every way I can – *provided* that you want me and will likewise put your weight behind things. But I can't possibly compete, and indeed won't, if you drag me down with despondency and hopeless pessimism. You will never get anywhere with that – either in your art or in anything else.

Robert's reply seems to have been to ask her to ask Phyllis Nichols for money. 'I will write', she told him, 'and try to fix a time to see them before they go away and have this horrible discussion – I'm not looking forward to it but I'm sure she will be kind and sympathetic.'[16]

Perhaps she was, but not to the extent of giving Robert £300 a year. Robert's brother and sisters were all solidly disapproving. His sisters, who were attached to Norah, refused to meet Vivienne, and Irene said that even with the £800 he expected from his father's estate he could not afford to marry her.[17] Phil seems to have misjudged the depth of Robert's affection for Vivienne, apparently regarding it as one more example of an infatuation of the Lesley Black type for a muse. Cynthia Noble, or Cynthia Jebb as she had become, was probably expressing Phil's view when she said 'She would make an excellent mistress, not a wife.'[18] Phil also played on a fresh source of anxiety. In March Robert's physician, Dr Eidinor, had warned him that Vivienne's thyroid condition made it unlikely that she should conceive, and he too advised him not to marry her but simply have an affair.[19] Robert found these cynical counsels distasteful. But her condition, Dr Eidinor said, also roused sexual cravings and he feared that if Vivienne could not have a child she might be unfaithful. Other doctors were more optimistic on the question of fertility, but Robert believed that his own sexual powers would decline after the age of fifty. He hardly needed Phil to remind him in September that he was nineteen years older than she.[20] When he was fifty-three and impotent and she was still a lusty thirty-four, he felt sure she would leave him.[21] Henceforth the spectre of infidelity joined hands with his other chronic fear: that if he married, the need to earn money would interfere with his writing.

Helen Shell, Vivienne's great-niece, who was perhaps closer to her than any other surviving relative, has suggested that there may have been grounds other than expediency for viewing the match with apprehension. Though Vivienne's letters seem reasonable and realistic, her temperament, in Miss Shell's opinion, was as excitable and erratic as Robert's, and the combination of two such unstable people might have been terrifyingly precarious.

In the autumn of 1935 Douglas Fairbanks was in London. Robert and he renewed their friendship and Robert introduced Vivienne to him, hoping that jobs might be found for both of them, for her as an actress and for him as a writer. Earlier in the year he had been negotiating with Korda, and at RADA Vivienne had known David Lean and watched Eisenstein films with him.[22] But people were more easily found to attend to Robert's health than to give him employment. In the winter of 1935-6 he went to Morris Robb for analysis and to Mathias Alexander for his posture.

In February 1936 Robert and Vivienne met in Aldous Huxley's Albany flat and agreed not to see each other for a year, and then, if they felt like it after that interval, to make a fresh start. It was not the first and would not be the last time that they tried this way of ending Robert's agonising indecision. In May, hoping to recover the inspiration he had had on his Spanish cruise, Robert left London to stay for the summer at the Hotel Portmeirion. In June Vivienne went to Corsica. The summer was a bright interval for both. Vivienne thrived in the Corsican sun. Robert wrote a lyric, 'Evenstar', which he included in *Such Was My Singing* and made progress with *Komuso*. He also found stimulating company. The Bertrand Russells were there and Robert improved his acquaintance with the philosopher. He amused him with

> my story of Augustus John's dream. 'You know, Bob,' (deep voice, broody eye) 'I feel very bad this morning.' 'What is it, Augustus?'
> 'I had a dream – a horrible dream.' 'What was it? - We all have

bad dreams now and again.' 'Not as I dreamed, Bob; not as I dreamed.' 'It must have been frightful, Augustus, but what was it?' 'It was frightful. You know that chap Epstein?' 'Yes, I know that chap Epstein.' 'Well, Bob, he appeared to me last night in the form of a beautiful damsel in a diaphanous garment. And I desired him – her. I think I'd better go to a psychoanalyst, don't you?'[23]

Russell told Robert that he used to see Vivienne – he called her 'Miss Wilkinson' of course – shooting with a revolver in the woods round Portmeirion. 'What are you doing?' he asked her. '"Just practising," she answered. But I thought to myself, "One never knows. Perhaps she is thinking of killing herself."'[24] Those were the days before firearms control.

While Robert was on his own this year he showed that he had not lost whatever attracted such writers as Sheila Kaye-Smith and Edith Sitwell to him as a correspondent. He had written in April to a young American writer, Catherine Whitworth, who was in hospital. She responded like a drooping plant to water and sunlight, and talked artlessly about herself in a series of friendly letters during 1936.[25] In December she wrote 'Are you feeling sad? I would dearly love to comfort you were I near you.'[26] It was perhaps just as well that the Atlantic stretched between them.

The final draft of *Komuso* is dated Cambridge 1943, but Robert's journal for 1936 says it was 'all but finished' that summer.[27] It was broadcast in 1954 and well received by listeners; but when it was put in stage at the Arts Theatre Club the following year (from 8 November to 11 December), the press notices were uniformly poor.

The play is set in Japan, in a house based on the building, formerly a temple, in which Robert and Norah had lived; and it contains three characters that are modelled rather obviously on the author. There is Ronald Chilvers, a young lecturer in English Literature who dislikes Japan and wants to go home to his fiancée. He is a minor figure. Then there is Augustus Peach, known as Peachy, a middle-aged English merchant who after many years in Japan has run to seed and drinks too much. In his youth he had been a painter and he is portrayed as remaining an artist at heart. Finally there is a thirty-eight-year-old scientist called Dr Eliot Ballentine who is doing research into poliomyelitis and who is married to Karin, the central figure of the play. Karin is a beautiful woman of twenty-four, 'slim, virginal, broad-browed'. Her beauty 'is not the pure lines of the flesh only, – indeed it is the extraordinary limpidity of her expression that most impresses you, ... that, and, when she speaks, the gentleness and sweetness of her voice.'[28] She was played on the radio by Googie Withers and on the stage by Honor Blackman, and although the performances of both were warmly acclaimed, neither had much in common with the original of Karin, who was certainly Norah.[29]

The theme of the play is Robert's failure with Norah. Ballentine is totally devoted to his work: he offers no passionate love to Karin and tells her that they cannot at present afford a child. She is seduced into a one night stand with a man not unlike Clem Gresswell (played at the Arts Theatre by the young Paul Eddington). This results in a pregnancy and a showdown between her and her husband. He refuses to be responsible for another man's child and tells her she must either go to the father or have an abortion. She charges him with marrying her without loving her, and now proposing 'I should go to a man you know doesn't love me and whom I don't love.' This, except for the pregnancy, is what happened between Robert and Norah, and remarks which Robert puts into Ballentine's mouth must have come often from his own: 'I have denied myself a child. ... My work is more important to me than any child.' Norah, however, not pregnant and breathing the phlegmatic air of England, overcame her resentment, stayed friends with Robert, and typed out his works for him, *Komuso* included. Karin's crisis occurred in a house that had been built as a Buddhist temple, that still held the atmosphere of a past tragic death, and that was haunted by a mysterious mendicant penitent, the *komuso* of the title, who seemed to be a legacy of that tragedy. Under these influences she hangs herself in the last act. The story is complicated by Peachy, who loves Karin and despite his alcoholism plays the part of friendly sage and philosophical commentator. He too speaks with Robert's voice, not only when he talks about the meaning of life and the seven fundamental forms in nature (Act I) but also when he relates the story of how his own life has been blighted (Act II).

In his journal for 1936 Robert said he believed *Komuso* 'to be a masterpiece and one of the deepest and finest plays since the Jacobean'.[30] It is not as good as that, but neither is it as bad as his critics said. The way in which he spreads out his own weaknesses and shufflings without any exculpation is impressive. Guy Verney, who produced it, wrote to Norah that he was 'unable to understand the viciousness with which most of the critics dismissed it contemptuously as if it were some cheap bedroom farce. ... If it had been a translation from the French or the Italian the reception would have been vastly different.'[31] The main trouble, no doubt, was the same as with *Guilty Souls* and *Wings Over Europe*: it needed more cutting. In the autumn of 1936 Robert consulted his friend Harley Granville Barker and received some kind words but also some critical advice.[32] The play was much too long and there was too much Peachy in it: 'The business isn't Peachy. He's a *mirror*, no more – though a most interesting mirror.' Although there must have been some cuts in 1955, with no author there to stitch up the incisions they may have been inadequate. At least the stage directions, very detailed in the Cambridge typescript, were reduced. Honor Blackman remembers that in the seduction scene some thirty lines of Robert's beating about the bush were abbreviated to: 'He strokes her breast. She has an orgasm. Her shoe falls off.'[33]

While Robert was putting the last touches to *Komuso* his local doctor diagnosed a duodenal ulcer. At the end of August he entered the War Memorial Hospital, Edenbridge, Kent, for six weeks' treatment. Vivienne returned from Corsica at the beginning of September and went to see him. 'I was delighted to see her,' he says in his journal,[34] 'and kissed her in high spirits. And at once she proposed we get married directly I was out of hospital. I pointed out that I might have to go to America.' The trip to America would have been to get *Komuso* performed, but this was rather a remote possibility and thereafter the meeting went badly. In her Recollections she says 'We lived in a fog of disapproval, and he would not marry me which would have settled it. In all his long letters to me he always made excuses when it came to the point.'[35]

Although Robert was not prepared to take any kind of paid employment, he had no objection to removing the financial obstacle to marriage by some profitable invention. In July 1934 when he was trying to decide between Vivienne and Lesley Black, he hoped to make a fortune out of what he called a 'commercial idea'.[36] This was to set up a chain of eating places beside filling stations along main roads, where lorry drivers should be served good meals cooked by electricity. That, of course, is exactly what has now everywhere been done; but it was moonshine to imagine anyone would enrich him just for the idea without any of the detailed planning or capital needed to bring it into actuality.

In September 1936 he had another idea, this time for a way of defending Britain against attacks by air. The Nichols Bob, as he called it, was to be a shell with a time fuse which on explosion released something like a giant jellyfish: a parachute trailing metal 'filaments' in which the enemy flying machines would be entangled. Bobs would be used in place of conventional anti-aircraft guns and barrage balloons. A fence of them could be put up at a height and with a density calculated to protect a target against any airborne threat; yet a 'wicket' could be left open to allow friendly fighters to pass in or out. Depending on the nature of the aggressor, Bobs could release parachutes of different sizes, from little puffs of silk armed with piano wire to vast, cloud-sized leviathans trailing massive chains.[37]

Inspired with this vision as lay in the Edenbridge Hospital, Robert asked Eddie Marsh to summon Winston Churchill to his bedside to hear all about it. Marsh knew Robert too well to be put out by this staggering request. Instead he arranged for Robert to be invited to Chartwell for lunch.

In 1918 Robert had written to his father: 'I was introduced to Winston Churchill yesterday and hated him instinctively.'[38] His reception on this occasion made him sing a different tune.[39] 'Just returned from Winston. By God they treated me as if I were a distinguished confrère! They were simply *marvellous*. They sent a car for me, they had special food cooked, she looked after me all the time because I was exhausted from being in bed.'

After lunch he and Churchill had a *tête-à-tête*, in which Churchill undertook to send him and an engineer friend called E. E. Leigh Scanes along to his trusted scientific adviser, Professor Lindemann. Churchill in action impressed him enormously: 'I beheld Winston ruffled (not by me) but by things in his mind, and it was a memorable experience – a cross between a scowling cherub and a red hot coal rolling up and down the room. But it was great to feel the energy and will coming off him like a subaqueous upheaval of tropic waters.'

This happy meeting was followed by a lunch in London on 22 October that did not go quite so well. Robert described it[40] in the ingenuous way in which he had described his memorable conversation with James Joyce.

You know, Eddie, I'm awfully bad at parties unless I know the people. Even if I appear to get on all right the strain is *terrific* because I am so impulsive. I don't know when to butt in and when to stay out and since my ideas are always forms of intoxication I get into difficulties as to when to stop, dry up suddenly, am encouraged to proceed and then can't stop.

He thought he antagonised Churchill by staring at him. 'You see he's the only *really* great man-of-action I've ever met and I have brooded on the nature of such men for years.'

The subject came up of Lindemann's standing for the university seat of Oxford. Robert asked Churchill whether he thought Lindemann would get it.

Unfortunately the presence of the other people made me so nervous in addressing the great man across the table that my voice had a sound of challenge which I by no means intended. He said 'I really don't know.' Whereat the wretched voice answered 'A. P. Herbert' [with whom Robert had been talking the night before] says Lindemann will get in – and he ought to know!' for all the world as if I was telling W. C. where he got off.

Robert's uncle Lord Braye was trying to start an Independent ginger group on air defence in the House of Lords, and had asked Robert if he could persuade Churchill to see him. Robert now asked Mrs Churchill if he might tackle her husband about this, and she thought he might:

(You know, Eddie, she really is a most extraordinarily kind woman for she was already *literally* blushing for my first mistake.) By this time W. C. was sitting back, *glimmering* like a sulky baby, sunk in his chair, and I could see that he regarded me as a cross between a Bounder and a Bloody Nuisance. However the shade of my little tubby uncle – and the feeling of how awful it was for my uncle to have had to ask something of *me* – you know how one feels this of elder relatives whom one respects – drove me on. By this time the whole table was watching the Bard-in-difficulties-on-his-trick-tricycle and so I was more inept than ever. I began 'I have an uncle who's a peer...' and it sounded as if I was a snob of the first water, whereas all I meant was 'There's a chap in the Lords who might be useful in a small way...' Winston didn't answer – he simply doddled his head after a few more of my sentences and I retired in confusion. Moral (since drawn!) 'If there's one more awkward thing to do than ask a favour of the great, it is to try to help them. I was endeavouring to do both at once.'

Mrs Churchill's heart must have bled for Robert, since a couple of days later she wrote to Marsh:

Dearest Eddie,

I'm so sorry Mr Nichols was upset by Winston. He, Winston, likes him very much, but I think he finds him rather overwhelming. He has written very interesting but unreadable and copious letters to both Winston and me and we can neither of us read his handwriting!

I think he is probably a unique human being and he does bear on him the marks of physical and mental suffering. What happened was that Mr. Nichols asked Winston suddenly if he would see Lord Braye. You know how mapped out W's time is and how he hates seeing new people! I'm sorry to say that he replied 'No, certainly not!' It made my hair stand on end with shyness but it really was rather funny.

Winston is much touched by Mr Nichols wishing to give him his beautiful Nelson bust [a peace offering injudiciously tendered] but he says please he does not think he could accept so valuable and unique a gift. Do reassure Mr Nichols – I like him so much. He is a winged creature.

It does not appear that the Nichols Bob brought Robert a heavier shower of gold than the transport café idea.[41] He was hard up, and a letter to the Heads, undated but probably belonging to November 1936, speaks of selling his letters from Robert Bridges and W. B. Yeats to raise cash. But in December Vivienne decided to move things along. She summoned Robert to her room in 160 Piccadilly on the pretext of discussing a possible job in Cambridge. After some conversation she asked him to turn on the radio. While his back was turned she slipped out of her clothes and folded Robert in an embrace. 'I must go now' said he. But she 'pressed closer than ever saying "I love you – I love you. I want you. I want you *now*,"'[42] with the inevitable result. A couple of days later Maria Huxley told him that she wanted marriage straightaway. The Huxleys thought he ought to marry her. So did the Joneses, so did Bertrand Russell. But in spite of this formidable weight of opinion Robert stalled.

He spent Christmas 1936 at Lawford with his sisters and their husbands:

This place is absolute poison to me – or rather not this place but

one personality and the atmosphere he exudes... Every one of us –
save Harry – undergoes a moral transformation for the worse
here: Irene goes more sarcastic, being the more driven to sustain
herself by a sort of scurrilous bonhomie and bravado at the
expense of life and what is fair and honest and beautiful in it;
Anne becomes moodier. Even George deteriorates and one sees
him finessing all the time.[43]

With all members of the party except Harry Strauss committed athe-
ists, there must have been a fine Yuletide atmosphere. It may have
contributed to Robert's decision, when he got back to London, to bring
his relationship with Vivienne to an end, though what he told himself
was that he was sacrificing personal happiness to his duty as a poet. In
any case he wrote to her saying that marriage was impossible, and
before she could come round and remonstrate, fled for a week to his
doctor in North Wales.

Vivienne, meanwhile, had found a pleasant flat on the Chelsea
Embankment at a rent which would allow them to live there on their
present joint incomes. Day after day she wrote imploring him at least to
look at it. At length her determination prevailed over Robert's weakness. He proposed to her on 30 January 1937 and was accepted.

But within a couple of weeks he was having misgivings, and then on
14 March Vivienne confessed to him that the previous night she had
slept with another man. Robert was now in psychoanalysis with Dr
Graham Howe. The analyst and Vivienne disliked each other and Vivienne thought him a fraud who was being used to separate Robert from
her – he certainly seems to have been in communication with Philip
Nichols who paid his bill.[44] But whatever it was that led Vivienne to
this infidelity, it naturally reinforced Robert's apprehensions about their
long-term future. He broke off the engagement but they continued
seeing each other and flat-hunting.

In May there was a possibility of Robert's income being supple-
mented. Myrtle Farquharson, a common friend, suggested to Evan
Morgan, now Lord Tredegar and receiver of a large income, that he
might give Robert some paid literary work. Tredegar offered him £100
a year to write (or ghost) his biography. Robert found the offer 'somewhat hair-raising' since Tredegar 'proposed to treat fully of his personal
relations with Aleister Crowley and Lord Alfred Douglas' and also to
'relate his doings with the Windsors' – a mission to Mrs Simpson, the
composition of the attempted 'King's Party', etc.[45] Robert considered

the work *infra dig*[46] but did not refuse it. £100 was a significant sum, and on 3 July he told the Heads he was about to announce his engagement in *The Times*.

But then his nerve failed him. He got disgustingly drunk.[47] On 16 July he wrote in his journal 'I become more and more afraid I shall kill myself.' He must have peace to think things over. Dr Howe, who had given him the matrimonial all-clear, suggested that he and Vivienne should go abroad. Vivienne was still under contract to Piguet and in the autumn also had a part in a play, but a Mrs Mary Baker said she had a palace in Venice on the Grand Canal where Robert could work on *Don Juan*, and Robert went there by himself in August.

Within days he was experiencing 'piercing sadness',[48] and in September he painted for the Heads a desperate picture of his situation. His room looked over a noisy street, not the Grand Canal. Mrs Baker kept a tyrannical and half-mad mother in the palace, and she herself was being blackmailed. At the end of October he escaped to Asolo, about forty miles inland, where Mrs Stark, a cousin of the Wilkinsons and mother of the traveller Freya Stark, took charge of him. She was worried about her daughter, then in Arabia. She said she was glad of Robert's company, and she suggested that he and Vivienne should live in Freya's empty villa near Ventimiglia at a nominal rent. She would throw in a chaperone, a Mrs Reid, who would housekeep for Robert until Vivienne arrived.

There followed 'a terrible five weeks' at the Stark villa.[49] 'Robert was wretched, cold and uncomfortable with a horrible stove that smoked'.[50] But it gave him a base from which to look for somewhere better, and by the end of January 1938 he had found a charming house just outside Menton. He wrote to Phil: 'I feel it is just possible you may be annoyed by this letter', and asked for a loan of £2,700 with which to buy it. Phil naturally refused, pointing out that the political situation in Europe made the speculation particularly risky.

In February Robert found a house to rent for three months at Vence, and Vivienne came out to him. He nearly sent her home after three days because he felt depressed, but Mrs Reid prevented this.[51] They had three months of happiness,[52] in spite of the daunting proximity of Nancy Cunard and Norman Douglas.[53] But on 1 May he wrote that they had parted 'entirely due to the realization that we couldn't marry and have a baby on £600 a year'.[54] In fact this was Robert's unilateral decision, but Vivienne's mother was in Italy and wanted her company.

Robert remained in the vicinity of Vence, pining for Vivienne and searching for a permanent home. He could not write. In the winter of 1938–9 he found a house called Le Piol in St Paul de Vence, a place that had caught his eye when he went to D. H. Lawrence's funeral. An elderly invalid called Lady Jane Gathorne-Hardy who was living at Vence wrote on his behalf to his brother saying 'it might be really disastrous for him if it were snatched from him'. Phil approved the project and the money was obtained, after some delay, from the Nichols estate. Robert shifted his anxiety to doing it up.

Lady Jane was an important new friend. She set Robert up with a car, though he had still, it appears, not learnt to drive – his generation did not have to take a driving test. She also came to replace the Heads as his chief correspondent. After the summer of 1938, though Henry was not to die until 1940, Robert's weekly letters ceased. This was partly because of the advancing nature of Henry's disease, but partly because Ruth, the active correspondent, had since Norah left Robert become increasingly unsympathetic to his self-pitying outpourings. In February 1938, for example, she wrote: 'Yes, I began by feeling poor, poor Robert, wishing to console, but as I write on I end by longing to give you a good nursery shaking and say "For heaven's sake, Master Robert, get up and *do* something, don't sit there looking a proper little misery with tears dripping over your nose!"'[55]

On 2 June 1939 Bowyer Nichols died. Robert had been summoned a little earlier but arrived in time only for the funeral. The admiration and affection for his father which had appeared in his earlier letters had withered in the deterioration of his character after 1932, and in the last few years he had been wishing (in a way he knew to be shameful) for his father's death. He wrote to Lady Jane from Lawford: 'Down here he seems not only dead but his presence wholly evaporated. Only when Phil laid his two watches and the little jade cuff links he enjoyed wearing on the table did his presence – all that was most delicate, gentle (there was much that was gentle) and forlorn – seem near.'[56]

Robert expected to inherit £800-£1,000 a year, and was pleased to learn that he had been left £4,000 in addition to his third share of the estate. Lawford was to go into hotch-potch, but Phil and Phyllis intended to buy it in from the estate. A couple of weeks after the funeral Robert met Vivienne at Portmeirion and again proposed to her. He was accepted, her parents approved, and a wedding was scheduled for early July.[57]

Then he discovered that his computations had been too optimistic.

He had forgotten about income tax, and the £4,000 which was to pay off his debt to the estate for Le Piol (and reimburse Lady Jane for the car) was not immediately available. A July marriage was impossible. In justice to him it should be recognised that he was under pressure from his family. Sir George Gater summoned him to his presence and told him he should give up Vivienne and go back to Norah. Robert asked Lady Jane to write to Phil[58] and sent her a draft of what she ought to say, but Phil replied that Robert and Vivienne were 'unsuited'.[59] He too was in favour of Robert's being reunited with Norah – in which case, of course, the burden of subsidising him would revert to the Dennys. At the end of July Robert went back to St Paul without Vivienne.

The work on Le Piol was unfinished and Robert could not bear to be alone. Lady Jane took him in for fourteen weeks.[60] During this time war broke out.

Vivienne enlisted in the FANYs. Robert after Christmas moved to Le Piol where he had a housekeeper, Mme Prebin. Vivienne decided on a last throw: when she was due leave and before her exit permit expired she would go out to Robert and face the storm at his side. He told her not to. So did Phil, and Irene (who had seen Vivienne only once, at a large reception for the new King and Queen in 1937[61]) wrote to Lady Jane saying that Robert must not marry her with only £500: if he did 'he cannot expect to get any help from his family as we are *all* strongly opposed to the marriage.' Vivienne was undeterred. She and her friend Elizabeth Montagu (daughter of the second Lord Montagu of Beaulieu) went out to France in May 1940, and despite the worsening military situation she reached Nice. Robert met her with a white rose and black looks. He would not hear of her marrying him or even living at Le Piol with him unmarried. He lodged her for the night with Lady Jane and then put her on a train back to Paris. She departed resentfully and wrote from her Paris hotel:

> I may not have made it clear to you what was in my head that made me decide definitely to come out to you – even when you wrote and told me not to. I am absolutely *convinced* it is of no use whatever going on depending on material values. Things now, and after the war, will be down to the very brass tacks of living.[62]

She was lucky to get out of Paris before the Germans came in.

Back in England she urged Robert to leave Le Piol at once and escape if possible to America.[63] In fact he escaped to England. Although stationed in Cheshire she came down to London. He refused to see her.[64] She wrote to him: 'I think you are the most unkind person I have ever met. *No one* has any money or any future but at least the people who love each other stick together – but you can't because you just haven't got the guts. Well, it means nothing to me now either, because I can neither love nor respect you any more.'[65]

19

The Second World War

After sending Vivienne back to Paris Robert remained in St Paul de Vence for a month. That was partly to stay with his house. Expecting the Second World War to be a replica of the First, he imagined that the German advance would be halted more or less at the line of the Western Front, and that hostilities would not get to the Côte d'Azur. But he had also given himself the duty of looking after Lady Jane Gathorne-Hardy and helping her out of France should that be necessary.

By 18 June 1940 France had capitulated and the Germans and Italians were swooping down like raptors on the plump English residents of the Riviera. The only way of escape was by sea, and the only transport from Cannes was two aged coal ships. Robert and Lady Jane embarked with 681 other refugees on the SS *Ashcrest*. There were no beds, very little food and only two lavatories. The refugees hoped to obtain more food at Marseilles, but since there was no British representative left there they were not allowed to land. Initially they had the benefit of a convoy, but a pump failed, their speed dropped to 4 knots, and they were left behind. They put in for repairs at Port Vendres near the Spanish border. After a few hours' work they proceeded towards Gibraltar but in the night the *Ashcrest* was attacked by an Italian submarine. Captain Anderson, the commander of the ship, laid down a smokescreen and ordered a sharply zigzag course. Two torpedoes and three shells were fired at them but missed. They gave the submarine the slip and reached Gibraltar intact. From there most of the passengers including Robert and Lady Jane were transferred to another coal ship and reached Liverpool nine days later. Robert thought Captain Anderson ought to be decorated and sent an account of the voyage to Mrs Churchill. Captain Anderson did in fact receive a commendation.[1] As for Lady Jane, she said of Robert's staying with her and maintaining morale on the ship: 'I can't begin to tell you what I think of you. I hope your brother will realise what your work on the collier was.'[2]

From Liverpool Robert took a train to London and was met at Euston by Norah. She took him to Phil's house in Chester Square. But the brothers grated on each other and a few days later Vivienne's friend

Paula Tennant found him lodgings in Clarges Street. A long and painful quarrel came to an end when he met Osbert Sitwell and they shook hands.[3] But he felt unhappy and ill.[4] Although his brain teemed with inventive schemes to help the British war effort – the Nichols Waterspider (a flying-boat bristling with cannons),[5] a new kind of searchlight, standby pipes for pumping oil into the sea that could be set alight to repel invaders[6] – his resolve not to see Vivienne made him miserable, and although Norah was at hand to minister to him, she could not allay fears that he had an ulcer or even cancer. A fortnight at the West London Hospital in Hampstead failed to disclose anything seriously amiss but London was not suiting him. Mrs Boulton carried him down to Porlock on the north Somerset coast and lodged him first in a hotel and later at private houses.

There he stayed throughout the winter, writing and hoping eventually to get work with the Government or with the BBC. He was spared the main heat of the Battle of Britain, but trained as a machine-gunner for the Home Guard[7] and later recalled with satisfaction 'the sight of an enemy machine pursued at the height of a hundred or so feet by a demonic Spitfire which shot it down into the offshore shallows, both machines travelling above the idyllic scene at some three hundred miles an hour.'[8] He was also pleased by a radio report which suggested that his oil-pumping idea had been used, and wondered if he might get a reward. '£60,000 would not be too little' he mused optimistically.[9]

In August Lady Gater had written to Lady Jane Gathorne-Hardy 'I think the "little creature" has at last shifted from his affections.'[10] From their first acquaintance in 1934 Robert had used 'the little creature' to refer to Vivienne as an expression of endearment, and his brother and sisters adopted it as an expression of scorn. But Lady Gater was wrong if she thought that Robert was not seeing Vivienne because he had ceased to love her. Letters that autumn[11] show him pining for her, and throughout the winter of 1940–1 he was immersed in a work he intended to be his memorial to her, *Solitudes of the Sun*.

He gave this the subtitle *The Poems of Prince Axel*, and it was to contain that alter ego's reminiscences and conversation on a variety of topics literary, moral and political – one short piece was on 'His Dislike of Germans'. Axel has a sweetheart who is Vivienne renamed Yvette but otherwise unchanged, and his reminiscences are a kind of autobiography of what Robert took for the Dr Jekyll in himself. This prose component, of which 100 pages of typescript are extant, would probably have gone into what Robert calls an 'excursive introduction'.[12]

The body of the book was to consist of his mature work as a lyric poet, divided into several sections. *A Spanish Triptych*, described above, would have formed one of them. Two sections, entitled *Consolations* and *Leaves from a Notebook of a Prince in Disguise* were to contain fairly short lyrics. Four poems destined for these sections were published in *Such Was My Singing* and Robert intended to include also the seven line 'Sunvassal's Evensong', 'The Palmer' (published in *Time and Tide*[13]), 'Night Song for a Solitary', composed in 1935 off Tenerife, and a short, untitled piece that begins 'Everything seems softly sighing'. All but one of these works were composed after he met Vivienne. Another section was to be taken up by a long narrative of a visit to the Island of Flowers, 'an imaginary island but founded on the landscape of the Grand Canaries.' It would be 'essentially *comédie* in character', and 'the verse should be characterised by an unusually high degree of the *sans gêne* of manner that I now seek'; but the mountain would symbolise 'eternal verities etc.', and the city 'everyday life'. The fragments of this run to about 200 lines. And a further section would consist of two long 'idylls of happiness'[14] recalling good times with Vivienne/Yvette. It was with these that Robert was chiefly occupied in the winter of 1940–1.

'Marseilles Elegy' describes in veracious detail their meeting at Marseilles in 1934. It starts:

> She had written: 'Why ask me whether
> I'd come? – how very peculiar!
> Of course I'll come, should you really need me,
> Whenever you wish, wherever you are.
> First make quite sure. Then send your wire.'

Robert sent his wire and next day had her answer: 'Arriving tomorrow. Meet five thirty.' He continues:

> I took two rooms in an inn by the harbour
> And turned hers into a blossoming arbour –
> She should have a feast of flowers.
> It was June. I kept going back for more –

and ended with laying a gardenia on her pillow. He describes his impatient waiting for the train and its arrival:

> With soaring sunbeams, with sinking sunbeams,
> With trumpets, with triumph, with rolling gold,

With whirlpools of cloud among the girders,
With whirlpools of cloud along the floor ...

and

> there she stood at a sun-dappled door –
> A Robin Hood hat with a pheasant feather;
> Silvery tweeds, a crocus glove,
> A pair of huge eyes under the hat,
> Eyes full of beseechment, fatigue and love.

She had had, she tells him, some misgivings on the train:

> the sing-song train kept rocking,
> Always knocking the same mocking
> Sing-song deeper into my brain:
> *Clitter-clatter you mad-hatter*
> *What are you doing? Why d'you do it?*
> *You will rue it; you will rue it –*
> *You are going to your ruin.*
> *Ruin. Ruin.*

Nevertheless when they reached the hotel she took the initiative:

> 'You've taken two rooms haven't you? Why?
> Have I come all the way from Florence
> To lie as chaste as that gardenia?'

Robert describes with a vividness to which excerpts hardly do justice
her exuberant chatter as they go about Marseilles:

> 'Lord what a bluster! Hold my hat.
> Only the Mistral? Only! ... what? ...
> Kiss me, darling, again, again...
> Or am I looking too frightfully plain?
> I don't? Hurrah! I adore Marseilles.
> Where are we off to? The Inner Harbour?
> Shall I be able to see the sails?
> Is this the Canebière we're in? ...
> What's in that jar? What's in those bales?
> Pickled pirate? Puppy-dog's tails?
> Which does one eat here – frogs or snails?
> Where shall we dine? Am I invited?'

This gaiety contrasts with the softer character of her words in the bedroom:

> 'It's you, it's you! It's I, it's I!
> Kiss me; let me kiss you! ...
> Is my hair soft? D'you like my mouth?
> How do girls kiss here in the south?
> Darling ... darling! But why so few?
> Softly. Softly. I know; I know.
> No, don't cry, for if you do,
> I shall cry, I know I shall.'

Robert avoids the mistake of giving the physical particulars of their encounter, but lets the heroine's voice speak to the reader's imagination.

The poem is unfinished but it runs to more than 500 lines and has an ending of a sort: in the morning sunshine the lovers regard each other with a tacit understanding in which happiness and sorrow and consciousness of parting are mixed. Robert conceived the poem as an 'idyll of happiness' but he entitles it an 'elegy', that is, a song of mourning, and the heroine's fears on the train were in reality all too prophetic.

The second poem, 'Together', is much less advanced. It was based on Vivienne's stay with Robert at the rented villa in Vence in the spring of 1938. Robert intended it to describe 'the general position of the villa,' the rising of a pair of lovers and their taking a day-trip into the country, their return and evening on the villa's terrace. 'The poem is to be steeped in nature: the most Delius-like of all my compositions. Nature undying. Surface beauty – light, clouds, breeze – all that – and underneath two continual presences: the mountains and the sea.'[15] Although 170 lines are extant they contain only some of Vivienne's fanciful vivacity and some descriptive passages for the opening scene. 'Note new style,' he said to Marsh, 'characterised by very free handling of rhythm and lavish use of assonance, interior rhymes etc. (I 'rock' in them, use them as pivots, cannon off their echoes etc.)'[16] This style is in fact already visible in 'The Virgin of Joy' in *A Spanish Triptych*.

Vivienne that winter was stationed in the north of Scotland. According to her Recollections[17] she despaired of Robert because he never wrote, and became engaged to someone called Angus Maclean, a 'splendid young doctor who looked like a Greek God'. The news of this reached Robert from Mrs Boulton on 21 March[18] and had an electric effect. Frantic with loss and despair he hastened up to London and on to Hove where Mrs Boulton was living and planted himself on her as a paying guest.

The BBC now gave him some work, but he developed a gastric ulcer which required treatment in London in June.[19] From there he went to Lawford for the summer. On 19 July he heard from Vivienne that her engagement was off. The godlike Angus was 'far too unreliable and unsettled in his way of life', something that Semele and others probably complained of in Zeus. Robert immediately proposed marriage himself and suggested that in any case she should come and live with him at Lawford. Unfortunately Phil had an ulcer too. Although Phyllis might have endured this addition to the household, he certainly could not, and Vivienne was forbidden even to visit.[20] Robert himself was expelled, with an allowance of £100-150 a year, in September. For a couple of weeks he lodged in Ladbroke Gardens, London, with Mrs Reid, the lady who had chaperoned him and Vivienne in 1938. She was too busy, however, to cook for him, and had a cat whose mouldering food made him queasy. His doctor said he was suffering from starvation. He was also cold, the windows never being shut because of the smell from the cat-food.[21] Unable to bear these discomforts (or, perhaps, the stress of London life), he went to Cambridge and found a couple of rooms in 12 Newnham Terrace. They left something to be desired in the way of beauty,[22] and Robert's books and other cherished belongings were in German-occupied France, but his landlady provided board and these two rooms served as his home for the rest of his life.

During the later months of 1941 Robert was working on his last major publication, *Such Was My Singing*. In May Mrs Boulton's friend Herbert van Thal had offered to look for a publisher for a collection of Robert's poems. He found one in Collins and in spite of wartime austerity they brought out an attractive volume in June 1942. The first third consists of selections from *Invocation*, *Ardours* and *Aurelia*. Robert kept only four of the war poems in *Ardours* for which he was best known; he preserved more from *A Faun's Holiday* and much more from *Aurelia*. The rest of the book, apart from some pieces chosen from *Fisbo*, consists of poems now appearing for the first time, or for the first time, at least, in book form. There is a *Wreath of Iron* section and a section of fragments from *Don Juan* and from the projected *Solitudes of the Sun*.

The reviewers seem to have been rather surprised at this evidence that Robert was still alive and composing poetry, and some of them had so far forgotten his idiosyncrasies as to say it has a long introduction.[23]

It is nothing to the prefaces to *Guilty Souls* and *Fantastica*, running to a mere twenty-five pages. Half of these, since he felt at a distance from poets like Eliot and Auden, Robert devoted to defending his aims. The first was comprehensibility: a poem's general drift should become apparent at the first reading. In the interests of this and of 'energy of expression' he avoided allusiveness and reliance on familiarity in his readers with an extensive range of ancient and foreign literature. On the other hand he did not agree with those who would banish classical allusions altogether and treat ignorance as 'a virtue to be cherished'. Though not a scholar he was widely read, and always wished to write in the tradition of European civilisation. These principles explain features of the poems in *Such Was My Singing* which may have displeased some critics: his retention of rhyme, his choice of traditional subjects, his talk of Eros and Olympus. Finally 'I have aimed at variety.' He believed that a poet who can work in two genres is by that very fact superior to a poet who can work only in one; though he admits that he has heard this disputed, and 'it is an uncommon long while since I noted variety accounted a virtue at all.'

Such Was My Singing was the last book Robert saw published that was all his own work; but the following year Nicholson and Watson brought out an *Anthology of War Poetry, 1914–1918*, chosen by him. He must have started putting this together immediately the 1939 War broke out; it had been accepted by December 1939, though many months of negotiation over permissions and fees lay ahead, and the Preface is dated January 1940. If Robert stinted himself over the Preface to *Such Was My Singing*, here he gave himself a holiday. There are 82 pages of Preface to 51 of poetry. Although G. W. Stonier, reviewing in the *New Statesman*, said 'the proportions seem wrong'[24] Desmond MacCarthy declared that the Preface 'is in itself the best piece of prose Mr Robert Nichols has written, and extremely interesting'.[25] The appearance of disproportion arises because the book came out three years too late; it was finished, and Robert intended it to be published, early in 1940, when the Preface would have been very much to the point.

It takes the form of a dialogue between Robert and his friend Julian ('Dooley') Tennyson who in 1939 is twenty-four and has just been called up. Robert tries to explain to Julian's generation the spirit that animated poets like Rupert Brooke and Charles Sorley in 1914, and how the mood and attitude of poets changed as the war progressed. But interwoven with this piece of literary history (extensively drawn upon in chapters 4 and 5 above) is a pamphlet addressed to the Allied war leaders at the beginning of the new war. Robert acknowledges the influence of Alfred de Vigny whose *Grandeurs et Servitudes Militaires* brightened his first days in Japan.[26] But what he says seems perfectly topical today.

'Battles', he declares (p. 46), 'are won by the collapse of enemy morale' and by nothing else. It follows that psychological factors are of paramount importance in warfare. But the General Staff commenced the 1914–18 War 'in a state of palaeolithic innocence as to the importance' of such factors. 'There existed excellent psychiatrists who would have made thoroughly practical recommendations just as there were intelligent junior officers, both medical and other, with trench experience who could have provided from personal observation supplementary and illuminating data as to the sort of conditions and events which make such advice necessary.' But 'not till the last months of the war was Authority persuaded to consult those who could most enlighten it' (pp. 45–6).

Under the pretext of saying how poets might lose faith in their cause, he offers quite general analyses of the two kinds of fatigue, physical tiredness and exhaustion generated by psychical stress, to which junior officers are exposed (pp. 76–8). He also analyses the psychological effects of two kinds of mechanisation (pp. 79–83). One is the development of weapons of mass destruction. He is thinking of conventional machine-guns, shells and bombs, not of nuclear devices, but his point is that even these have an effect on those who use them quite different from the effect of wielding the weapons of chivalry and primitive warfare, the bow, the spear and the sword. The other is the social or institutional mechanisation, in which the unit is no longer the individual warrior or group of comrades, but the division, the army, the army group; 'And each division, employing several thousand men, is in part a mass-production plant engaged in converting fragmentary material, a horde of tiny bipeds, into entities which later prove to be anonymous strangers unable to get up and who have begun to putrefy where they sprawl.' (p. 81) Military leaders in the 1939–45 War did learn to employ expert advisers for keeping up the morale of their own side and damaging that of their opponents; but Robert's remarks have wider implications which neither that nor any succeeding generation has been prepared to take on board.

Dooley Tennyson read the Preface for the first time in October 1943 when he was serving 'in the middle of the foulest jungle in India'. He wrote: 'I have enjoyed it immensely, Robert. The thoughts contained in it are admirable and the writing excellent. The speeches to which I subscribe are from my point of view unexceptionable, and I disagree with hardly anything that I say myself nor that you say, for that matter. You have put "my" ideas into your own words, but the ideas are very largely mine.'[27]

Sir Charles Tennyson, Dooley's father, says in his book *Life's All a Fragment* (pp. 25–6) that when the news reached Dooley of Robert's death in 1944:

He felt it deeply, for their friendship had been a source of great pleasure and encouragement to him. He did not know that one of Robert's last acts had been to write to Lord Wavell, asking him to see if some work of a literary kind at Headquarters could be found for Julian, whose talents, he felt sure, were being wasted in the merciless routine of the Burma front. Lord Wavell made enquiries about Julian, and was told that he was an exceedingly good regimental officer doing very well with his Battalion. He then wrote to the D. P. R. on the Commander-in-Chief's staff, putting forward Robert's suggestion. The D. P. R. happened to be away and the letter lay unopened in his office for some weeks. Before action could be taken on it Julian had been killed.

Robert's contributions to the Allied war effort were by no means exhausted by this Preface to his *Anthology* and by the devices mentioned earlier. He was intensely interested in propaganda. By 14 September 1939 he had prepared a long memorandum of proposals on the subject. In July and December 1940 he was pressing the Ministry of Information for broadcasts to France. He also sent the Ministry a memorandum on dropping pamphlets by air over Germany.[28] In February 1941 he sent the BBC a short radio play about the murder of Matteotti in 1924. It was entitled 'Two Who Cannot Sleep', the two being Mussolini who ordered the murder and Dumini the hitman who carried it out. Val Gielgud rejected this, but invited Robert to a meeting which resulted in a series of literary talks he gave that spring.[29] He heard from two men working for the BBC European service that they could be more effective in enemy-misdirection if they had more coordination with RAF Operations and in August 1941 arranged for them to meet Air Marshal Sir Wilfrid Freeman.

In January 1942 he drew on his experiences of 1921–4 to give a broadcast on Japanese psychology in which he warned his hearers both of the bravery of Japanese soldiers and of the difference, much greater than was then generally appreciated, between the ethical codes of Japan and Christian Europe. He also contributed detailed notes on Japanese psychology to a government pamphlet for internal circulation,[30] and wrote an article for the *Star* on Japanese atrocities.[31]

Later in 1942 he submitted to the Ministry of Information the scenario for a film that would reveal to English and American audiences the character and extent of Nazi educational propaganda. The Ministry turned it down on the slightly odd grounds that 'it would over-tax the resources even of the largest Hollywood producers' – it would have been quite an inexpensive and simple film to make – and that it might arouse sympathetic feelings for the Germans who were victims of the Nazi system: 'It is perhaps best to avoid stories about Germans except those in which they appear quite straightforwardly as "the enemy".'[32]

Robert had an odd response also when he advised the Ministry to consider how they would accommodate their allies' policy of racial segregation when American troops arrived in Britain. 'My own impression', said Mr J. S. Lowe, 'is that if you told English girls tactfully that it was unwise for them to walk out with black troops they would by no means take it amiss, but I dare say it would be far simpler if black American troops were detailed for work in countries like Egypt.'[33]

But the cause closest to Robert's heart was wired wireless. Conventional wireless, as the word implies, transmits messages without wires, by propagating radio waves. But as early as in 1932–3 Robert's friend Peter Eckersley, a cousin of the Huxleys, was demonstrating the possibility of broadcasting through wires. Various methods were possible, either relaying broadcasts through wires set up for the purpose or using telephone wires or the conventional electrical grid. The modern internet is an example of the kind of thing envisaged. Robert had the benefit of Eckersley's technical advice, and support from, among other people, H. G. Wells and Julian Huxley.

On 23 October 1939 Robert sent a memorandum through Phil to the Ministry of Information on the merits of relay broadcasting. In further memoranda in 1941 and in an article in *Time and Tide* that October[34] he urged the value of wired wireless for educating Europe to democracy when the war should be over and reconstruction replace victory as the main task. In January 1943 he asked Phil to approach R. A. Butler. Phil being unable to do so, he wrote to Sir George Gater, then at the Colonial Office, arguing that education would be needed to hold together the

Empire and the Colonies (the future Commonwealth), and that wired wireless would be a perfect instrument not only for dispelling ignorance and indifference in Britain, but for 'bringing whole communities into familiar touch'.[35] *The Wireless World* opposed wired broadcasting in its issue of September 1943, and Robert replied in November with a memorandum to Lord Woolton, newly appointed Minister of Reconstruction, and also wrote to Mrs Churchill asking her to enlist her husband's support.[36] Mrs Churchill found it 'not possible to lay your memorandum before Winston'[37] – they were both then out of the country – but Robert continued to plead his case throughout 1944. In February he sent updated memoranda to Sir Henry Tizard, and in September he was receiving some help from Walter Elliot, MP, whose wife, later Lady Elliot of Harwood, was a Tennant and a friend of long standing.

Robert emphasises in his memoranda that he has no financial interest in wired wireless and in fact, apart from his broadcast on Japanese psychology, he received no reward at all for these patriotic activities. But he needed paid work, especially if he was to redeem his promise of marriage to Vivienne, though as time went on it became harder to believe that that would ever happen. When he thought Vivienne unattainable he was clear that he wanted to marry her under any conditions; when she was attainable the conditions always seemed wrong. Mrs Boulton said he had two personalities, one generous and loving, the other timid, indecisive and calculating,[38] and that as soon as Vivienne broke off from Angus Maclean the second started to predominate.[39] Certainly he had time for reflection while Vivienne was being boarded out of the FANYs on medical grounds. His computations then showed that he had only £300 a year, which even Mrs Boulton agreed was too narrow a basis for marriage,[40] and Vivienne, once released, took a job with the American Red Cross in Basingstoke. But in August 1941 Robert was perceptibly seeking full-time employment.

Besides urging the Ministry of Information to take up wired wireless, he asked for a job for himself. Harold Nicolson replied 'I do not think you would be good in an office chair. You would become impatient at civil service caution.'[41] Philip Nichols had a further try with Nicolson on Robert's behalf in October, but Nicolson remained smoothly unhelpful: 'There are very few administrative chairs vacant,' he said, and 'Poets very seldom make good civil servants.'[42] What about the BBC, in which his word was all-powerful? 'The BBC, as you probably know, do not like roving commissions.' Likewise 'The National Theatre, I fear, is far beyond me.'[43]

The possibility of a National Theatre had been mentioned when Robert met Val Gielgud in March. Robert was extremely enthusiastic. He wanted the Government to set up a National Theatre Nucleus right away under the directorship of Harley Granville Barker, with intention of building an actual, bricks and mortar theatre after the war as part of Reconstruction.[44] But he received a douche of cold water from Val Gielgud's brother John in March 1942:

Dear Nichols,

I'm afraid I think that your schemes are madness, and I will have no part in them. You can have no conception of the appalling difficulties under which the stage is labouring, and they get worse each month ... Barker is ill with eczema, I hear, and has given up his work at the University in America – less than ever would his wife allow him to come back... For heaven's sake leave Keynes and his money and goodwill till the end of the War, when the theatre might well be glad of them and some kind of representative body of the best people working in the theatre could be got together – we are now without producers, playwrights, actors and technicians, and only holding on by a thread. There are not more than a dozen first rate players left – each of these is keeping some 100 people in work and entertaining thousands. Try and collect them in one place and you would make them all dissatisfied and deprive the public of such few plays as they are getting and are eager for.[45]

The BBC was a more practical proposition, and though Harold Nicolson was not prepared to support Robert, he had less Olympian friends within the Corporation such as Stephen Potter, Val Gielgud and Andrew Stewart. He was interviewed for a full-time post on 11 February 1942, and decided to ask for a salary of £600 a year. The interview went badly and on the 13th he heard that the Appointment Board 'has decided, with reluctance, that we are unable to offer you an appointment on our staff. This decision has been made chiefly in recognition of the fact that the strenuous nature of our work would make too exacting a demand on your health.'[46]

Presumably the BBC was scared of Robert's reputation, and his manner at the interview failed to reassure them. Nevertheless they expressed a hope that they might keep him as an occasional contributor[47] and Robert did in fact make contributions over the next three years. He appeared on the Brains Trust at least three times (March

1942, June and November 1944). He selected and introduced Elizabethan poems in the 'What the Poet Sees' series.[48] During the summer
of 1942 he composed a long appreciation in dialogue form of Arnold
Bennett. This was not what the BBC had asked for, but Stephen Potter
got a version broadcast in September. And the same month the BBC put
on a short light-hearted play, *Portrait of a Smiling Woman*, which is
credited to him jointly with his agent Milton Waldman but all the material is recognisable as his. The setting is the island of Madeira, taken
from his 1935 trip. Living on it is the smiling woman, in appearance
and character resembling Vivienne. A cruise ship puts in and from it a
man comes ashore, less attractive in appearance than Robert but
unmistakably he. We learn that he is her former husband, and that he
lived with her in a town like Winchelsea until he caught her in a careless
infidelity and threw her out. Now, two years later, her smiling noncha-
lance makes him want her back; but she will not come.

In 1944 he found a new opening. He had always been interested in
music. It was a bond between him and all the women he loved, from
Daisy Kennedy onwards; many composers, conductors and performers
were his close friends, and he had written about music in the *Japan
Advertiser* in the 1920s. In 1944 he gave three long broadcasts, one on
meaning in music, one on Delius and one on music and poetry.[49] Delius
had been a particularly honoured friend, and the Delius broadcast
contains some personal recollections which preserve Robert's feeling
for him:

> It was very still out there on the stream in the summer twilight – so
> still that I could just hear the tiny sounds made by Delius, blind
> and paralysed, half singing, half sighing some fragment of his
> music to himself. He was lying back, a crumpled figure under a
> rug, in a special chair in the middle of the little boat. Weighed
> down by Delius, Mrs Delius, my wife, myself and the houseboy,
> the boat was stealing, as if asleep, down the bosom of the little
> French river. Overhead the leaves of the lofty alders idled softly
> together. Now and then a single leaf flashed or some sigh, coming
> one knew not whence and travelling one knew not whither, set a
> thousand leaves shivering ... and then a leaf would dilly-dally
> silently down. One such alit on the rug beside Delius' nerveless
> hands – a leaf so green it was like a flake of emerald in which a
> sunstar lay imprisoned. Delius did not see it. It seemed hard that
> he – he who had loved nature with a more exquisite passion than

any man I have ever known – he, the poet of human love and separation, for whom the presence of nature had been the supreme
consolation – it did seem hard that he could not see that leaf. Yet
my solicitude wronged his serenity. The sound that issued from his
throat didn't, so far as I could catch it, seem unhappy, and his face
was as calm as the golden light which illumined his stern and
wasted features.

I recalled his face as it had been when I first knew him – the face
of a distinguished technician, severe but debonair. I contrasted my
memory of that face with the face I saw before me now. That face
had been handsome; this was beautiful. Two qualities were
common to both; extreme sensibility and a signal serenity.

These broadcasts brought Robert something, but not a livelihood. In
July 1942 Kenneth Clark asked him to write the introduction to an
illustrated Penguin book on William Nicholson.[50] The task was congenial – Nicholson was an old friend and Robert had a collection of his
woodcuts – but the fee was only £50. In December 1942 he had an
offer from the British Council which might have put an end to his financial anxieties. 'The Foreign Office', he was told, 'have recently informed
the Council that a Professor of English is urgently required for the
newly instituted Farouk University in Alexandria.' Might they put his
name forward as a candidate?[51] Robert declined. His reasons are not
hard to surmise. He had hated being a professor in Japan; Vivienne had
by now arrived in Cambridge; and since September, at least,[52] he had
some kind of job with the RAF. His papers do not contain details of the
engagement, but it was to do with public relations and involved spending time on RAF stations and flying in various kinds of aircraft, with
the hope that he might write a book about the Pathfinders and perhaps
some fresh war poetry. Robert was a little distressed that he could
produce nothing that satisfied him.[53] But Vivienne said: 'I'm pleased
and desperately proud that at last you have something really worthwhile to do.'[54]

20

The Bell Sounds down in Dedham Vale

Robert's personal life after he had settled himself in Cambridge at the end of 1941 was rather desolate. His mother died on 2 March 1942. He wrote to Mrs Boulton about this, and she replied 'I am sorry to think what a distressing and indeed heart-tearing time you must have had; the picture of your mother forgotten and buried years and years in her madness, and much more painful moments of sanity, is a fascinating and terrible one.'[1] Fascinating and terrible indeed, as she was not visited by any of her children for the last two decades of her life. Her daughter-in-law Phyllis Nichols insisted on a meeting, but it came about only the day before she died.

Vivienne was working for most of the year either in Basingstoke or in London, and she and Robert were officially supposed to be attempting life apart. Mrs Boulton and her partner Peter Eckersley (soon to be forsaken for Sir Francis Rose), who had formerly been advocates for marriage, were now against it. Vivienne was too 'featherbrained' said Mrs Boulton,[2] and when Vivienne got into financial difficulties she told Robert not to help her.[3] Robert nevertheless sent her a cheque. That was the end of the separation. In December Eckersley told Robert, then at RAF Officers' Mess, Oakington, to sit down, write to Vivienne and say 'No'.[4] Robert's version of what actually happened is set down at some length in his journal for 1 August 1943. In November 1942 she appealed to him and he sent her some money. He did not want her to come to Cambridge but not only did she arrive, she wanted to live under the same roof at 12 Newnham Terrace. He found her a room elsewhere, and though supplying small subsidies, tried to keep her at arm's length. But this policy broke down on three occasions. Vivienne's Recollections have a different emphasis. The American Red Cross sent her to Cambridge to 'organise the offices for the Regional Commissioner' (p. 60). She saw hardly anything of Robert, both being hard at work. But at a Polish Exhibition at the Senate House she met an interesting officer called Zalesky who had been Paderewski's private secretary, and he recruited her into the Polish Ministry of Information, which was based in Cambridge. Vivienne and Robert agree that this caused Robert intense jealousy. Zalesky's office was visible from Robert's window. Vivienne was maintaining a centre of communication for Poles throughout Britain, and the sight of her bicycle outside at all hours tormented him. 'It does not even occur to her', he says in his journal (p. 104) 'to spare me by leaving her bicycle and walking the less than half mile that separates him from her.'

Jealousy was probably the main force that led him to open communications in July with a lady called Primrose who had recently separated from her partner and who was the only person he had met since Vivienne entered his life that he could consider marrying. He set up a meeting with her in London for September when he was to do his broadcast on Elizabethan poetry, auspiciously entitled 'Lovers' Meetings', and for two or three days he was happy. But this soap opera affair was over before it had begun. 'A nightmare weekend in London,' he told his journal (pp. 124–5). He saw Prim, but 'it was all too evident I meaned [sic]* nothing to her.'

A more dignified project which engaged Robert at about this time was the preservation of works of art in southern and central Italy, at risk from the advance of the Allied forces and the attendant fighting. Robert wrote to *The Times* urging that the staff of AMGOT (the body officially charged with this matter) should be 'reinforced by experts – for not only knowledge of the whereabouts of such masterpieces but of the technique of preservation is required – who shall assist whatever Italian public servants, charged with the care of such works, remain.'[5] This cause had the pleasant effect of bringing him into alliance with D. S. McColl, an Oxford friend of his father now aged eighty-four. McColl wrote to *The Times* supporting Robert, and his letter elicited an approach from Squadron Leader J. E. Dixon-Spain, an architect then serving as Air Liaison Officer on the Commander-in-Chief's staff at Portsmouth. They had questions asked in the House of Commons by E. H. Keeling and Sir Percy Harris. The point was that while troops were being warned off major classical remains and cathedrals, humble buildings and works of art in smaller towns and villages were in danger of being damaged irreparably by the general disruption of war.

Robert's chief desire during his time in Cambridge was to finish his play *Don Juan*. He counted on it to ensure an unassailable reputation; and it would also prove that he had been right to put poetry before everything else in his life. When one considers the number of years, and

*Robert always insisted on this spelling.

the amount of time within those years, which he devoted to this one work, it is tempting to say that Don Juan was his evil genius. He admitted to starting it in February 1926,[6] but there is evidence that the project had been in his mind five or six years before that.[7]

'The play', wrote Robert in *Such Was My Singing*, 'is on a large scale and panoramic in design, resembling in this [Eugene] O'Neill's *Strange Interlude*, albeit its action, being in the romantic tradition, is more varied, picturesque and violent. As in the case of O'Neill's play a dinner interval is postulated.'[8] *Strange Interlude* is a trifle compared to Don Juan, the true models for which are Ibsen's *Peer Gynt*[9] and Goethe's *Faust*. In 1944 Robert deposited with his bankers 225 pages of double-spaced typescript, but this is only half of what the completed work would have been. Mozart's *Don Giovanni*, he noted, is defined as 'a *dramma giocoso*, that is to say, a comic opera'[10] and he calls his play 'a tragi-comedy'. It is in poetry throughout and enriched with scenes of Hogarthian turbulence and spectacular borrowings from the Italian *commedia dell' arte*.

Like *Faust*, *Don Juan* was to have a prologue in Heaven.[11] The terrestrial action is set in a territory ruled by a duke, but otherwise undefined as regards epoch and geographical location. In the opening scenes Don Juan flirts with girls in a public garden and so humiliates a young poet that he goes off and commits suicide. Act II takes place in the graveyard where he is being buried. Maurice Barrès, in an essay which Robert had translated for the *Japan Advertiser*,[12] identifies the Don with a seventeenth-century debauchee, Don Miguel Manara Vicentello de Leca, who underwent a conversion and joined (or perhaps founded) a religious order for laymen, the Caridad, that buried executed criminals and suicides. Robert brings the Caridad to the graveside and gives the Don extended conversations about the meaning of life with the Prior, who represents ascetic Christianity, and various other 'emblematic figures': a gigantic gravedigger, a dwarf, 'old Mo', a character who doubles the roles of Mr Punch and the Judaeo-Christian God, and Narcissus Misanthropos, an Oxford philosopher now dead but supposed to be interred at the speakers' feet. He must have turned in his grave when Don Juan proclaims it as the sum of his own philosophy

> To conjugate the verb 'to be'
> In the mood joyful and the present tense. (p. 100)

And when Old Mo explains that Hell is

When being feels again the thirst to be
And cannot find the wherewithal to slake it.

The real Oxford philosopher J. L. Austin made fun of those who conceive being or existing as an activity 'like breathing, only quieter'. Robert evidently imagined it as like breathing, only noisier.

In the next act the Duke is giving a masked ball, and Don Juan attends incognito. Seven years previously he had been in love with a lady now married to the Duke, and had been exiled for his lawless behaviour. He now plans at one stroke to wreak vengeance and to satisfy his amorous passion by possessing himself of the Duchess. But a party of aggrieved husbands, fathers and brothers are conspiring to murder him. The Duke has engaged a troop of *commedia dell' arte* actors and the conspirators hope to mingle with them undetected. Their plots are overheard, they are nabbed by ducal halberdiers, the Duke greets Don Juan magnanimously, and the act ends with the Don's standing between the ducal couple in a triumphant reconciliation.

The finished typescript stops here. In 1932 Robert told the Heads: 'Then there is Act IV which will be *fearfully* difficult, and after that – what a job – the Desolation Scene, the Revelry Scene, and the Last Scene of All.'[13] The 'fearfully difficult' act is set a few months later and was to show Don Juan trying to seduce the Duchess. The final act takes place after a lapse of years and the Duke's death. In the Desolation Scene Don Juan, discovered in a desolate place by moonlight, is offered a chance of happiness with the Duchess if he submits to the Church, a condition which of course he refuses. The notes on the Revelry Scene make it sound Hogarthian. There are to be three harlots (who had appeared as flighty girls in Act I), the gigantic grave-digger of Act II is transformed into a Leper King, and Don Juan fights a duel. In the Last Scene he was probably to have gone mad and killed himself, though not without addressing some fine lines to his god the Sun. And there might well have been an epilogue outside the gates of Heaven along the lines sketched in 1930: the dwarf Lobito pleads that 'though the Don has thrown his life away he was at least trying to give humanity an example... An example of what? Of an attempt at joy.' Then a 'Chorus of Heavenly Powers is heard again... They inform man that they exist but they only exist for those who are willing to make a movement of the will toward them .... In time the spirit of every one of us may become a Heavenly Power ... *Explicit credo Roberti Nicholsi*.'[14]

In 1935 Robert sent Eddie Marsh Acts I and II, and Marsh wrote back: 'It is certainly a most remarkable and individual work which no one else could have written.'[15] That is an understatement. The ambitiousness of the plot is breathtaking and both the level and the variety of the extant poetry are extremely impressive. Robert's facility for imitating Shakespeare is unimpaired, and he provides a varied feast of pastiche, ranging from blistering curses to clowns' songs like the samples included in *Such Was My Singing*. He even adds German drinking songs. Don Juan's 'Song to His Rabble' begins:

> Who in this world-bordello
>   Fancies his pot and punk, sir,
> Come let him roar beside his whore
> And be, as we are, drunk, sir![16]

He had proved himself a master of the heroic couplet in *Fisbo* and he plunges boldly into rhyming couplets from the start. Act I Scene 1 opens with a characteristic conversation in the public gardens:

> VIOLET [fourteen] What swarms of moths!
> GRANDFATHER   Mayfly, they call these things.
> VIOLET The white ones, Grandpapa?
> GRANDFATHER   Yes.
> VIOLET   Have they stings?
> GRANDFATHER No, sweet. The mayfly never hurts a soul.
>   It dances, loves and dies. – That is the whole
>   Of its existence.
> VIOLET   Lucky, lucky fly.
>   Tonight I feel like one – gay warm and shy
>   And utterly happy and I can't think why.

As the play continues, Robert varies the rhyming scheme, but hardly ever withdraws into completely blank verse. These lines, from Act I Scene 2, show the energy with which he uses the medium:

> DON [to Prior of the San Caridad]: Why, beyond limbo, where
>   your Twaddle chatters
> To Clap and Trap, those fratricidal brothers,
> Where the Giant Gooseberry prophesies disaster
> To Snarks and Boojums, March Hares and Mad Hatters,
> Where Nightmares nest on the Sea-serpent's knee
> And he who is not his imagination's master
> Becomes the helpless bondslave of another's! (p. 61).

If the poetry in *Don Juan* left some professional critics cold (the reviewers had little to say about the selection included in *Such Was My Singing*), it appealed to musicians. Sir Edward Elgar was encouraging, and may have been present when Frank Schuster's garden inspired the setting for Act II.[17] So too was Sir William Hamilton Harty: 'It seems to me powerful and fantastic and also very painful – all very definite qualities.'[18] Robert had wanted Heseltine to do the music for it. After Heseltine's death van Dieren volunteered. 'I told him it was pastiche work,' said Robert, 'and would have to be measured out by the bar like a frankfurter sausage. This didn't seem to put him off.'[19] The play never reached the stage at which music would have had to be written, but Jack Moeran did set a piece from it to music, and his setting, under the title 'Nocturne' was performed at the Norwich Festival in 1935.[20] This was Don Juan's 'Address to the Sunset'. In the Preface to *Such Was My Singing*[21] Robert singles it out as the poem which, along with 'Prison Calvary', comes closest to fulfilling his mature poetic aspirations. Vivienne, too, thought it shows him at his best.[22] It runs:

> Exquisite stillness! What serenities
> Of earth and air! How bright atop the wall
> The stone crops fire and beyond the precipice
> How huge, how hushed the primrose evenfall!
> How softly, too, the white crane voyages
> Yon honeyed height of warmth and silence, whence
> He can look down on islet, lake and shore
> And voiceless woods and pathless promontories,
> Or, further gazing, view the magnificence
> Of cloudlike mountains and of mountainous cloud
> Or ghostly wrack below the horizon rim
> Not even his eye has vantage to explore.
> Now spirit, find out wings and mount to him,
> Wheel where he wheels, where he is soaring, soar,
> Hang where now he hangs in the planisphere,
> Evening's first star and golden as a bee
> In the sun's hair – for happiness is here.

At the rate at which it was proceeding, *Don Juan* seemed unlikely ever to be completed. But Robert had shown, once *Fisbo* was accepted by Heinemann, that he could work fast under pressure. The trouble was that the time in which adventurous producers or publishers might press him to finish *Don Juan* was running out.

In December 1943 Charles Morgan as 'Menander' of *The Times*

Literary Supplement wrote a complimentary piece about Robert which gave him, he says in his journal, 'a happy day'.[23] Such days were becoming very rare; indeed, he wrote the following September 'One cannot go on year after year hating every day of one's life.'[24] His work with the RAF seems to have come to an end with a second stay at Oakington in May 1943, and although he was offered the opportunity to visit a different station in January 1944[25] he declined. He had his occasional BBC broadcasts in 1944 to take him up to London, but he seems for the most part to have stayed in Cambridge and even retired into his journal. When it was suggested that he visit Lawford he felt that the contrast between his brother's situation and his own was too painful: 'I cannot look at Anne and Jojo [Phil's two small daughters] without being in danger of bursting into tears.'[26] In Cambridge there was Vivienne, someone whom, in spite of jealousy, he never ceased to love, and Bertrand Russell, who returned from America that summer, had him to his house about once a week.[27] But he knew few of the new generation of dons and for the first time in many years he seems to have had no correspondent in whom he could confide. Lady Jane had died in January 1943 and a certain coolness developed between Robert and Vivienne and their friend Mrs Boulton after she became Lady Rose. He felt lonely; the boarding house food and cramped quarters at Newnham Terrace depressed him; he had insomnia and relied increasingly on Luminol.

In the autumn the Allies drove the Germans out of the south of France, and Robert heard that Le Piol was safe. He will have been pleased also that Trinity College, Oxford, showed a belated interest in their old alumnus and invited him to a guest night dinner and a night in college.[28] But throughout 1944 his health must have been failing. Those close to him had heard him complain about his health for many years. His valetudinarianism was part of his persona, which is why, no doubt, Richard Pennington made the slightly cruel selection from his letters in *Peterley Harvest* – the letters printed on pages 115–16 and 124–5 are real letters from Robert, though they read like parodies and were not, of course, written to David Peterley who did not exist.[29] Even Vivienne had learnt to ignore his cries of 'Wolf!' But then, as she says in her *Recollections* (pp. 63–4), in December 1944

> The agonising and dreadful thing happened. I received a 'phone call from his landlady telling me he was ill and for two days owing to pressure of work I did not go to see him and then I called and he

was strangely silent and concerned about himself. He showed me the blood on his handkerchief, only a speck, and then he said he felt tired and must go to bed early. I tried to comfort him and cheer him, but left feeling very concerned and frightened. Apparently he woke in the night and went downstairs and knocked on his neighbour's door saying he had a frightful pain in his left arm. He complained of this before I left. They did not get up.

He went to 'phone the doctor who also did not come, but promised to come in the morning, and then he must have returned to bed and died of a thrombosis. They called me in the morning. I saw him lying with his hands over his chest dead. He was the first person I have ever seen dead, and the person I cared most for in the world.

Robert died on 17 December 1944; the cause, said the doctors, was 'acute heart failure' resulting from coronary disease. Vivienne performed the task of summoning Phil, Phyllis and Norah, and they seem to have taken charge of Robert's body and belongings without much attention to her, since it was left to the Bertrand Russells to invite her to stay with them that night. 'They earned', she says, 'my everlasting love and gratitude as a result. They were so kind and comforting.'[30]

Norah, at least, wrote to Vivienne afterwards, since on 1 January 1945 she replied:

Dear Norah,

I am grateful for your letter and I should be glad to see you when you come – I am sure you are feeling stricken and desolate and I send you my real sympathy. It has been dreadful. I had no idea things could happen like that, and I know how you feel when you say the world is empty and dead for you. For me, it will never be the same again.

I don't know how to send you comfort. Thank you for telling me about the memorial service, but excuse me please if I don't attend it. I find I can best endure things alone. Please don't think I bear any ill will towards you. I never have done and know what a large part you had in Robert's life and how deeply he cared for you. Life is a cruel business and I am sorry for all the hurt I must have caused you. Perhaps there is small consolation in thinking that Robert is free and whole and in good company – I think the best have gone from this earth – and that he is no longer wearied by his frail body. Norah, I know that he wouldn't want you to grieve. I only wish he had had more happiness in this life before he left. I feel he needs prayers. The fact that his work wasn't finished is tragic and disastrous and I should like to talk to you about this when we meet, as well as other things. Please let us remain impersonal but meet as friends.

Both women cherished the memory of Robert throughout their lives. Vivienne never married; Norah did not marry again. Norah continued on good terms with the Nichols family until her death in 1960. She made preparations for writing Robert's life after his books and papers were recovered from France in the 1950s, but the undertaking was too much for her advancing age and failing health. Vivienne outlived Robert by fifty years, dying only on 13 March 1997. She was never received by Robert's generation of Nicholses, nor does it appear that she and Norah ever became friends, but there was a reconciliation with the next generation of Nicholses before she died. She became a Catholic in her later years, and her niece, Helen Shell, believes that this was because of Robert's persistent though never satisfied search for God.

Robert left the income of his estate to Vivienne for her life and thereafter to the Royal Literary Fund, expressing the wish that it be used for the benefit of young poets, and especially young married poets. His name is now in Poets' Corner, Westminster Abbey. His bones, however, lie in the churchyard at Lawford near the end of the lime avenue which he loved. The trees he knew have all died or been cut down since 1944, but the avenue has been replanted and in another hundred years they should be

> Diffusing dizzy fragrance from their boughs,
> Tasselled with blossoms more innumerable
> Than the black bees, the uproar of whose toil
> Fills their green vaults[31]

to inspire another poet.

Not having been much written about in his later years, Robert received tributes in many journals at his death. One that showed particular warmth was from Charles Morgan. He wrote another long appreciation for *The Times Literary Supplement*,[32] and when this appeared in book form in *Reflections in a Mirror: Second Series*[33] added some personal reminiscences.

One day, when I was crossing Regent Street, not having seen him

[Robert] for more than a year, my arm was taken by his, and his voice began to pour out the thought on dramatic poetry of which his mind had been full when he sighted me. In Burlington Street he interrupted himself to ask where I was going. 'To my tailor's.' He would come with me. If I had answered 'To Valparaiso', he would have taken the same boat train, but Hanover Street was nearer; the tailor's fitting did not impede or exhaust the flow of his mind, and afterwards he drove home with me, drank tea which he allowed to grow cold, ate dinner which he seemed not to notice, for he was hungry and thirsty only for ideas. He would leap from his chair, pace the room while he talked, stand in mid-floor with clenched fists thrown up to shoulder-level, thrust his hair back from his forehead, hold us spell-bound. Triviality was impossible to him. If he spoke of outwardly trivial things – a dance, an escapade, a fashionable woman – he would say something never said before on land or sea, would strike them with lightning; and if he spoke of poetry and the drama, he made not the least pretence of taking them easily, of being a man of the world who could shrug indifferent shoulders at them, but spoke of them with the torrential passion of one who was, and knew that he was, both their master and their slave; their master, and yet not fully so, for he was not his own; their slave who suffered. Suddenly he would remember his listeners, shake his head violently like a dog emerged from a stream, hunch his shoulders and say, with the smile of a boy caught in recurrent wrong-doing: 'I am talking too much,' and fight his way back into silence. The restraint was agony. While others spoke, he looked from face to face, his lips trembling with muttered speech, until at last his ideas burst from him again; and yet he gave no impression of being what is ordinarily called a talkative man, for words, which come from the talkative in a perpetual dribble, came from him under pressure; you could be battered but never bored by him. Nor was his seizure of the conversation felt to be discourteous, for it had authority, and in all else his courtesies were gentle, elaborate, of another age. Of what age? Never was a man freer of the centuries. As an artist, he was an innovator, and, particularly in the theatre, in advance of his time; as a man, he was so strange a mingling of seer with gentleman of fashion that, when you met him, you had to decide by his mood whether he had been walking with Blake at Felpham or dining with Byron at Melbourne House.

Morgan's book was reviewed by Sir John Squire.[34] Squire, who had printed so much of Robert's work in the *London Mercury*, quotes nearly the whole of this passage, and says it is good portraiture. But he adds:

A man like Nichols, extraordinarily sensitive and aware, shows different sides to different people. I knew him well for nearly thirty years and should have said, not only that he was 'a talkative man', but that he was the most voluble man I ever knew. To me he was: probably because he had a completely sympathetic listener, who was willing to hear a Niagara of talk in which sense and nonsense, grandiose imaginings and preposterous theories, beautiful images, sharp witticisms, flat jokes, penetrating and wild criticisms all poured out helter-skelter.

Robert was at his best with his literary friends; his siblings saw a different man. Phil and Anne both said that in his last years it was unbearable to be in the same room with him. Living in lodgings, separated from his possessions, without wife or child and forgotten, as he felt, by the public, he accumulated great reservoirs of self-pity and when he saw them it gushed out in tears, complaints and pleas for money. From an early age he had evaded the responsibilities of an oldest son. When difficult guests appeared he absented himself; when his sisters were getting married he played no part but that of a perceptive and articulate chronicler; he never acquainted himself with the needs of Lawford Farm or Nichols Square in London or the details of the Pusey inheritance. But it was not through impatience at having these duties thrust upon him that Phil did not offer him a home in the war years, and still less through hardness of heart, but rather because he was himself too sensitive to stand the proximity of Robert's misery.

Robert's personality was composite, and the elements did not fuse into a homogeneous whole. In his own affairs he could be quite irrational. He believed that he was born to be a poet, which was not, perhaps, untrue, but he inferred from this by a monstrous *non sequitur* that he should do nothing else but write poetry. He never gained an academic qualification because he cared to work at nothing but English literature. No needs of his own, no ties he had or made with other people, would ever place him under the slightest obligation to take a paid job. When he was engaged to marry Norah he wrote with shocking brutality to the Heads: 'I shall certainly chuck Norah if she comes between me and my work.'[35] He justified his courtship of Lesley Black by saying that she provided him with poetic inspiration. He refrained from marrying Vivienne because if he did he would have to work for the cinema or become a teacher or journalist.

It is impossible to say how far Robert's failures with the women in his life were due to his early separation from his mother and her progressive mental ill health. His compulsion to write and his jealousy over the time he set apart for writing could have grown out of proportion to fill this lack or to cover these traumas. That would explain why his unreasonableness was confined to his own personal affairs. On other matters his justness of vision is one of his strengths. When he volunteered in 1914 he was under no illusions about what lay ahead, his reasons were well thought out and he kept them in view till the end. In the 1920s and '30s when many people who should have known better were deceived by Mussolini and Hitler, he saw through them from the start. He rebuked the Heads for saying the rise of Nazism was not his business, but he avoided the fallacy of believing that Russian Communism was significantly different. He saw the evils of capitalism and the shallowness of social Darwinism, and called himself a socialist; but he mistrusted easy solutions and disavowed any belief in the imminence of the Millennium.

In all his social and economic ideas he was a rock of sanity; and in literature and the arts and sciences again and again, as Morgan says, he was ahead of time. He was right to espouse the cause of a national theatre, and it is pity that his pleas for a British Film Corporation were unheeded. In his religious plays he was a decade before T. S. Eliot. His novel of the future, *Golgotha*, is a decade before Aldous Huxley's *Brave New World* and untainted by Huxley's infatuation with compulsory eugenic planning.[36] In the cinema he foresaw the rise of the animated cartoon and looked forward to developments that have got under way only in very recent years. His play *Wings Over Europe* anticipates the splitting of the atom and predicts the military use that would be made of it. His advocacy of wired wireless when it was pooh-poohed by the broadcasting establishment has been vindicated by television and the internet. His ideas for the British war effort in the Second World War, the Nichols Bob, the oil-pumping scheme and so on, though they have their comical side, demonstrate the continued fertility of his invention.

Robert's inconsistencies will not appear exceptional if he is seen as an Englishman of privileged background to whom waywardness was a birthright. 'Robert Nichols', said Arnold Bennett in 1923, 'was brought up in an atmosphere of ancient houses and connoisseurship; he imbibed taste and the historic sense as simply as babies imbibe milk.'[37] And he had an ineradicable pride in his national and family past. His roots, however sickly and straggling his branches, went deep into the streets of literary London and the bricks and soil of rural Lawford. This enabled him to define himself in two words he often used and directed to have cut into his tombstone: the words 'English poet'. It accounts too for his ability to mix extravagance with good sense and unite extreme tiresomeness to the tender consideration with which he decked Vivienne's Christmas tree and wrote well over 400 letters to the stricken Henry Head.

Edmund Blunden was a loyal friend, and hit Robert off well in these lines he wrote after his death,[38] quoting from his war poem 'Farewell to a Place of Comfort':

> I think of Spring, cold-pure and venturous youth,
> Snowdrop to bluebell, leaping from the undergrowth,
> Brief spring! What poetry taught us not that truth?
> And you, inspiring visitant, fragile-strong,
> Desirous messenger and source of song,
> Were Springlike, and I reckoned not 'how long?'
>
> 'The bell is sounding down in Dedham Vale',
> And merry Robert in his snow-wrapt grave;
> O come again, join star and nightingale –
> But truth turns wintry now. Let tempests rave.

Source Notes

I · BACKGROUND AND CHILDHOOD

1 25 January 1945, pp. 109–10.
2 Letter dated 26.12.44.
3 Written for John Gawsworth: *Ten Contemporaries*.
4 *The Times Literary Supplement*.
5 Letter to Henry and Ruth Head dated 20.8.31.
6 Letter to the Heads dated 14.1.33.
7 Letter to the Heads dated 30.7.30–3.8.30.
8 Letter to the Heads dated 10.10.31.
9 Letter to the Heads dated 1.9.29.
10 Published 24.12.22 under the title 'An Episode of Carols on Christmas Eve'.
11 From 'A New Life', address to a Japanese planting society.
12 Letter to the Heads dated 10.10.31.
13 Oxford, Basil Blackwell, 1943. Mackail drew on two volumes produced by himself, Nichols and another Balliol friend, H. C. Beeching: *Love in Idleness* (1883) and *Love's Looking Glass* (1891). Robert possessed quite a substantial volume of his unpublished poems (now in the hands of the present writers).
14 Journal of 4.11.44, p. 128.
15 Oxford, printed for private circulation, 1907.
16 Letter dated 21.1.07.
17 In 'Notes on the poem "Arrogant Eros"', sent to Marsh 25.11.33.
18 Letter dated 26.8.15.
19 Letter to the Heads 1.9.29.
20 *Ibid.*
21 *Poems by Bowyer Nichols*, Introduction, p. iii.
22 Letter to the Heads, 1.9.30.
23 Letter to the Heads, 20.9.31.

2 · PRE-OXFORD POETRY AND SCHOOLING

1 Letter dated 8.3.35.
2 Journal of 8–9.12.39, pp. 20–1.
3 Letter to the Heads dated 10.10.31.

4 Letter to the Heads dated 16.5.31.

5 Letter to the Heads dated 15.2.31. In the last year of his life Robert acquired a fine copy of the 1748 edition of this book.

6 Journal of 5.4.44, pp. 43–4.

7 *Guilty Souls*, Preface, p. xl.

8 Letter dated 3.8.18.

9 Editorial note in No. 3; letter from Robert to Mrs Nichols postmarked 25.4.10.

10 Letter to the Heads dated 10.10.31.

11 Letter to the Heads dated 20.8.31.

12 *Guilty Souls*, Preface, pp. xl–xlii.

13 Letter to Edward Marsh dated 3.12.25.

14 Letter dated 23.11.44.

15 Letter to the Heads dated 8.11.30.

16 Letter postmarked 22.1.10.

17 Letter to Mrs Nichols postmarked 1.2.10.

18 Letter to the Heads dated 8.11.30.

19 Letter to the Heads dated 4.2.27.

20 Letter dated 11.8.12.

21 *Guilty Souls*, Preface, p. xlii.

22 Memoir of Philip Heseltine, RN's typescript p. 9.

23 12 July 1917; it also got a favourable mention in *The New Witness* of 16 August from Charles Scott Moncrieff.

24 7 August 1917.

25 London, Jonathan Cape, 1952, pp. 240–2.

26 For example 'Shame' and 'Fear'.

27 London, Cassell, 1956, chapter 6.

28 Copy supplied by Michael Bristow-Smith.

29 London, Cassell, 1937.

30 p. 69.

31 p. 78.

32 At best she gave only the day and month and not the year; this results in some uncertainty about the order of the letters in Robert's collection.

33 29.8.12.

34 *All the Books of My Life*, p. 93.

35 p. 79.

36 *All the Books of My Life*, p. 93.

3 · OXFORD 1913–14

1 *Peter Warlock: a Memoir of Philip Heseltine*, London, Jonathan Cape, 1934.

2 Letter to the Heads dated 29.11.31.
3 *Memoir of Philip Heseltine.*
4 Her part in this is attested in Robert's letter to his mother dated 27.6.17.
5 The composition is described in a letter to the Heads dated 29.11.31.
6 21.6.17.
7 Letter to his father dated 12.7.15.
8 London, Heinemann, 1919, p. 53.
9 Robert Graves, *Collected Poems*, London, Cassell, 1938, p. xv.
10 *Guilty Souls*, Preface, pp. xlii–xliv.
11 'E. M. M.' in *Occult Review*, November 1917.
12 12.7.17.
13 *Westminster Gazette*, 20.7.17.
14 *Art and Life*, November 1917.
15 Letter to the Heads dated 9.3.30.
16 Letter dated 5.7.17.
17 Letter to the Heads dated 12.7.31.

4 · THE EARLIER WAR POEMS

1 *Guilty Souls*, p. xxviii.
2 Letter to the Heads dated 27.8.30.
3 *Ibid.*
4 Letter to Mrs Nichols dated 27.12.14.
5 p. xlvi.
6 Preface, pp. 34–5.
7 Letter, no date or addressee, among letters to his mother, written in September 1915.
8 Letter to the Heads dated 27.8.30.
9 *Anthology*, pp. 42–4.
10 Letter to Bowyer Nichols.
11 Undated letter to Heads, January or February 1933.
12 *The Times Literary Supplement*, 12.7.17.
13 Prometheus, Amsterdam.

5 · THE LATER WAR POEMS

1 Letter dated 29.10.15 to Miss Bernard, possibly the Cristina referred to in chapter 4, n. 7.
2 Letter to Mrs Nichols dated 5.9.16.
3 Letters to Norah Nichols, 25.1.45 and 29.1.45.
4 Letter from Dr D. J. Frick, dated 11.8.26.

5 Letter to Siegfried Sassoon, 25.1.17.
6 Undated letter to Basil Liddell Hart, October 1943.
7 Vivienne Wilkinson, Tape 2.
8 *Diaries 1915–18*, London, Faber, 1983, p. 52.
9 'Plaint of Friendship by Death Broken'.
10 Letter to the Heads dated 20.4.30.
11 Letters to his father dated 7.6.18 and 5.7.18.
12 Letter to his father dated 3.4.18.
13 Letter to Mrs Nichols dated 23.12.17.
14 Letter dated 2.1.18.
15 Letter to his father dated 5.7.18.

6 · NEW FRIENDS

1 Letter to the Heads dated 29.11.31.
2 Letter to Robert from Ruth Head dated 11.2.25.
3 Letter to Henry Head of 26.1.25, mistakenly dated 26.1.24.
4 *The Times*, October 1940.
5 Letter to the Heads dated 21.11.16.
6 Robert's typescript memoir of Heseltine, p. 33.
7 *Ibid.*, pp. 34–5.
8 Hugh Kingsmill, *D. H. Lawrence*, London, Methuen, 1938, quoted in *The Spy's Bedside Book*, ed. Graham Greene and Hugh Greene, London, Hart-Davis, 1957, pp. 203–5.
9 Letter to the Heads dated 2–3.12.33.
10 Quoted by Nigel Heseltine in *Capriol for Mother*, London, Thames Publishing, 1992, p. 101.
11 Nigel Heseltine, *op. cit.*, p. 31.
12 Letter to Mrs Nichols dated 15.9.17.
13 Letter to the Heads dated 17.7.17.
14 Letter to Edward Marsh, 26.7.17.
15 Letter to Marsh, 17.10.17.
16 Letter to the Heads dated 3.5.17.
17 Letter to his father dated 3.4.18.
18 Letter to the Heads dated 27.11.32.
19 Letter to Henry Head, 9.9.17.
20 *Siegfried Sassoon Diaries 1920–1922*, ed. Rupert Hart-Davis, London, Faber, p. 233.
21 RN's typescript, p. 19.
22 *Fairies and Fusiliers*, London, Heinemann, 1917, 'To Robert Nichols'. Graves's pencil manuscript of a longer version is enclosed in Marsh's letter to Robert dated 30.6.27.

23 Letter dated 10.10.31.
24 *Robert Ross, Friend of Friends*, ed. Margery Ross, London, Cape, 1952, p. 305.
25 Letter to the Heads dated 31.5.31.
26 Letter from Marsh dated 28.12.16.
27 Letters from Marsh dated 22.6.17 and 7.7.17.
28 Christopher Hassall, *Edward Marsh, Patron of the Arts*, London, Longmans, 1959, p. 413.
29 Christopher Hassall, *op. cit.*, p. 447.
30 Letter to Siegfried Sassoon dated 7.4.26.
31 27.8.18, from North Cornwall.
32 Letter dated 16.1.18.
33 Undated letter.
34 Letter postmarked 19.12.17.
35 Remarks quoted by Ann Thwaite, *Edmund Gosse, A Literary Landscape 1849–1928*, London Secker and Warburg, 1984, p. 1.
36 Hassall, *op. cit.*, p. 58.
37 Letter of 31.10.17.
38 Ann Thwaite, *op. cit.*, p. 471.
39 *Ibid.*
40 In his first letter to Robert, dated 26.10.17, he asks to be remembered 'to your father'.
41 Letter dated 17.7.19.
42 Sassoon, *Diaries 1923–1925*, p. 222.
43 Letter of 21.11.17; *Diaries 1915–1918*, p. 195.
44 Letter of 7.12.17; *Diaries 1915–1918*, p. 196.
45 Letter to Marsh dated 29.1.32.
46 Letter to Julian Huxley in *Letters of Aldous Huxley*, ed. Grover Smith, 1969, quoted by Ann Thwaite, *op. cit.*, p. 471.
47 *Enid Bagnold's Autobiography*, London, Heinemann, 1969, p. 134.
48 *Ibid.*
49 *Op. cit.*, p. 80.
50 There is a warm letter from Enid dated 8.11.29 and Robert could call on Sir Roderick's help over local politics in 1930, according to a letter to the Heads dated 11.5.30.
51 Undated; postmarked 7.8.18.
52 Letter dated 22.8.18.
53 Letter dated 12.12.18.
54 Letter dated 4.12.18.
55 Following a contribution by Robert on 12 December 1936 of a dialogue between Weimar and Wasteland.
56 Letters to Head dated 13.10.29, 12.12.30.
57 *The Japan Advertiser*, 25.12.21.

58 Letter to the Heads dated 16.8.27.
59 *Ibid.*

7 · NEW POEMS

1 Letter to Marsh dated 7.8.18.
2 Note to 'Table of Intentions'.
3 Letter to Marsh dated 25.10.19.
4 Letter to Head dated 3.8.29.
5 Poem entitled 'The Living Dust'.
6 *Guilty Souls*, Preface, p. xlix. Pusey was his mother's great-uncle.
7 Card dated 13.5.18.
8 Letter to Head dated 21.6.18.
9 Letter dated 20.2.19.
10 Letter dated 30.3.19.

8 · FIRST VISIT TO AMERICA

1 Letter to Head dated 29.6.17.
2 Letter to Head dated 5.7.17.
3 Letter to Head dated 6.12.18.
4 Letter to Bowyer Nichols dated 7.6.18.
5 Letter to Bowyer Nichols dated 17.10.18.
6 Letters to the Heads on 19.11.33 and to Marsh 19.11.33.
7 Newspaper report dated 23.10.18.
8 Letter to the Heads dated 5.12.31.
9 Letter to Marsh dated 17.1.19.
10 Undated letter, possibly 1930 or 1931.
11 Most of what follows is documented by M. A. DeWolfe Howe in *John Jay Chapman and His Letters*, Boston, Houghton Mifflin Co., 1937.
12 Hollywood C.V.; letter to Bowyer Nichols dated 21.4.19.
13 Letter to Bowyer Nichols dated 21.4.19.
14 Undated cutting from *The Banner*.
15 22.3.19. Aiken wrote to the paper saying 'this lunatic piece of fooling was never intended for the horror of print.'
16 Letter to Marsh dated 2.3.19.

9 · AURELIA

1 The first stanza of 'Hymn', undated.
2 Letter to Marsh dated 20.10.19; he had asked his father for an allowance in a letter dated 2.5.19.

3 Letter to Head of 4.11.19.
4 Letter to Marsh dated 1.11.18.
5 Letter to Marsh dated 13.11.19.
6 Quoted in Anne Chisholm, *Nancy Cunard*, London, Sidgwick and Jackson, p. 56.
7 Quoted *ibid.*, p. 55
8 Letter dated 26.4.20.
9 6.6.20.
10 1.7.20.
11 Letter to Robert Nichols from Marsh dated 13.8.20.
12 30.7.20.
13 25.1.20, p. 109.
14 July-August 1951, p. 200.
15 30.12.44.
16 Letter dated 3.1.45.
17 Quoted in *Nancy Cunard*, p. 56.

10 · MARRIAGE

1 Notes accompanying manuscript poems.
2 Notes accompanying manuscript poems.
3 Letter dated 3.3.43.
4 *Four Songs and Lyric Intermezzo*. The volume has no publisher's name and may have been privately printed. She gave Robert a copy in August 1918.
5 Letter to Head dated 13.6.27.
6 There are no letters in the Head correspondence from 1920. Could there originally have been letters discussing Robert's relationship with Norah which Norah destroyed?
7 Letter to the Heads dated 24–5.7.32.
8 Letters to Bowyer Nichols dated 15.11.19 and Easter 1920.
9 Journal for 8.9.44, p. 103.
10 The article was probably for *The Japan Advertiser*.
11 Letter to Richard Tolson Esq., postmarked 3.4.57, in Mr Tolson's possession.
12 *Goodbye to All That*, London, Jonathan Cape, 1929, p. 366. The words of Sir Edmund Gosse may be found in *Some Diversions of a Man of Letters*, London, Heinemann, 1919, pp. 279–80. They are 'There could hardly be a more vivid contrast than exists between the melancholy passion of Lieut. Nichols and the fantastic high spirits of Captain Robert Graves.'
13 Letter to the Heads dated 24.11.29.
14 Letter dated 3.8.20.

15 Letter to the Heads dated 14.4.35. The story was revised in the 1940s but never published.

16 Letter to the Heads dated 'Round about Christmas Eve, 1932'.

17 Letter to Marsh dated 10.10.20.

18 Letter dated 29.12.20.

19 Letter to Head dated 16.2.21.

20 Letter dated 7.4.21.

21 Letter dated 9.5.21.

22 Letter to Head dated 9.9.21.

23 Or so he declared to an audience in California between 1924 and 1926.

24 Letter dated 24.11.29.

25 Diary for 19.4.22.

26 Letter to Marsh dated 24.4.23.

27 Robert's publishers.

28 Letter to Marsh dated 27.3.23.

29 *In Broken Images*, p. 144.

30 Letter to Head dated 9.5.21.

31 Article in *The Star*, 27.8.28.

11 · JAPAN

1 Entitled 'Hero Song', Robert seeing himself somewhat as a hero going to his doom. The poem appeared in *The Observer* of 10.4.21.

2 Dated 6.1.25 and addressed to Miss Stephens.

3 Enclosed in a letter to Marsh dated 2.2.21.

4 Letter dated 30.3.21. He had arrived in Tokyo on 12.3.21. The same points are made in a letter to his father dated 20.4.21.

5 Letter to Miss Stephens, cited above.

6 From a broadcast on Japanese psychology written by Robert in 1942.

7 Letter dated 5.6.21.

8 Letter to Bowyer Nichols dated 26.5.21. Robert does not say who translated this from the Japanese.

9 *Diaries 1920–1922*, London, Faber and Faber, 1981, p. 142.

10 Journal of 8.10.35, f 26r.

11 Letter to Head dated 2.6.27.

12 100 copies were printed in Tokyo round about Christmas 1921.

13 10.11.21.

14 11.12.21.

15 18.12.21.

16 25.12.21.

17 1.1.22.

18 8.1.22.

19 Letter dated 7.4.21.

20 Letter to Marsh dated 22.3.22.
21 *Fantastica*, Preface, p. 26.
22 Letter to Head dated 3.9.21.
23 Article, written under the name June Lawford, in *The Sketch*, 18.9.29.
24 Letter from Robert to his father dated 5.9.23.
25 Letter from Norah to Bowyer Nichols dated 15.5.23.
26 19.11.22.
27 10.12.22.
28 23.12.22.
29 4.2.23.
30 22.4.23.
31 23.5.23.
32 20.5.23.
33 25.5.23.
34 Letter from Maurice Browne to Robert dated 19.4.23.
35 Letter from the SS *Tyndareus* on his way back to Japan in September.
36 *Diaries 1923–1925*, London, Faber and Faber, 1985, p. 61.
37 Letter to Bowyer Nichols dated 23.9.23.
38 Letter dated 16.1.24.
39 6.3.24.

12 · *GUILTY SOULS* AND *GOLGOTHA*

1   Letter to Robert dated 22.6.22; Robert had evidently sent him a copy of the book.
2   Letter dated 5.7.22.
3   Letter dated 26.4.20.
4   1.6.22.
5   26.5.22; cutting dated but no source.
6   Letter dated 12.12.20.
7   See *Fantastica*, p. 307.
8   Letter dated 20.12.24.
9   *Ibid.*
10 Letter dated 20.12.24.
11 Letter dated 7.1.25.
12 *The Nation and The Athenaeum*, 2.5.23, p. 305. The review was not what one might reasonably expect from a friend, and Sassoon sent Sitwell (without comment) a copy of a generous letter Robert had written to *The New Witness* in defence of him, Sitwell, when he had been attacked by C. K. Scott Moncrieff (*Diaries 1923–1925*, p. 34).
13 Letter dated 17.6.23.
14 Undated letter from SS *Tyndareus*, September 1923.
15 Letter dated 3.12.23.

16 Letter dated 26.5.23.
17 Letter dated 16.1.24.
18 Clippings without date or source.
19 Undated clipping.
20 *The Observer*, 20.5.23.
21 Colin Grant in *Eve*, 30.5.23.
22 *The Saturday Review*, 2.5.23.

13 · HOLLYWOOD

1 Letters from Lee dated 15.8.23 and 21.8.23.
2 Undated letter from SS *Tyndareus*, September 1923.
3 *Diaries 1923–1925*, p. 171.
4 Letter dated 25.7.24.
5 Letter dated 11.12.26.
6 Exclamation at the end of a letter about Leopardi dated 7.8.24.
7 Letter dated 12.10.24.
8 Letter dated 28.10.24.
9 Phrases from Robert's letter.
10 Letter dated 8.12.24.
11 Article for *The Sketch*, 11.9.29.
12 Letter to Bowyer Nichols dated 13.8.24.
13 Letter of rejection dated 4.9.24.
14 Letter to Marsh dated 5.9.25. In a letter to his father dated 3.12.25 he speaks of $150 a month.
15 Letter to Marsh dated 2.10.25.
16 Article in *The Times*, 1.9.25.
17 Poem dated 21.7.25.
18 Letter to the Heads dated 29.11.29.
19 *Hollywood Life*, June 1926.
20 Letter from Marsh dated 17.9.25.
21 The *New York Times* printed a digest of them in its Magazine Section.
22 Letters dated 8.9.25 and 3.11.25.
23 Letter to Marsh from SS *Tyndareus*, September 1923.
24 Programme note, printed at the Gate Theatre Press May 1928.
25 Letter dated 28.12.26.
26 Letter to the Heads dated 1.9.27.
27 Letter to the Heads dated 20.5.1928.
28 Letter dated 12.5.26.
29 'Variation on a Well-Known Theme' and 'Sir Horace Wiseacre's Waggery', *The London Aphrodite*, 1928.
30 Edited with an essay of appreciation by Horace Bridges. Robert's

dialogue appeared in *The Literary Digest International Book Review*, pp. 302–5.

31 Translated with Introduction and Notes by Jacob Zeitlin. Robert's dialogue appeared first in August 1925 according to a letter to Head dated 15.8.25.

32 *The London Aphrodite*, December 1928, pp. 222–3. Robert wrote a sketch of Mrs McPherson's career for *The Star* in September 1928.

14 · YEW TREE HOUSE, EARLY YEARS

1 Letter from Ruth Head dated 13.7.26.

2 Postcard from Sassoon dated 17.9.26.

3 Letter to the Heads dated 25.4.31.

4 Letter to Marsh dated 21.2.28.

5 Letter dated August 1930.

6 Letter dated 7.11.26.

7 The letter (dated 31.1.27) survives.

8 Letter dated 18.1.27.

9 Note, dated 18.7.38, attached to revised typescript given to Evan Morgan (Lord Tredegar).

10 Letter dated 4.4.28.

11 Letter dated 6.5.28.

12 Letter dated 27.7.30.

13 Issue of 20.5.28.

14 Letter from Robert to the Heads dated 20.5.28.

15 Letter from Romer Wilson dated 30.1.26. Lady Head too speaks of it in letters dated 1.12.26 and 2.12.26.

16 'Notes on Rake's Progress', accompanying typescript and letter to Robert Helpmann dated 19.11.44.

17 Letter to Helpmann dated 19.11.44.

18 *Ibid.*

19 *Ibid.*

20 Review 19.5.28.

21 Letter to the Heads dated 13.9.31.

22 Letter dated 6.3.28.

23 Letter dated 24.2.27. A play 'on release of energy in atom' is on the list of dramatic projects drawn up in America (see p. 149).

24 In a letter to Marsh dated 5.10.27 he says he has finished it but is revising it.

25 Letters from Preusler dated 3.8.27 and 29.12.28.

26 Letters from Leroy MacLeod dated 21.11.28 and Donald Friede dated 16.1.29.

27 Letter dated 16.5.32.

28 Letter dated 2.8.29.
29 *The Sketch* 4.5.32; *The Tatler* 4.5.32; *Daily Mirror* 7.5.32.
30 Letter dated 2.10.28.
31 Entitled 'The Excursion'.
32 Issue of 30.12.28.
33 Letter (from The Harvard Club) dated 17.1.29.
34 Letter to the Heads dated 27.8.30.
35 Letter to the Heads dated 24.1.30.
36 Robert writes harshly of him in a letter to the Heads dated 1.11.31.
37 Letter to the Heads dated 24.10.34.

15 · DEATHS AND QUARRELS

1 Letter to the Heads dated 3.9.30.
2 Dated 13.4.30.
3 Letter dated 29.7.29.
4 Letter to the Heads dated 31.7.30.
5 *Ibid.*
6 Letter dated 25.1.27.
7 Letter dated 31.1.27.
8 Letter dated 29.7.28.
9 Letter dated 6.10.29.
10 Letter dated 10.8.28.
11 Undated letter from Gruyères.
12 Letter dated 8.2.30.
13 Letter to Lady Jane Gathorne-Hardy dated 28.2.41.
14 Letter to the Heads dated 22.12.29.
15 Letter postmarked 12.12.29.
16 Letter to the Heads dated 22.12.29.
17 Letter postmarked 28.12.29.
18 Letter to the Heads dated 24.11.29.
19 Letter dated 31.12.29.
20 Letter dated 28.2.30.
21 Letter to the Heads dated 28.2.30.
22 Letter dated 9.3.30.
23 Letter to the Heads dated 24.11.29.
24 Letter dated 11.5.30.
25 Letter to the Heads dated 8.2.30.
26 Letter to the Heads dated 27.7.30.
27 Undated letter to the Heads, probably of 9–10.8.30.
28 Letter to the Heads dated 13.4.30.
29 Letter to the Heads dated 26.9.30.
30 Letter to the Heads dated 30.1.30.

31 Letter to the Heads dated 12.12.30.
32 Letter to the Heads dated 25.6.32
33 Letter to the Heads dated 26.8.33.

16 · MORE FRIENDS LOST

1 Draft of statement for the British Museum.
2 Letter dated 30.11.30.
3 Letter from Captain J. Richards dated 29.10.15.
4 Letter to Robert dated 26.11.34.
5 Letter to the Heads dated 5.12.30.
6 Letter dated 27–28.12.30.
7 *Ibid.*
8 Letter dated 28.2.31.
9 Letter to the Heads dated 16.8.27.
10 Letter to the Heads dated 23.8.27.
11 Letter dated 26.5.31.
12 Copy in the possession of the writers.
13 Letter to the Heads dated 27.7.30. Leslie's *The Epic of Jutland* was published by Benn later that year.
14 Letter to the Heads dated 13.11.30.
15 Letter to the Heads dated 5.2.31.
16 Letter dated 12.12.31.
17 Undated letter from Yew Tree House, probably in 1930.
18 Letter to the Heads dated 20.8.31.
19 Letter to the Heads dated 13.9.31. Robert was also friends with her sister Beatrix, who had acted in *Twenty Below*, and her brother John.
20 Letters dated 29–30.1.32 and 12.2.32.
21 Letter to the Heads dated 28.6.30.
22 Letter to the Heads dated 8–9.6.30. In giving this hostage to fortune, Robert did not foresee that Gielgud would be acting with scarcely diminished vigour in his nineties.
23 Letter to the Heads dated 31.5.31.
24 Letter to the Heads dated 7.1.34.

17 · AUSTRIA, ITALY, BAVARIA 1932–4

1 Letter to the Heads dated 25.6.32.
2 Letter dated 2.7.32.
3 Letters to the Heads dated 7.8.32, and, for the sexual dimension, 19.10.34.
4 Letter dated 23.6.34.
5 Letters to the Heads dated 3.11.29, 11–19.7.31, 30.8.31.

6 Letters to Marsh dated 24.4.23, to the Heads dated 16.10.30, cf to the Heads 29.11.31 and 21.6.34.
7 Letter to the Heads dated 17–18.9.32.
8 *Ibid.*
9 *Fenby on Delius*, p. 122.
10 Letter dated 1.10.32.
11 Letter to the Heads dated 30.10.32.
12 Letter to the Heads dated 2.5.33.
13 Copies of five letters to Fenby supplied by Mr R. Tolson.
14 Letter to the Heads dated 6.11.32.
15 Letter to the Heads dated 1.1.33 (continuation of letter dated 'around Christmas Eve 1932').
16 Letter to the Heads dated 26.2.33.
17 Letter to the Heads dated 12.2.33
18 Letter to the Heads dated 6.3.33.
19 Letter to the Heads dated 11.3.33.
20 Letter to the Heads dated 17–18.3.33.
21 Letter to the Heads dated 2.4.33.
22 Letter to the Heads dated 17.6.33.
23 Letter to the Heads dated 23.1.33.
24 Letter to the Heads dated 29.4.33.
25 Letter dated 31.5.33.
26 Letter to the Heads dated 2.6.33
27 Letter to the Heads dated 28.7.33
28 Letter to the Heads dated 5.8.33.
29 Letter to the Heads dated 7.10.33.
30 Letter to the Heads dated 6.7.34. This mentions the 'Address to Fame' quoted below and the lines to Courage.
31 Quoted in letter to the Heads dated 25.6.33.
32 Letter to the Heads dated 5.8.33.
33 Letter dated 19.11.33.
34 Letter to the Heads dated 20.11.33.
35 Letter to the Heads dated 17.1.34.
36 Letter to the Heads dated 14.1.34.
37 Letter to the Heads dated 17–20.1.34.
38 Letter to the Heads dated 9.2.34.
39 Letter to the Heads dated 21.6.34.
40 Letter to the Heads dated 6.7.34.
41 Letter to the Heads dated 21.6.34.
42 Letter dated 15.5.34.
43 Letter from Koteliansky dated 17.5.34.
44 Letter to the Heads dated 17.6.33; there is a similar rhapsody in a letter to Marsh dated 25.11.33.

45 Letter to the Heads dated 16.10.34.
46 Recollections, pp. 26–7.
47 Letter to Robert dated 19.7.34.
48 Journal, vol. 1, p. 21.
49 Letter to the Heads dated 28.6.34.
50 Letter to the Heads dated 8.7.34.
51 Letter to the Heads dated 1.7.34.
52 Letter to the Heads dated 28.6.34.
53 Letter dated 1.7.34.
54 Letter from Bowyer Nichols dated 31.8.34.
55 Letter dated 14–15.9.34.
56 Letter to the Heads dated 4.11.34.
57 Letter to the Heads dated 4–5.11.34.
58 Letter to the Heads dated 1.12.34.
59 *The Poetry Review*, October 1942, p. 279, reviewing *Such Was My Singing*.
60 *The Manchester Guardian*.
61 20.10.34.
62 January–February 1935.
63 Letter to Marsh dated 18.6.34.
64 Letter dated 14.10.34.
65 Letter dated 14.11.34.
66 Letter to the Heads dated 8.1.33.
67 Letter to the Heads dated 29.4.33.

18 · VIVIENNE

1 Journal for 29.3.37, 79a rev.
2 Letter to the Heads dated 25.7.37.
3 Recollections, p. 37.
4 Recollections, p. 39.
5 Letter dated 14.12.35.
6 Letter to Lady Jane Gathorne-Hardy dated 11.7.40.
7 Letter to the Heads dated 14.9.33.
8 Letter dated 25.8.36.
9 Letter to the Heads dated 23.2.35.
10 Letter to the Heads dated 2.9.36.
11 Letter to the Heads dated 28.4.35.
12 Letters to the Heads dated 4–5.5.35, 6.5.35, 10.5.35.
13 Note in *Such Was My Singing*, p. 138.
14 Undated letter, presumably summer 1942.
15 Letter from Dorothy Boulton to Robert dated 26.6.42.
16 Letter postmarked 20.9.35.

17　Letter to the Heads dated 23.6.35.
18　Journal, vol. II, 40b obv. She was a closer friend of Phil than of Robert.
19　Letter to the Heads dated 26.3.35.
20　Letter to the Heads dated 23.9.35.
21　Journal, vol. II, 68a obv.
22　Recollections, p. 21.
23　Letter to the Heads dated 13.5.36.
24　*Ibid*. Russell's suspicion is confirmed in Journal for 12.9.44, p. 107.
25　Originals at Trinity; tcc file.
26　Letter dated 11.12.36.
27　Journal for 19.7.36, vol. II, 49a obv.
28　Act I, p. 5.
29　Pencil dedication by Robert.
30　Vol. II, 49a obv.
31　Letter dated 13.11.55.
32　Letter dated 11.12.36.
33　Private communication from Miss Blackman.
34　Vol. II, 51b rev.
35　p. 42.
36　Letter to the Heads dated 6.7.34.
37　Descriptions and drawings in possession of the writers.
38　Letter from The Hut dated 21.7.18.
39　Letter to Marsh dated 30.9.36.
40　Letter to Marsh dated 23.10.36.
41　Letter from the Air Ministry dated 16.11.36.
42　Journal, vol. II, 56a rev–56b obv.
43　Letter to the Heads dated 26.12.36.
44　Letter to Lady Jane Gathorne-Hardy dated 2.4.41.
45　Letter to the Heads dated 28.5.37.
46　Letter to the Heads dated Derby Day, 1937.
47　Letter to the Heads dated 16.7.37.
48　Journal of Venice, 23.8.37.
49　Letter to Philip Nichols dated 23.2.38.
50　Vivienne Wilkinson, Recollections, p. 43b.
51　Letter to the Heads dated 12.3.38.
52　Letter to the Heads dated 28.4.38.
53　Vivienne Wilkinson, Recollections, p. 43b.
54　Letter to Philip Nichols dated 1.5.38.
55　Quoted reproachfully by Robert in a letter to her dated 12.2.38.
56　Letter dated 6.6.39.
57　Letter to Lady Jane Gathorne-Hardy dated 29.6.39.
58　Letter dated 20.7.39.
59　Letter from Philip Nichols to Lady Jane dated 7–8.8.39.

60 Letter to Lady Jane dated 27.12.39.
61 Letter to the Heads dated 28.5.37.
62 Letter dated 20.5.40.
63 Letter dated 7.6.40.
64 Letter to Lady Jane dated 26.10.40.
65 Letter dated 26.7.40.

19 · THE SECOND WORLD WAR

1 Letter to Lady Jane Gathorne-Hardy dated 15.10.40.
2 Letter dated 7.7.40.
3 Letter to Lady Jane dated 7.2.41. Sitwell writes of Robert in a not unfriendly way in the last of his autobiographical books, *Noble Essences* (London, Macmillan, 1950).
4 Letter to Lady Jane dated 29.7.40.
5 Plans dated 10.7.40.
6 Letters to Sir George Gater dated 27.5.40 and to Sir Henry Tizard in February 1944. The correspondence with Gater also refers to certain cruiser-cars or 'see-sees'.
7 Letter to Lady Jane dated 3.3.41.
8 Letter to N. J. O'Conor dated 1.9.42, printed in *Arizona Quarterly* 4.3, Autumn 1948, pp. 214–15.
9 Journal for 4.2.41, p. 17.
10 Letter dated 5.8.40.
11 Letters to Lady Jane dated 12.9.40; 18.11.40.
12 *Such Was My Singing*, p. 135.
13 6.6.42.
14 Note dated 2.9.39, attached to 'Together' typescript.
15 Note dated 2.9.39, attached to 'Together'.
16 Letter dated 27.10.40.
17 p. 58.
18 Letter to Lady Jane dated 23.3.41.
19 Letters to Lady Jane dated 12.5.41 and 5.6.41.
20 Letter from Vivienne dated 1.8.41.
21 Letter to Lady Jane dated 10.10.41.
22 Letter to Lady Jane dated 15.10.41.
23 Richard Church in the *New Statesman* 25.7.42; Austin Clark in the *Irish Times* of 5.9.42.
24 Issue of 28.8.43.
25 Review in *The Sunday Times* 8.8.43.
26 Note in his copy of the Huard translation.
27 Letter dated 30.10.43.
28 Dated 14.10.40.

29 Letter from V. Gielgud dated 25.3.41.

30 14.3.42.

31 6.4.42.

32 Letter from Jack Beddington, Director of the Films Division, dated 10.8.42.

33 Letter dated 16.7.42.

34 11.10.41.

35 Letter dated 10.2.43.

36 Letter dated 16.11.43.

37 Letter dated 7.1.44.

38 Letter dated 26.5.41.

39 Letter postmarked 25.7.41.

40 Letter dated 26.1.42.

41 Letter dated 21.8.41; also letters from A. S. Hodge, 19.8.41, and Nigel Law, 22.8.41.

42 Letter dated 23.10.41.

43 Letter dated 4.11.41.

44 Memorandum sent to the Ministry of Information.

45 Letter from John Gielgud dated 15.3.42.

46 Letter from B. D. Freeston, Assistant Recruitment Director.

47 Letter from A. C. Cameron dated 23.2.42.

48 Broadcast August 1943; see Journal, vol. 2, p. 123.

49 Dates 16.4.44, 4.6.44 and 19.11.44 respectively.

50 Letter dated 20.7.42. The book was not published until 1948.

51 Letter from Harold Orton, Deputy Educational Director, dated 5.12.42.

52 Letter to N. J. O'Conor dated 1.9.42, printed in *Arizona Quarterly* 4.3, Autumn 1948, p. 213.

53 Journal (vol. II, p. 64) for 6.5.43.

54 Letter postmarked 26.11.42.

20 · THE BELL SOUNDS DOWN IN DEDHAM VALE

1 Letter dated 5.3.42.

2 Letter dated 21.7.42.

3 Letter dated 17.8.42.

4 Letter dated 22.11.42.

5 Letter printed 17.9.43.

6 Letter to the Heads dated 15.7.43.

7 Letter from John Masefield dated 24.11.20; letter to the Heads dated 27.11.32; undated poem 'Don Juan in Hell'.

8 *Such Was My Singing*, p. 154.

9 Letter to the Heads dated 12.2.38.

10 'Don Juan in Music', projected BBC broadcast.

11 Letter to the Heads dated 28.2.30.
12 3.2.23.
13 Letter dated 6.3.32.
14 Letter to the Heads dated 28.2.30.
15 Letter dated 8.3.35.
16 *Such Was My Singing*, p. 109.
17 Letter to Robert dated 7.10.31.
18 Letter to Robert dated 31.8.36.
19 Letter to the Heads dated 15.2.31.
20 Letters from Moeran to Robert dated 30.12.34 (on the change of title) and 26.3.35.
21 p. 17.
22 Recollections, p. 64.
23 Journal for 6.12.43, vol. III, p. 11.
24 Journal for 12.9.44, vol. III, p. 108.
25 Letter from R. Dangerfield dated 20.1.44.
26 Journal for 12.9.44, vol. III, p. 115.
27 Journal for 6.9.44, vol. III, p. 99.
28 Letter from Philip Landon (Bursar) dated 10.10.44.
29 Letter from Milton Waldman to Norah dated 23.10.59.
30 Recollections, p. 66.
31 From 'The Sprig of Lime' (changing 'your' to 'their': in the poem Robert is apostrophising the limes).
32 31.12.44.
33 London, Macmillan, 1946.
34 *The Illustrated London News*, 27.4.46, p. 450.
35 Letter dated 6.6.21.
36 See *The Hidden Huxley*, ed. David Bradshaw, London, Faber and Faber, 1994, pp. xiii ff.
37 William Rothenstein, *Twenty-Four Portraits*, 'with critical appreciations by various hands', London, Chatto and Windus, 1923. The (unsigned) appreciation of Robert is by Bennett.
38 *The Listener*, 22.2.51.

Select Bibliography

Published Works by Robert Nichols

BOOKS AND PAMPHLETS

Invocation: War Poems and Others, London, Elkin Mathews, 1915.

Ardours and Endurances also A Faun's Holiday and Poems and Phantasies, London, Chatto and Windus, 1917.

The Assault, Chatto and Windus, 1918 (the war poems from *Ardours and Endurances* with a new Introduction).

The Budded Branch, London, Beaumont Press, 1918.

Invocation and Peace Celebration, Hymn for the British Peoples, London, Hendersons, 1919.

The Smile of the Sphinx, London, Beaumont Press, 1920.

Aurelia and Other Poems, London, Chatto and Windus, 1920.

A Year's Grain, 1920–1921, Tokyo, privately printed, 1921.

Guilty Souls, A Drama in Four Acts, London, Chatto and Windus, 1922.

Fantastica, being The Smile of the Sphinx and Other Tales of Imagination, London, Chatto and Windus, 1923.

Winter Berries, Hollywood, Youthland Press, 1924.

Twenty Below, being a Drama of the Road, with Jim Tully, London, Robert Holden, 1927.

Under the Yew, New York, Covici Friede, n.d. [1928]; London, Martin Secker, n.d. [1928].

Wings Over Europe, A dramatic extravaganza on a Pressing Theme, with Maurice Browne, New York, Covici Friede, 1929; London, Chatto & Windus, 1932.

Hamlet and Don Quixote, an essay by Ivan Turgenev, translated by Robert Nichols, London, Hendersons, 1930.

Robert Nichols, Benn's Augustan Books of Poetry, London, Benn, n.d. [1932].

Fisbo, or, The Looking-Glass Loaned, London, William Heinemann, 1934.

A Spanish Triptych, London, Rampant Lions Press, 1936.

Such Was My Singing, London, Collins, 1942.

Anthology of War Poetry 1914–1918, assembled by Robert Nichols, London, Nicholson and Watson, 1943.

William Nicholson, London, Penguin 1948.

PRINCIPAL CONTRIBUTIONS TO BOOKS AND JOURNALS

Oxford Poetry 1914, 'Prophecy'.

Oxford Poetry 1915, 'The Prince of Ormuz Sings to Badoura', 'The Tower', 'Midday'.

Oxford Poetry 1916, 'Leonore', 'Shut of Night', 'Song of the Princess beside the Fountain'.

Georgian Poetry 1916–17, 'The Assault', 'Fulfilment', 'The Naiads' Music', 'The Philosopher's Oration', 'The Prophetic Bard's Oration', 'To – ', 'The Tower'.

Oxford Poetry 1917, 'The Man of Honour'.

New Paths 1917–1918, 'Reply to an Imaginary Invitation', Spanish Folk Song.

Oxford Poetry 1918, 'Polyphemus'.

Georgian Poetry 1918–1919, 'The Sprig of Lime', 'Seventeen', 'The Stranger', 'O Nightingale my Heart', The Pilgrim'.

A Miscellany of Poetry 1919, 'Paean on Seeing a Portrait of Blake'.

The London Mercury, 1919, 'The Smile of the Sphinx', 'Night Rapture'.

The London Mercury, 1920, '12 Sonnets to Aurelia', 'November'.

The Sackbut, August 1920, 'Of the devil who would learn Gregorian'.

The Observer, 10.4.21, 'Aspiration'.

The London Mercury, 1921, 'D'Annunzio'.

The London Mercury, 1924, 'Night Song'.

The Calendar of Modern Letters, August 1925, 'Petrarch, D'Annunzio, Solitude and other matters'.

The Times, August–September 1925, nine articles on the cinema.

The London Mercury, 1926–7 'Lines by a Person of Quality'.

The London Mercury, 1927, 'Passers By', 'To the Unknown God'.

The London Aphrodite, 1928–9, 'Variation on a Well-known Theme', 'Sir Horace Wiseacre's Waggery', 'The Rake's Progress', 'Paean in Honour of Los Angeles'.

The Best Poems of 1929, 'Epic Wind'.

The Times, 30.5.31, 'The Souls of the Righteous'.

The London Mercury, 1931, 'For the Eve of Palm Sunday'.

The Best Poems of 1932, 'Song of the Jester Dwarf'.

The New Statesman and Nation, 25.7.36, 'Prison Calvary'.

The Best Poems of 1936, 'Virgin of Sorrows'.

Time and Tide, 1942 'The Palmer'.

Other Works Referred to

Bagnold, Enid, *Enid Bagnold's Autobiography*, London, Heinemann, 1969.

Bradshaw, David, ed., *The Hidden Huxley*, London, Faber and Faber, 1994.

Chisholm, Anne, *Nancy Cunard, a Biography*, London, Sidgwick and Jackson, 1979.

Fenby, Eric, *Delius as I Knew Him*, London, Faber and Faber, 1981.

——, *Fenby on Delius*, London, Thames Publishing, 1998.

Fielding, Daphne, *Emerald and Nancy*, London, Eyre and Spottiswode, 1968.

Fussell, Paul, *The Great War and Modern Memory*, New York and London, Oxford University Press, 1975.

Gosse, Edmund, *Some Diversions of a Man of Letters*, London, Heinemann, 1919.

Graves, Richard Perceval, *Robert Graves 1895–1926*, London, Weidenfeld and Nicolson, 1986.

Graves, Robert, *Collected Poems*, London, Cassell, 1938.

——, *Fairies and Fusiliers*, London, Heinemann, 1917.

——, *Goodbye to All That*, London, Jonathan Cape, 1929.

——, *On English Poetry*, London, Heinemann, 1922.

Gray, Cecil, *Peter Warlock: a Memoir of Philip Heseltine*, London, Jonathan Cape, 1934.

Hassall, Christopher, *Edward Marsh, Patron of the Arts*, London, Longman, 1959.

Heseltine, Nigel, *Capriol for Mother*, London, Thames Publishing, 1992.

Howe, M. A. DeWolfe, *John Jay Chapman and His Letters*, Cambridge Ma., Riverside Press, 1937.

Kaye-Smith, Sheila, *All the Books of My Life*, London, Cassell, 1956.

——, *Three Ways Home*, London, Cassell, 1937.

Lamont, Edward M., *The Ambassador from Wall Street*, Lanham, Maryland, Madison Books, 1994.

Nichols, Bowyer, *Poems*, ed. J.W. Mackail, Oxford, Basil Blackwell, 1943.

O'Prey, Paul, ed., *In Broken Images, Selected Letters of Robert Graves 1914–1946*, London, Hutchinson, 1982.

Roberts, John Stuart, *Siegfried Sassoon (1886–1967)*, London, Richard Cohen, 1999.

Ross, Margaret, *Robert Ross, Friend of Friends*, London, Jonathan Cape, 1952.

Sassoon, Siegfried, *Diaries 1915–18*; *Diaries 1920–23*; *Diaries 1923–5*, ed. Rupert Hart- Davis, London, Faber, 1981–5.

Sitwell, Osbert, *Noble Essences*, London, Macmillan, 1950.

Tennyson, Sir Charles, *Life's All a Fragment*, London, Cassell, 1953.

Thwaite, Ann, *Edmund Gosse, A Literary Landscape 1849–1926*, London, Secker and Warburg, 1984.

Webb, Barry, *Edmund Blunden, a Biography*, New Haven and London, Yale University Press, 1990.

Wilson, Jean Moorcroft, *Siegfried Sassoon*, London, Duckworth, 1998.

Index